Robin Barbosa

I AM REVEALED

 AM REVEALED

Behind The Ashram Door

Robin Barbosa

Full Court Press
Englewood Cliffs, New Jersey

First Edition

Copyright © 2016 by Robin Barbosa

Published in the United States of America
by Full Court Press, 601 Palisade Avenue
Englewood Cliffs, NJ 07632
fullcourtpressnj.com

ISBN 978-1-938812-70-5
Library of Congress Catalog No. 2016933952

Visit us at revealedbook.wordpress.com
facebook.com/BehindTheAshramDoor
twitter#RevealedBook.com

*Book design by Barry Sheinkopf for Bookshapers
(bookshapers.com)*

Cover art by Silverio Barbosa

Colophon by Liz Sedlack

I AM: The Beginning

Deuteronomy 29:29: *"The secret things belong to the Lord our God, but the things revealed belong to us; and to our children forever..."*

DEDICATION

This book is dedicated to my husband, who heard me typing these words through my apartment door, even before we ever met, and who has been consistently supportive throughout this writing process.

ACKNOWLEDGEMENT

"He will bring our darkest secrets to light and will reveal our private motives" (1 Corinthians 4:5).

I am grateful to my two darling daughters, who have always been my motivation.

I am forever grateful to my mother, who never gave up on me as her daughter, and to my father, who was my role-model of my heavenly father. I am grateful for my son-in-law Alex, who has always been curious about me and my life, and my son-in-law Lee, whose knowledge of law makes for enjoyable repartee. Special acknowledgement to Peter Tembo, a man of God, who instilled in me the measure of faith for this story to take book form. My soul-sister Christiana Morgan read through this manuscript in one day and validated its efficacy. Melanie Swaim made constructive comments, which ushered in the sequence in which this story is told. I am grateful to Elenice Persaud and Crystal and Tony Telesco, who listened to me throughout this process and embrace me as family.

DISCLAIMER

This account is not meant to reflect any particular organization or institution in any way but does reflect the overall cult phenomenon, and it is based on actual experiences which will offer an opportunity to gain insight into the fictitious organization being dubbed the World Organization for Righteous King Service (WORKS), its internal structure, and the mentality I assumed as an adherent.

Any explanation of the philosophy or the lifestyle is not intended to be critical, or to convince or persuade the reader. It is offered simply to lend glimpses of what life became for me as a "worker" (also referred to as an "agent") who was persistently overwhelmed and entwined in an illusory ideology. As a worker, my lifestyle was fashioned through adherence, and inspired by the intense loyalty, dedication, and service required having as their source the tenets and precepts of the philosophy preached within the WORKS. The airports are arbitrary settings, as they were used by political and religious groups for fund-raising in the 1970s and 1980s.

PROLOGUE

It would be impossible to write about getting involved in a cult without mentioning that cult members are seeking spiritual truth. I thought I had found it as I was led on gradually to believe that it could only be found in the cult. Over time, in order to reap spiritual benefit, mandatory obedience and full immersion in the lifestyle was the requirement.

I had this manuscript stashed in a briefcase under my bed for over three decades before venturing through the manually typed pages to retype on a computer. I had pecked out each page on a manual typewriter so many years earlier as a purging, a catharsis, as the memories came vividly to mind, flooding my days with what had transpired for me as I relived many incidents from the three years I lived in a Righteous King Center as one of the soul-saving agents who would elicit donations from anyone willing to give. I did this with passion and fervor.

"As the King had commanded his servant Moses, so Moses commanded Joshua. And Joshua did as he was told, carefully obeying all the commands that the Lord had given Moses" (Joshua 11:15).

Like Joshua, I did what I was told, but unlike him, it was not the

God of the Bible I listened to. I had succumbed to the deception of well-crafted persuasive techniques that promised spiritual fullness through the special knowledge found only in the cult. For three years, I was a tunic-wearing, bead-thumbing, Righteous King-reciting agent on a mission to save my soul and to benefit all mankind.

My two daughters, Mahlia and Saadya, attended Jesuit colleges. I knew something was different about them after they graduated. My daughters had peace, and I could see they didn't let their feathers get ruffled. They noticeably allowed things to roll off their backs, keeping everything in perspective. I knew they studied the Bible in college as a requirement, and I overheard many of their conversations. I intentionally did not question them on the specifics. It was obvious to them that I was guarded. Mahlia and Saadya did not know why. But they are about to find out.

"There, in a foreign land, you will worship idols made from wood and stone—gods that neither see nor hear nor eat nor smell. But from there you will search again for the Lord your God. And if you search for him with all your heart and soul, you will find Him" (Deuteronomy 4:28-29).

GROWING PAINS

As a child, I often contemplated how big God would have to be if He had the whole world in his hands—the song I sang with enthusiasm as a youngster, jumping up and down transforming my bed into a trampoline.

I grew up in a Jewish neighborhood. I knew I was Jewish, but I didn't know what that meant, other than going to synagogue all dressed up on the Jewish High Holidays of Rosh Hashanah and Yom Kippur. I also wore a dress on the Jewish holy days that did not require going to synagogue. I always liked being in synagogue, but when the service was over, I couldn't understand how the people who had just been there could carry on and simply resume their activity as if God no longer mattered.

Another thing confounded me. The majority of my schoolmates were also Jewish. Some of the girls wore dresses on Saturdays while others did not. These girls spent all day on Saturday at the neighborhood synagogue in observance of the Sabbath while others carried on as if it were just a day off from school. Some girls didn't even wear a dress on the High Holidays. Yet we all considered ourselves Jewish without question.

As a teen, I began to question how this could be, and what did it really mean to be Jewish. I grappled with how, on Yom Kippur, I was being cleansed from sins committed throughout the previous year. I even fasted. I shuddered at the notion that I would need atonement the following year, and so on. This made me realize my sins would always be an obstacle between me and God.

I pondered what I would have been if I had been born into a different family. I would have been me, but I would be of a different religion. I realized that I had been rubber-stamped a Jew. This was not satisfactory, so I concluded that to be Jewish meant I had to do more Jewish things. So I began attending an early Sunday morning youth group in one of the local synagogues for a bagels-and-cream-cheese breakfast. I would stay for the Hebrew dance practice to learn the dance steps and then put them together to music as we danced in a circle.

I enjoyed all of this. But again, when I left, my feeling Jewish dissipated. I began to make a practice of reading the English translation in the Siddur—the Jewish liturgy book. I read along with the Hebrew praising and acknowledging the God of Israel, the Melech Yisrael, the King of Israel. This enlightenment helped me understand that I was worshiping the God I already knew existed.

As a senior in college, I became interested in Eastern philosophy, and I began to consider myself as spiritual, more as a new-ager, yet I felt like an outsider looking in. As a twenty-one-year-old college graduate, I already acknowledged the existence of God, yet I wanted to know more. That did not change for me even after being set loose of the cult's tentacles that had been intricately woven in and around my brain for the three years I was in the WORKS.

I have been hoping, for over the past thirty years, to see this story told, as my beautiful daughters have grown into independent, intelligent and successful women. My heart's desire is for my daughters, and those who think they know me, to know me more.

My hope is for these words to convey what I am unable to say.

BEGINNING

DREAM WORKS

"Nothing in all creation is hidden from God's sight. Everything is uncovered and lain bare, before the eyes of him to whom we must give an account" (Hebrews 4:13).

In my dream, I am running away as fast as I can. "Running away from *what?*" Mahlia wants to know. *What* is what I am about to tell you. I am speaking to Mahlia, one of my dear darling daughters. The fact that I was running to get away makes this dream no different from all the other recurring dreams I have had over the years after my rescue from the high-demand group known as the World Organization for Righteous King Service—WORKS. I had Mahlia's attention as she stared at me wide-eyed, with disbelief that her own mother had this story to tell of her past.

"Who has believed our message, and to whom has the arm of the Lord been revealed?" we are asked in Isaiah 53:1.

AT THE TIME, I DIDN'T have the answer. But they did in the WORKS. This was written soon after I was rescued out.

We had no rest or peace within, separate from our obligation—to satisfy King's desire and that of those to whom we answered. In my search I sought those answers Absolute. Now it seems my life and search have only just begun. I panic when I am not absorbed in prayer. Now I pray and pray not to turn away, being torn as to whom and what to believe. So as never before, I seek, I must know for myself and truly understand, what is involved and how I should see; black and white do not exist, but shadows and shades cast by people with minds, minds that work or overwork, and analyze to be, so I pray to know what is involved in mind-control, and not being me.

HITTING THE ROAD

THE ORDEAL I HAVE EXPERIENCED, wondering when it will reach completion, began in the winter of 1975. I made plans to travel across the country from as far east as Connecticut to as far west as California. I felt no responsibilities or obligations to deter me from my determination to do so. My story begins in 1975 going into 1976, when as a college graduate I had an opportunity to travel across the United States, in my case in a Volkswagen minibus just like the ones used to travel to Beth El, in New York State, and Yasgar's Farm, heading for Woodstock. This is exactly what I was determined to do—travel west to California. When the opportunity presented itself, it was a feasible alternative to accepting a job offer in journalism right after college. I was told about someone who was planning to travel. He was a friend of a friend's brother, an older fellow who was taking the winter months off from his landscaping business. My parents had the landscaper over for dinner and, after meeting him, were satisfied that this would be nothing other than a road trip to California. My plan was to visit my pen-pal cousin, who was a student at the University of San Bernardino, and that I would be staying at her apartment for a visit before flying back east. Two years earlier, my parents had agreed to one of my brothers backpacking through several countries in Europe with three of his fraternity buddies, so this was just to be my adventure before getting a job and settling down. There would be plenty of time for that. In the meantime, the journey seemed innocent. So my parents agreed to the trip.

I would bring my racing bicycle with me. I sold my car and walked away from a prospective job offer. "You mean *drove* away," Mahlia points out, and I know I have her attention. I will provide her with some background while I wait for her sister Saadya to get home. Yes, I drove away with only my rolled-up sleeping bag and the duffel bag I had prepared for my journey. We took off right after the New Year and hit the road in preparation for me to "hit up" everything that moved. Mahlia exclaims, "Were you like Bonnie and Clyde, Mom, did you hold up banks, or something?"

I tell her, "Not banks, but people," and my story begins to unfold.

BONE CHILLING

THAT FIRST NIGHT ON THE ROAD, I nearly froze with cold. Mahlia is again in disbelief as I continue. The threat was real; it terrified me that I had nowhere to go, nowhere to turn for warmth, and remained this way throughout the night. When the first rays of sunlight ushered in the dawn of a new day, I ran through the brush along a winding creek, wishing to be totally embraced by the warmth of the brisk morning sunshine. I'm lost in this memory when I hear Mahlia exclaim, "No way!"

Yes way. It must have been at the first stop, in Kentucky, after driving all day from Connecticut, and it was a seriously cold night. The landscaper and I stopped at a general store in the evening, and when we said good-night to the owner, I was secretly wishing I could just stay in the store and roll out my sleeping bag in front of the warm pot-bellied stove. But this was not to be. It was back into the VW minibus that would be the only roof over my head that frigid night. Or so I thought. Instead, I was forced to take other measures, while the landscaper slept in the van. Turns out, I took shelter in the Kampgrounds of America (KOA) campground restroom and tried to get comfortable in one of the bathroom stalls. "But, Mom, I had no idea," I hear Mahlia say. It has taken me a long time to be able to tell her. Still waiting for Saadya, I tell Mahlia to listen. And she does.

I used all my mental faculties, while I still had them, to keep from going crazy with cold. I reminded myself that the sun would be up in a matter of hours. I just needed to make it until then. I wrapped myself in a blanket and my sleeping bag, and huddled in fetal position to maintain as much body heat as was possible—though, in reality, impossible; my efforts were in vain. It simply was not possible for me to keep warm in the unheated facilities at the campground. "Mom, I can't believe what you're telling me," Mahlia offers. "Why do I have the feeling I haven't heard anything yet?" She's on board when she commits by adding, "I have no idea where all this is going."

I hesitate, not knowing how she will take what I have to tell her and her sister, yet I know this is the right time. Saadya will be home any minute.

I situated myself in the women's restroom at the camping grounds, and that is when I knew I had to take my mind off the icy air. Feelings of safety and security began to seep into my consciousness. However, they did not alleviate the severity of the frigid air penetrating my bones.

Now I glance up at the clock on the wall. Mahlia reads my mind and assures me, "I just got a text from Saadya. She's on her way." I plan to fill Saadya in as soon as she comes home. The entire four-week trip to California offered me breathtaking scenery, landscape, and a myriad of views of the wide-open space throughout the lands of Kentucky (brrr!), Missouri, Tennessee, and Ohio. I saw lands bountiful with nature's treasures. From the minibus, I could see rolling hills, ribbons of highway, fields rich with tilled top-soil, and farm houses, each with a story of its own. All this offered me the inspiration to continue on until my journey's end, which was in itself only the precursor for another adventure. Shortly after arriving in San Bernardino, I met up with my cousin. I bade farewell to the landscaper, and we parted ways.

IN GOD WE TRUST

SAADYA HAS JUST COME HOME from visiting with Emma, her best friend from high school, and finds us in the kitchen, after a light casual dinner, washing dishes, drying them, and placing them in their designated places. My girls knew that we made a game of clean-up when they were small children by singing, "Pick up and put away." As youngsters they delighted in scurrying around the house to pick up a toy and put it in its proper place. So it is no wonder that Saadya begins to tidy the kitchen counter to lend a helping hand. It's Tuesday evening of a long Thanksgiving weekend, and my precious daughters have come home for a family gathering. We will be guests at Mahlia's in-laws on Thursday.

"What are you guys talking about?" Saadya asks matter-of-factly.

Before I say a word, Mahlia answers, "Mom is just telling me about when she froze her *tuchus* off in Kentucky."

"*What?*" Saadya squeals.

I now have an audience with *both* my daughters. After all these years, I couldn't have arranged this any better.

Mahlia wants to know why, and why *now*. Why am I about to reveal this about myself from the past? You are adults, and I adore you. *I know I can trust you with what I am about to tell you.* I recite lines from a poem written long ago, soon after living on my own:

> *If perchance you wonder how and why, as I do many times, Perplexed and vexed, In a state confused, It's silly now, I was cultivating the intuition of my mind, My life eternal, Free of ego obstacles, distractions for my soul, Reciting, so I could be pure enough to live forever in a state of bliss.*

As Saadya begins to prepare herself a plate of dinner and munch on reheated broccoli spears, I continue. My destination, along the way across the United States, was Barstow, California, for a visit with my cousin Arlene. Her father and my father were brothers. While her father was in the navy, he was stationed in San Diego, where he met his future wife. After getting married, they remained in California to raise their family. So Arlene and her older sister Brenda grew up on the West Coast. I only saw them when they came east on several family vacations. We would have a good time during their visits, and it was always sad when they left. As preteens, Arlene and I became pen-pals. Therefore, it made sense to everyone for me to visit her in Barstow, since I would be traveling to California. After making it across the country, I drove up the coast with the landscaper, through San Diego, Santa Barbara, Carmel, Monterey, San Bernadino, and finally reached my destination, Barstow.

There, I was to join a King Center and remain for three years as a loyal and diligent worker. I was to internalize all doctrines and to assume all the characteristics of a loyal agent of the World Organization for Righteous King Service. "You belonged to *WORKS!*" exclaims Saadya. She is now definitely part of this conversation.

Not only that, but I dressed like a worker, talked like a worker, walked like a worker, and could think only as a worker was trained to think. Mahlia confesses, "I'm confused about the part with you thinking only as you were trained to think." That's because I stopped thinking for myself. I even became a model worker out of my intense desire to actualize spiritual ideals. I thought that I had found a group of people who shared my principles and were turning their faith into action.

I had no idea then of the repercussions of my conviction to my ideals, and the pliability with which I would be manipulated and molded to formalize those ideals according to the lifestyle and internal structure of this religious affiliation. Subsequently, I became a world missionary, out to benefit all mankind as a humble servant and representative of the spiritual monarch of the World Organization for Righteous King Service. I was on a worldwide mission in the name of King and on his behalf to reach people, all lost souls who otherwise would be doomed to incur the reactions of their unspiritual behavior due to having selfish and physical desires separate from the wishes of King.

"But how could you?" Saadya asks.

Mahlia comes to my defense. "This is exactly what Mom wants to tell us about." In short, I stayed, taking one day at a time, getting hoodwinked and beguiled by various means used at the Center by everyone, even the ashram girls. The basic premise was that the ends justified the means, and I fell for it hook, line, and sinker.

This meant that the leadership in the Center had the license to do or say anything that would keep a person there. They practiced deception for the sake of indoctrinating us into the King Service mindset. We all believed what we were hearing and what we told each other. So I went from one Superior Text class to another, from one meal to another, and by the first week, I was already fervently reciting Righteous King phrases for salvation and purification, and quoting verses from the Superior Text.

BACKGROUND IN BARSTOW

I HAD BEEN STAYING AT MY COUSIN Arlene's apartment in Barstow after parting ways with the landscaper. She had grown up in California and was a student at the University of California at San Bernadino. As I started to tell you, though we were cousins, living so far from each other had previously prohibited direct contact, so as a preteen I had initiated a pen-pal relationship. Arlene knew I was en route to California and would be staying at her apartment temporarily. When I arrived in San Bernadino, I called her.

I had been at Arlene's house only three days. During that time, I was looking into the possibility of attending graduate school. I really did not know what to do with myself now that I was in California, what to do with the future, and the future did not know what to do with me, or so I thought.

But my main concern was with the present. I had been riding my bicycle all over the college town of Barstow, not far from San Bernadino. One evening I rode to a graduate school meeting to determine which requirements I had to meet to apply to graduate school at the University of California. The evening was a bit cool, calm, and balmy. It started to rain unexpectedly during the meeting, and I had to ride my bicycle through it back to the apartment. By then, it was a light rainfall and made the street glisten with alternating shadows and reflections from the light beams bouncing off the rain-washed pavement. I couldn't help but think how clean the streets were. The pavement sparkled black and shone, lending the entire town an incandescent look. The ambiance was magical.

I rode my bicycle back to Arlene's apartment feeling discouraged about the possibility of graduate school, which was not what I wanted at this time. I had just graduated college and was taking time off, prepared to live one day at a time as part of the adventure.

One day, while walking through Barstow on my way back from the bus stop where I had gotten off after a trip earlier that day into downtown San Bernadino, I was stopped by a poster board, with photographs of some farmland and communal life, being displayed on a table. A slogan on the poster board announced, *we have done what others only talk about doing.* I was stopped by the pleasantries with which a blonde, bright-eyed young woman greeted me as I was walking near the table. I briefly conversed with her. We were joined by a young man, boyish in appearance, who was also manning the table, on which also lay some literature. The blonde girl warm-heartedly invited me to visit their house, said I'd be welcome. She told me that, in the evening people usually sat around, played various instruments, and sang songs. I thought she was a bit spacey, and I was not attracted to the prospect of spending time with others like her. I didn't, in fact, feel particularly attracted to anything except the appeal of the farm.

I must have left them with the telephone number to my cousin's apartment, although I didn't recall having done so.

NOT TAKING THE BAIT

I RECEIVED A PHONE CALL that evening and also on the following evening from the boy whom I had spoken with briefly at the recruiting table. I thought this was odd, since I'd had more of an exchange with the young woman. My cousin's response, when I described the incident to her, was that these people were "Jesus freaks." When I heard that, I automatically refused to consider going over to the house they'd spoke of. On the second phone call, I asked the boy if he indeed was a Jesus freak. I sensed my question scared him, almost as if I had found him out. It was evident that he was uneasy with my question, but I was not sure whether he was uneasy being confronted or because he was not at ease with what he was involved in.

I didn't know, at that time, that he was involved with the Church for All United Souls Eternal.

Mahlia thoughtfully says, "You mean he was in the CAUSE."

Saadya asks her, "How would you know about that?"

Mahlia asks in return, "Haven't you ever heard of the CAUSE?"

Saadya quickly replies, "I can tell it's not good."

Obviously, the boy was aware that the term "Jesus freak" had a negative connotation, so he was hesitant about revealing himself. Mahlia observes, "The bottom line was, he wasn't just some guy trying to be friendly. Clearly he had an ulterior motive to recruit you into whatever he was involved in."

I never heard from him again. It wasn't until sometime later, when I was already involved with King Service, that I came to realize that this boy was indeed recruiting for the Church for All United Souls Eternal.

"See? I *knew* it," Mahlia boasts. "I heard a little in college about the claim of their leader to be the messiah, and how they're recruiting college students here in the United States." At the King Center, I was told how King would not let us join CAUSE or any other false teaching because those other groups were cheating their members—because, still attached to their physical beings, they *wanted* to be cheated. King would not allow *us* to be deceived because we, being in the WORKS, were genuinely sincere about our spiritual advancement.

"So what exactly happened, Mom?" Mahlia asks, as if somehow giving me an opportunity to convince her that her mother is not a complete fool.

I first went to the Barstow Center one Wednesday afternoon with the intention of attending a Wednesday afternoon vegetarian dinner. I'd learned about this from an announcement I spotted that morning on a bulletin board on the San Bernadino Community College Campus, *Easy Living on Higher Ground*, with the address of the event. I was aware that the King Centers held these mid-week dinners, although I had never attended one before. Friends of mine in college had told me about plans they'd made to attend a dinner at a WORKS Center in Philadelphia. I had decided not to join them. No further mention had ever been made about the event.

Therefore, that Wednesday, I had no reason to be apprehensive. I had no indication that spending the afternoon at the King Center would prove to be such a momentous decision. I thought it would simply be an enjoyable way to spend the afternoon.

I intentionally rode past the WORKS Center earlier that day, so I would know where it was. I saw some boys attending to preparatory chores on the side of the building. I sensed them moving about with earnestness, so I lingered for a moment as a witness, beholding the unusual sight. I spotted two of them, clad in T-shirts and tunics secured at the waist. They were clean-shaven, and this included their scalps. They were carrying large plastic buckets between the main building and a smaller structure situated on the side of it, in the rear of the parking lot. When the heavy door to this smaller building was opened, I could see that it was, in actuality, a large refrigerator. Although the sight was out of the ordinary on that particular day, I grew quickly and inextricably accustomed to it in the days that lay ahead.

From my perch on the seat of my bicycle near the sidewalk, resting my right foot on the curb, I sensed an air of purpose in the execution of these chores. There was sternness in their gaze as well, which I did not understand. I too would adopt that manner, which would burrow into my very demeanor as I became indoctrinated into the sacredness of the mission.

Mahlia remarks, "You of all people fell for this crock." Her anger is palpable. She is visibly shaken.

VISITATION

AT 3:50 P.M. THAT WEDNESDAY AFTERNOON, I rode my bicycle back up Fredericks Street from Ashby Avenue, where my cousin's apartment was.

I approached the building and wrapped my fingers around the steel-plated vertical door handles, contracting the muscles in my arm, elbow bent. The door swung open easily.

I stepped through the doorway into the edifice, rolling my bicycle alongside me. The King Service Centers are likened to "an oasis in the desert of the physical world." I didn't know it then, but I was stepping over that threshold, the demarcation between the physical and the spiritual.

I was greeted at the entrance by a boy whose welcome ushered me in. I answered several of his questions. He wanted to know if I had ever been to a King Center before, and where I was from.

He invited me to look at the book table where a display of titles appeared, arranged on a colorfully embroidered cloth shining with metallic sequins that draped the table down to the floor. He also said that it would be alright for me to leave my bicycle by the closet, where a pile of shoes was amassing having been left there by the other agents, first-time visitors, and guests, who were already spilling into the Center lobby.

I did not fully realize the subtly disarming effect removing my shoes would have. After all, I was just there to eat a vegetarian meal. "Or so you thought," Saadya remarks. "You were not alarmed at the fact that you were being disarmed."

Mahlia intercedes, "Let Mom go on."

I walked over to the table and picked up a small blue paperback embossed with bold red letters that read *KING*. I looked at the back cover to see what had been written about the book, turned to the introduction, and began to read the words of Sir Supreme. As I did, I could hear the words already resounding in my mind while I mulled over the first paragraph, then the first page, and so on. I identified with, and related to, what I was reading and continued in this way with renewed interest. I read: *You are not this body. You are spirit soul.* The text offered an overview of the King Service philosophy. As spiritual beings, we have fallen from the spiritual world in a feeble attempt to enjoy King's physical energy. Since King fulfills all our desires, he has equipped us with a physical body and physical senses by which to try to enjoy. However, we quickly learn—some more quickly than others—that, as spiritual beings, we can never be satisfied in this way. Enjoyment in the physical world is fleeting and temporary. It is the purpose of this lifetime to purify our existence, so as to be able to return to the kingdom of God. Our Service should be cultivated with love of God. We should become so evolved that our awareness is fixed on King, who will carry us back to the spiritual world where there is eternal enjoyment. The key was to recite the King phrases.

I entered the lobby and proceeded beyond what I knew (now referred to as the physical realm), only to leave behind all its indecency. I stepped into a room that looked like no other place I had ever been in. It was magnificent. The air was hypnotic. The music was spellbinding. I could see two groups of people at the opposite ends of it. Upon closer scrutiny, I realized one group was made up of women and girls, and the other of men and boys. All their concentration was focused on a large plant situated in the center of each group. The agents were waving various objects in front of a large potted marigold plant adorned in a gold-and red sequined-trimmed skirt fastened around the planter it was in. The marigold plant, if offered love and devotion, would bestow her mercy, fondness, and favor in the form of prosperity. The marigold plant is regarded as the incarnation of Ora, the goddess of gold, fortune or money.

I was soon to learn that, each morning, the agents offer a marigold plant, incense, flowers, handkerchiefs, and candles in love and devotion, and pray for large donations.

"Wait a minute," Mahlia interjects. "Did I just hear correctly? They offered flowers to a *plant?*"

Saadya is quick to explain, "It's the goddess they're offering the flowers to."

Even more so, it is the love, devotion and sincerity being offered.

"That explains everything," Mahlia says sarcastically. In return, Ora, the goddess of money, in the form of the marigold plant, will favor the workers with big results in soul-saving activity. "Well, that is certainly the weirdest thing I ever heard of," Mahlia adds. "But I'm just saying!"

Well, there is a lot more of *weird* about to come your way. "Go on, I couldn't help myself."

"No worries," I tell her.

My attention was soon riveted on more singing and dancing. This was followed by a lecture and slide show conducted by one of the men from the Center. He showed images of established King Centers in the Philippines, explaining that the WORKS philosophy is founded on established beliefs and scriptures from an age-old culture and civilization that constructed those Centers with such intricately carved facades, extolling the glories of King.

The actual focus of the lecture was for us to consider that as alert, living beings we had to be aware of something at all times. Intelligent and spiritual, we would not be satisfied with anything but fixing our mind at all times on God. He explained that this could be accomplished by training the mind on one of the names of god, since God was no different from his name. If we simply recited the name of King, we set our mind on God.

"Mom, don't you think, I mean don't you just think, that the slide show was used to lend some legitimacy to what they wanted you to believe?"

"Yeah," I admitted, as if to say, "I reckon so."

And furthermore, the audience, including me, would then give up all its misconceptions and preconceptions and allow itself to experience the sound the phrases made when recited aloud. We were invited to join in singing and dancing and reciting in honor of this god. The lecturer led us in a recitation of the Righteous King phrases.

At first, we began reciting as we remained seated on the floor. We were forewarned to open ourselves up to receive the love of God that would soon fill the room and to allow ourselves to be carried away by the sound-vibration. Reciting the Righteous King phrases, we ended with: *The name of King is to be praised.*

I don't remember exactly how long, but not before too long, everyone in the room was up on their feet, and wild frenzied dancing ensued. I do remember feeling overwhelmed by the recitation. The sound-vibration indeed brought on a light-hearted feeling. After the frenzy dissipated, we were instructed to seat ourselves back to back in rows along the width of the Center room. A paper plate, plastic spoon, and Styrofoam cup were placed on the floor in front of each of us by a boy who continued hurriedly on his way down the entire row. I spotted the young man who had greeted me at the door upon my arrival. I picked up my plate, cup, and spoon, went over to him, sat down next to him, and spoke a few words of recognition. I sensed his uneasiness. It quickly became obvious that it was utterly uncomfortable for him to be confronted with having to chat with me or any woman.

"So they can chant, but they cannot chat," Mahlia sums up.

I had unknowingly created that predicament, which only lasted a minute. Almost immediately, a young woman, clad in a tunic encircling her entire body and reaching down to the floor, with a head scarf covering her head from just above her eyebrows, seemed to appear out of nowhere. She squatted directly in front of me. She introduced herself as Paula. Still squatting, she explained there was a smaller room where a bunch of women ate and talked, and where it wouldn't be so noisy. I followed her logic, weaving through several rows of cross-legged people, other workers and guests still bubbling with exhilaration from the dancing just moments before, now seated, anticipating the vegetarian dishes soon to be served.

There were seven or eight women, clad in tunics, seated along the edges of a rectangular oriental carpet in that room. There were also three other female guests.

Saadya comments, "But not for long."

"What do you mean?" Mahlia asks.

Saadya replies, "I can see this coming—she wasn't a guest for long." I admonish Saadya not to refer to me in the third person. "Sorry," she replies. My daughters have been taught not to refer to me in the third person in my presence, or to criticize me in public. I would not waver from that, no matter how many times they needed to be reminded.

That was the standard, and I would reestablish and reinforce it whenever necessary. When they were too old for me to have them take a bath and put pajamas on as a consequence for a misbehavior, I would consistently remind them, even when they were not so darling, of what I accepted, what I tolerated, and what I didn't listen to. I didn't have to scream. I reminded them instead of the standard. In contrast, I would assume a submissive role living at the ashram. As a dutiful agent in the WORKS, I had to live up to imposed standards laid out for me.

I continue: We were seated on the floor, with two or three girls dressed in tunics situated between each guest and the next. I declined the offer of a pillow to sit on.

However, a large pillow was being used by a guy in an orange tunic sitting across the room from me. He was dressed like the boys I had spotted outside earlier in the day. His attention was turned to me, and he asked me my name, where I was from, and what I was doing in Barstow.

"The sirens must have gone off in his head once he recognized you as a prime candidate for his spiel," Mahlia perceptively says. He also asked me how I'd liked the dancing and reciting. There was already a plate of food intended for me. The women were quiet while this guy, who introduced himself as Leo, directed himself to the other guests and answered their questions.

One female guest identified herself as a born-again Christian. I could not relate to what she was saying, or how she was quoting from the Bible. I took my plate of food to where Paula was seated and told her I would like to talk to her, since she was the only girl I had met. She advised me to return to where I had been sitting and to talk openly, as well as to direct myself, to Leo, who would answer any questions I had.

I complied, feeling this scene had been set up like a harem, and this Leo was some kind of an Ali Baba. I listened to the conversation between the Christian girl and Leo.

There was an awkward combination of acceptance, as well as judgmental authority, in his voice. He was sly, cunning, and beguiling.

"Well that sounds just like a snake," Mahlia blurts.

After a short time, I picked up on the discussion of the spiritual nature of things and began to express my interest in the conversation; I imagine Leo detected it, because he began to direct his comments to me. He spoke of God, spirituality, and a higher purpose for mankind. It awed me that he so confidently claimed to have knowledge about God. Leo seemed to hold the key to assuage my wonderment about God. I solicited him, saying, "You actually know what God looks like," and he boldly pointed to a poster on the wall depicting King posing in a lush green pasture with mountains, hills, and valleys in the background. Leo declared that this was just one picture of King, as he is in the spiritual world where he enjoys unlimitedly. Leo's tone had turned nonchalant, and he mentioned that, each and every morning, the Center held a class where I could learn more. I asked him whether I could return the following day to do so.

Little did I realize that the class was held before sunrise, and that the entire morning program and routine began at 3:00 a.m. Leo worded his response carefully, in such a way that I could not then consider the ramifications. He asked me if there was any reason why I couldn't simply stay overnight, since the first class was held so early. This way, I could get up early with the others, recite the phrases, and get a feel for the lifestyle.

Saadya boils it down. "So attending a class the following day to learn more about God had morphed into staying overnight to learn about the lifestyle."

Well, I was not as alarmed as I had been at the invitation to go to a CAUSE house. Instead, I told Leo that, no, I had no reason not to stay overnight. It wasn't until I had already said it that other things were mentioned to me—in no more than an off-handed manner.

I had thought only about whether I could stay overnight. I had no idea that my decision to remain would result in being isolated, with the only input I would or could receive would be from Leo, the other women, and the leaders of that very controlled and controlling group of the WORKS.

We walked the two blocks down Fredericks Street from the Center to the ashram, where the women slept. I was walking alongside Leo. One of the girls was walking ahead of us, maneuvering my bicycle down the street. She stopped, turned, walked briskly back toward us, and childishly asked, "Leo, Premier, is it alright for me to ride the bicycle?"

He said, "Yes."

I thought it was not his place to so blithely assume jurisdiction over my bicycle. It was puzzling that she asked his permission instead of mine. I said so to him. He explained that it was out of respect that Jayda asked permission, so she would not be acting whimsically or on impulse. In this way, she could make spiritual advancement.

Referring to being God minded, Leo explained Jayda's only concern was to recite Righteous King phrases. She need not concern herself with having to make decisions involving mundane matters. He told me I would come to understand more and more.

"*Oops!* That was a red flag right in front of you," notes Saadya.

I did not pay enough attention, it is true, or maybe I did, but I will tell you how all of that was handled each step of the way.

"Yeah, oops big time," chides Mahlia. "Leo was already thinking long-term. What were you thinking?" she wanted to know.

At the time, it also occurred to me that he had no right to give his permission to ride my bicycle without first conferring with me. When I mentioned this to him, it was only then that he asked if it was in fact okay. And I agreed. He was already maneuvering himself into position to gradually usurp my decision-making and natural instincts, in fact my autonomy.

"But he didn't want to make it so obvious or he'd scare you off," Mahlia accurately surmises.

THE FIRST NIGHT

WHEN WE GOT UPSTAIRS, I entered a bare room with wooden floors and curtains made of Oriental printed cloth hung over the windows, but no furniture. As soon as the girls entered the ashram, there seemed to be much purposeful scurrying about, and within minutes they were laying out their sleeping bags in two rows along the floor of what could be considered the living room. One girl was merely laying a few blankets down on the floor to lie on and cover her body.

I remained to the side, observing. Someone pointed to an area in the corner where a thin foam rubber pad, blanket, and sheet had been laid out for me.

When Leo told me the girls rise at 3:00 a.m. to recite, I had said I was worried about having to get up so early. He'd replied that I wouldn't mind because it was fun. I'd figured that getting up that early would not be utterly intolerable, so I had been willing to give it a go. After all, I had concluded, I have no intention of doing so more than this one time.

I had an extremely difficult, almost impossible, time falling asleep that night. I lay awake with my eyes open, and when you only have a few hours to sleep to begin with, and wind up staying awake for most of them—needless to say, I didn't get much sleep that first night at the ashram. I remained awake with so much to think about, which is significant, because after a time, I no longer thought.

"You just went along," says Mahlia, who has been paying close attention.

I was eager with anticipation, you see, to hear more about God. Yet I didn't feel as if I belonged there. I excluded myself from the group. I felt like an outsider. I was skeptical and cynical.

"Who wouldn't be, with that crock of baloney?" Mahlia says.

I also feared my attitude would be discovered. I felt like I stood out from the other women because, as I was led to believe, they were exalted souls.

The following morning, just as Leo had said, the girls awoke at 3:00 a.m.

THE WAKE-UP CALL

I MUST HAVE REMAINED AWAKE until the time the other girls were awakened by Leo stepping over and between bodies while he recited Righteous King in the dark of the pre-dawn hour. A frenzy of activity ensued. Most everybody was reciting Righteous King phrases or calling out, "King." I was still just watching, and I remember thinking that I was witnessing crazy behavior. The girls weren't talking to each other. They seemed shut off from any external stimuli, not even aware of their physical surroundings, shut off from themselves, not thinking at all about what they were doing. They were moving on automatic. I say "seemed" because I was still an observer, very tired and very over-stimulated. I watched as each girl 'popped up' from her sleeping bag, trying to make sense of what I was observing.

The girls were racing to roll up their sleeping bags and pile them into a back room. Some washed up and brushed their teeth at the kitchen sink. I saw others pacing the length of the floor, reciting, "Righteous King, Righteous King," oblivious to all else. One girl stood in the corner with her finger pressing on the tragus at the opening of her ear, to cut out any other sound. She kicked her feet out one by one as she rocked from side to side.

The girls were also waiting in turn to use the shower. I learned later that I was expected to take a cold shower just as the others had. This practice of taking a shower with only cold water lasted for three years. Saadya and Mahlia look at each other and pretend to shiver. Mahlia says, "No wonder the girls were on automatic. After a cold shower, their blood had probably coagulated." Nevertheless, they moved throughout the ashram deliberately and punctiliously.

As soon as each girl washed and dressed in a tunic, she left the ashram to go next door. Within minutes, the place was almost empty when Linda came in to assist me. She answered my questions and directed me through the ceremony of showering, dressing, and marking my body with clay. She explained that nothing belonged to us. Even our bodies were to be used in the service of King. By marking various areas with clay, we were decorating the body in recognition of our true spiritual identity, distinct from the physical body. Linda was very sweet and soft-spoken, and I just went along with it as a part of the experience. It meant nothing to me. I even wore a tunic and head scarf, concealing my true identity as an outsider.

I was then ushered into the adjoining apartment, where all the girls were assembled and reciting "Praise the Name of Righteous King," and so on. I immediately joined in. My goal for the next few hours was, not only to recite Righteous King phrases, but to stay awake during the ritual. It became my goal to meet this challenge. I felt that, if the other girls could function, then I could muster up enough stamina to at least stay awake. Leo called me over to where he was seated, on a large pillow adorned with fringes at each corner, in one corner of the room. He nodded to me as a sign of approval. My life's ambition was going to be redefined by Leo, to please him as a link and liaison to Sir Supreme, the spiritual monarch of the WORKS.

FOOD FOR THOUGHT

SAADYA PRODS, "TELL US ABOUT the spiritual monarch." But then she promptly gets distracted by a cell phone call from Emma. Saadya briefly excuses herself to confirm the next time they will be able to visit while Saadya was still in the area. Emma and Saadya share so much history, having been best friends growing up. Saadya recently flew in to be with Emma to attend her father's funeral. Emma's dad had been loved by the entire community and held in high esteem by all who knew him. He was reciting the "Sh'ma Yisrael"—Hear, O Israel, the Lord Our God is one God," up until taking his last breath on Earth.

"I'll get to Sir Supreme in a bit," I say in response to Saadya's request to hear about the spiritual monarch as she leaves to take the call. In the meantime, I tell Mahlia about the very first morning, and subsequent mornings, after the morning routine—how we all assembled for breakfast sitting on the floor "pretzel style," no chairs, no cushions, and no pillows except for Leo, who was seated on that large embroidered cushion big enough for just one. He was served first, and the girls, including me, sat in two rows facing each other.

Mahlia asks, "What did you eat for breakfast?"

"Cereal."

"Oh, you had a bowl of cereal?"

"Not exactly a bowl," I say.

"Then how did you eat the cereal?"

Not only wasn't it a bowl, it wasn't exactly just cereal. We were served it in empty cartons of milk cut in half, and the cereal was incredibly delicious.

Looking back, if that breakfast hadn't been so engaging, I might not have continued to stay.

"You must be joking!" Mahlia insists.

Since the cereal was so good, and because I hadn't eaten since the afternoon before, it certainly did contribute.

"Well, then, what was so special about it?"

Saadya has just returned and hears me describe it. I was eating cereal made with coconut, dates, and walnuts—it was so good, I was so hungry, I had an appetite, and it was my favorite combination—combined with oatmeal.

Saadya squints, furrows her brow, and quietly asks, "Is that why you like to put raisins and nuts in your gluten-free oatmeal?"

She is concerned. Yet I pull back from the suggestion that, because I like dried fruit and nuts, I still may be under the influence of mind-control.

But no; I like that combination of flavors and textures, so I ate it morning after morning, asked for seconds, ate the seconds, and my weight began to pile on. I ate—or should I say over-ate—breakfast and lunch, and though I was on my feet, walking back and forth in short spurts at the ashram while reciting, and long strides at the San Bernadino Airport while fund-raising, it wasn't enough to burn the calories.

Seeing that this lifestyle was not agreeing with me, I could have left then, but I confided in Belinda, who told me she was sure something could be worked out, and that it was something I needed to talk to Leo about, so I did. He agreed with my idea of eating "live food." I had suggested carrot and celery sticks.

So all the girls were given plastic baggies filled with carrot and celery sticks to take out on soul-saving. I began to limit my intake at breakfast, and I welcomed going to sleep "to rest up" without eating anything after the late afternoon meal. For added exercise, I began to walk fast—if you want to call it that. I, in fact, *darted* from one end of the wooden floor in the ashram to the other end in long, quick spurts while we were gathered first thing in the morning to recite King phrases. This served more than one purpose. It was meant for added exercise, but it also helped to keep me awake.

Saadya points out, "If you can call it being awake. It was more like you were in a stupor."

Mahlia adds, "That's just where they wanted you to be."

Consequently, I was more open to suggestion. I was up, and although slumber was on my brain and in my eyes, my legs were carrying me back and forth and back and forth and back again. But my mind was going in circles.

THE BRANDING IRON

MAHLIA IS STRUGGLING WITH THE PACE with which my story is unfolding. "You sound like you're talking in circles, too." I pause and realize I need to backtrack.

My speech and my mind were not the only things going in circles. I was reciting Righteous King phrases on the loop of an abacus apparatus. My right hand lay in the open side of an abacus board, which displayed a strand of beads strung together on a wire and secured at either end. There was another bead with which we could keep track of how many times we had completed the rod or line on the abacus.

We were to count eighteen times, which took a little over an hour, and we did this every morning. We'd started at 3:00 a.m. at first, recited several lines, gone to morning service, and then returned to the ashram to complete the required number of sequences.

But then, after several months, Leo decided that, in order for us to be out for soul-saving sooner, we should wake up at 2:00 a.m. After that, we finished all eighteen lines and could head out on soul-saving right after breakfast.

Reciting King phrases the first thing so early in the morning as a prescribed activity was the rule. The objective was to be hearing and speaking King phrases and fingering the beads so all our faculties would be fully engaging in activities for King. The importance of reciting King phrases could not be stressed enough. The purpose was for the sound vibration to engulf us in King Awareness, so we would remain steadfast throughout the day. I soon learned that this group of women was on a mission to save souls through daily fundraising. If we gave up or even faltered, we understood our eternity was at stake.

Saadya says, "Reciting was more like a branding iron used with the intention of leaving a mark on your brain."

Then, with little hesitation, Mahlia says, "Yeah, with the mark of the cult."

FACE ON THE MILK CARTON

Saadya exclaims, "Mom, wow—sleeping on the floor with no furniture, just the basics, like eating out of a cut-down milk carton, captured you?" She didn't expect to be hearing this because she had left the room. "You ate cereal out of a milk carton. That makes you the face on the milk carton!"

I bring us back to the point. "I was more than the face on the milk carton. I was the whole heart, mind, body, and soul."

"And *face* on the milk carton." Mahlia won't let go. Unlike the 1995 made-for-T.V. *Lifetime* movie *The Face on the Milk Carton*, my parents knew where I was. I was up front about that almost from the beginning. Only they couldn't get me or get to me. Saadya brings us back to the original question: "How did eating out of a milk carton, while sitting on a floor in an apartment with no furniture, win you over?"

It wasn't the milk carton. Remember, it was what was *in* the milk carton, and then both Mahlia and Saadya chide, "The very delicious cereal."

Saadya continues, "With dates, coconut, and walnuts."

I have to agree; it sounds pretty ludicrous.

Mahlia musters up some support, offering, "It reminds me of Jacob and Esau, when Esau sold his birthright and blessing for a bowl of stew."

"Maybe it was a milk carton of stew!" Saadya says and throws one more jab: "Mom, you *were* the face on the milk carton!"

It still intrigues me to retrace the steps it took to get me, a non-partisan observer, a skeptic, an outsider, to get to the point these girls at the ashram were at, to feel as they did, to behave in the same manner, and ultimately to feel cohesion with the women's soul-saving group, until it felt like I belonged. All of the activity and behavior I saw was explained to me according to the King Service philosophy.

And then it started to make perfectly good sense to me. My conversion was consistent with conformity within the solidarity that defined the group. I understood why the girls recited so fervently, never addressed each other by their first names without first saying, "Sister," "Lady," or "Premier," and had to ask permission for second helpings on food, as well as for almost everything else.

As time went on, and it did, so did I. I went along, accepting more of the lifestyle abandoning my skepticism and cynicism. I could adopt that seemingly peculiar behavior. Once I understood the rationale behind it, it no longer seemed peculiar. "But didn't you realize that the worst thing to do was to participate and cooperate?" Mahlia asks.

It seemed innocent enough, as part of the adventure, at first.

THE FAST FORWARD

THAT FIRST WEEK I STAYED at the ashram, I was left in the company of Linda, who took care of the upkeep of the ashram, while the other girls went out to fund-raise. One mid-morning, I unfolded my sleeping bag and lay down for rest. I felt physically and emotionally exhausted. With the thought of sleep on my mind, I sprawled out on my back in my sleeping bag on the floor. My nervous system was too over-stimulated, my mind too engaged, to actually fall asleep. Rather, visions began to appear in my mind's eye in accord with the ideological input I had been receiving over the past forty-eight hours. I watched with horror as the vision of the face of a young person grew old speedily. It was my face, and right before me I could see the skin wrinkle up.

I watched with revulsion as the skin began to sag. It happened so fast. This was in accordance with all I had been hearing about how fleeting and temporary is this physical existence of a mere eighty to ninety years, and how this span of time was so insignificant in relation to all eternity.

Mahlia shakes her head. "Sounds like you were in a time machine going on fast forward."

Saadya reflects, "It sounds gross, Mom, getting old so fast, but we do have something to look forward to that is better than here." All I can think of to say is, "I hope to God that's true."

"It is," she says. "Go on, Mom." I did not awake feeling refreshed. Rather, when I rose I felt dizzy, groggy, confused, and unsure of myself. I decided to go for a bicycle ride. I rode around Barstow that afternoon, thinking about the previous two days. I could see and feel all the ugliness I had been hearing at the Center about the physical world. I even agreed that the ugliness in the physical world being spoken of existed.

Saadya off-handedly remarks, "They messed with your mind."

Yes; but the more I rode around, the more the distinct demarcation between life in, and outside, the physical world began to disintegrate for me. I understood what they were saying at the Center about frustration through trying to satisfy the soul with material things, yet the WORKS was not for me. The grip on me had slackened.

I felt sure about my decision. I could breathe easily, and rode back to the Center to change into my jeans and out of the long skirt I was wearing. I cracked open the door of the apartment we recited phrases in, and slid the skirt across the floor into a corner. I closed the door and turned to leave. Linda, the girl who had helped me the very first morning, appeared at the door. She sweetly asked where I was going. I told her that I decided that this wasn't for me, and that I was leaving. She said she wanted to show me something, and that it would only take a minute. I followed her into the apartment and sat down on the bare wooden floor beside her.

That minute cost me three years.

I watched as she opened a Superior Text book and turned to a brightly colored picture of a staircase as she explained the choice I had to make in life.

I listened to her and looked at the picture while she went on to impress upon me the monumental scope and benefit of being King-minded. I could either choose the path toward spiritual enlightenment or be doomed to a life filled with greed, lust, anger, and envy, all viewed, accurately, as ungodly qualities. She informed me that, now that I had this knowledge about the true purpose of life, if I chose to do anything less than follow the spiritual path which existed only within the WORKS, I would be going backward on the spiritual path and would descend into an ungodly existence, doomed forever in the vicious cycle of birth and death, never to reach the kingdom of God.

Saadya asks, "Was *she* believing this?"

She was; I didn't, but it lured me back enough that I lost heart. It paralyzed me so, that I did not stand my ground and follow through with my decision to leave. Linda then asked me to just hang around until Leo got back. When he returned, he spoke convincingly for me not to feel as if I had to make a long-term decision, but to just take one day at a time. This compromise once again left me vulnerable to the clutches of coercive persuasion.

REFLECTION IN THE MIRROR

"DOES THIS HAVE SOMETHING TO DO with when you were a little girl and got scared of dying?" Mahlia has remembered me telling her a story about myself as a child, and asks me about it again. I repeat the scenario.

I would stand in the bathroom, looking into the mirror, and stare at my reflection while contemplating death or non-existence. By remaining fixated in front of the mirror, I would scare myself silly. I would cry hysterically to my mother. As I ran out of the bathroom, I was saying, "I'm *afraid* to die" or "I don't *want* to die." I remember catching her off guard this one time and her frantically asking where I had been. She asked my three brothers if they knew, in her attempt to understand my hysteria. Then she cradled me in her arms. However, her only offer of reassurance amounted to telling me that I had a long life ahead of me. It would calm me down temporarily, but the fear resurfaced and bubbled up the next time I stared at myself in that mirror. Living for eternity with God was a welcomed alternative to nothingness.

Although I was not cognizant of it then, being King-minded was the only solution I was ever offered to my childhood fear of death.

Saadya notifies me of John 3:16. "Mom, you know in the Bible we are told, 'For God so loved the world that He sent His one and only son, whosoever believes in Him, shall not perish but have everlasting life.'"

Instead of someone quoting bible verses, Linda spoke of how King fulfills all our desires, and how, since I was a writer, I could probably do some book editing. Then she brought to my attention how joyful I felt singing and dancing at the Center.

I remained awhile longer, feeling attracted to an opportunity to work on book editing, and I did enjoy the singing and dancing. So that night, when Leo spoke to me about not feeling I had to commit myself but should just take one day at a time, I considered this request and concluded it was harmless enough, not at all understanding the ramifications of what he was asking of me. I figured I had nothing to be apprehensive about.

If I wanted to leave, I was sure I was strong-willed enough that, having once made up my mind, nothing Leo could say would change it.

"Mom, that is just like you," Mahlia exclaims. "You're strong-willed and strong-minded. But not after *they* got through with you."

I could not know then what would happen to my mind. I could not know then that the outcome of my decision to agree to Leo's request, which seemed innocent enough, would keep me for three years in the WORKS. I was loyal, diligent, and dutiful to Leo as my immediate authority, to any of the other delegated girls in authority, and to the

WORKS soul-saving activities that kept the funds flowing in.

Mahlia is perturbed. "Mom, you were up against a behemoth and didn't recognize the curve ball being thrown at you, how Leo had the ulterior motive of preventing you from skipping out."

THE MISSION

As THE DAYS WORE ON, I would have to overlook many of the practices I was observing because they contradicted what I was led to believe about this group of people. There were discrepancies between why I thought I was there, based on my initial and very personal motives, and what I was seeing as the practical application being reflected in the lifestyle.

"You just thought you were making a simple sacrifice—not eating too much, not questioning authority," says Saadya, and Mahlia adds,

"But you weren't getting the bigger picture of what was happening."

Leo mitigated the personal sacrifice of austerity we needed to make in comparison to the benefit, not only to me, but to all my family members, generations past and in the future, would get. Leo had us convinced that our soul-saving service would guarantee us a place in the spiritual world. The harder I worked, the quicker and more expedient my purification. And now I was responsible for the spiritual outcome of my entire family. They too could be freed from the horrendous inevitability of taking on repeated lower life forms.

In the beginning, all I had to do was reconcile myself to staying one day at a time. Once I started going out on soul-saving and following the schedule like the others, I became like them. The challenge of the austerity became evident to me. This was not a life of simply reciting and dancing, as it had been presented to me at first. Actually, after only one full week, I was already being convinced of the ideas I was being indoctrinated in. Fitting in meant being like the other girls, and that meant hard work with little rest. But it was all supposed to be worth it.

Saadya nods. "You were trapped with no escape hatch."

Mahlia is sipping on some chocolate soy milk. Between sips she is struggling to grasp all of what I have been speaking about. "So the harsh lifestyle was balanced out with what?"

All of it was harsh, but it was also considered fun and possessed the element of excitement and adventure.

Mahlia probes some more. "How did you spend the days?"

Soul-saving was the only activity sanctioned wholly—that of fund-raising and gifting books. In fact, soul-saving was referred to as "book gifting."

Foremost, soul-saving was regarded as the highest service. Any other service threatened the worker to likely fall under the influence of physical energy. Additionally, soul-saving activity would protect us from the spell of the physical energy.

"So even fund-raising was spiritual," says Mahlia. "I am not asking you, I am telling you."

Engaging in soul-saving activity was a guarantee that we would return to the spiritual Kingdom. It was a sure-fire way of spending eternity with King.

Consequently, I was led to believe, in no uncertain terms, that I would be doomed if I maintained any attachment to my physical body. Under this category were included family, friends, memories, and any pleasure derived from the senses other than those sanctioned as "transcendental" pleasures of a higher nature. These included eating holy food, resting up, smelling flowers or incense offered to the carved figures, reciting the King phrases, as well as dancing and singing as worship to King. Having any other attachments would make it impossible, I was given to understand, to leave this world behind at the time of death.

"Ignoring family and friends, and negating your relationships, is not really all that spiritual," Saadya declares.

The point is that the mission, as it was presented, superseded our mundane attachments, and that meant the things we can see, touch, and smell. So cloaked in the guise of spirituality, the mission in the WORKS required us to dismiss people on the outside, even family and friends.

THE GUARANTEE

FURTHERMORE, SOUL-SAVING WAS MADE to be exciting and adventurous. Some of the funniest things happened as a result of our soul-saving antics, some of which are actually painful to remember, considering the conditions under which they occurred. Those efforts exemplify how there was nothing I would not do to advance the mission, nor was there any austerity I would not endure. There was simply no time allotted or allowed for thinking about what was being asked of us. We were only to follow the program.

Although, at the beginning, Leo presented spending time at the Center as light-hearted, there was another aspect that was downplayed. I was not to be left alone. Even after the first night, when I returned to my cousin Arlene's apartment to retrieve my belongings, Leo accompanied me and provided commentary about the worthlessness of playing tennis, which is what Arlene was going to do when we left. Being in the WORKS soon became a serious matter. "So how did you become such a willing a participant in the process?" Mahlia asks.

As a matter of course, I was being systematically indoctrinated, and there was no opportunity to step back from it to process the information anywhere apart from the ashram.

An analogy was frequently used to cultivate our docility toward and trust in the leadership—and the leadership was anyone in authority according to the hierarchy.

Mahlia asks for an example. "For instance," I say, "just as we follow a road map to reach our destination that takes us from one point to the next, as a WORKS agent, I was to follow the process being laid out, by complying with instructions." This process guaranteed to take me right out of this miserable physical world.

Thus, by taking one step towards purification at a time, I would reach the ultimate destination—God's kingdom. The only caveat was that I needed to be purified, and the WORKS was there for this purpose.

Mahlia contorts her face. "Ridiculous!"

KING OF THE JUNGLE

AFTER REGAINING HER COMPOSURE, Mahlia inquires, "Who was this character Leo, anyway?"

Meeting her gaze, I realize she has in fact posed a question, and now both she and Saadya are expecting a reply.

In short, Leo, whose name suggests "king of the jungle," was the fund-raising leader of the women's soul-saving group. It was his service to Sir Supreme, the spiritual monarch of the World Organization for Righteous King Service (WORKS), to be the person who would oversee all the activities of the women's soul-saving group. In the beginning, when the group was first organized, Leo saw to it that the vans were properly loaded and the girls assigned to various locations throughout the San Bernadino area. As the months wore on and the group began to grow in number, Leo began to interpret what King Service meant and how we were to be trained. He defined, over time, how we were to be effective, and what it would take on his part to make us effective on soul-saving activity.

Mahlia facetiously declares, "In his eyes, your effectiveness was based on how much money was collected."

"And you all did just what you were told to when it came to Leo," Saadya adds.

SUBSERVIENCE

LEO HAD A WAY OF MAKING us all function as a unit. The women directed all their queries toward him. It was understood that he should be served first, and served the best, at mealtimes. For example, his plate for holy food was stainless steel and always adorned with fresh flowers. More importantly, Leo was the only male we could speak to. I was told never to make eye contact with any of the other men at the Center. I had to fix my gaze on the ground and keep my head completely covered in their presence. It was a common practice for one girl to reach over to another and secure her head scarf to cover her hair completely and as a friendly reminder to avoid eye contact with the men at the Center, even incidentally.

However, we *could* make eye contact with Leo. Leo grew to be a friend and confidante, to an extent—yet we did not venture to *complain* to Leo, or we would be reminded how fallen we were and how much we needed to submit even more.

Having to thus revere Leo, the man in charge, was so distasteful at first. Nevertheless, I wanted to be a worker, and I wanted to recite Righteous King, because I wanted to make spiritual advancement. Although I could see how the other girls were being oppressed, I did not accept their submission as my own behavior. Yet in order for me to feel a part of the women's group, I too had to submit.

I fought against this blind submission until it occurred to me that to submit was what it meant for me to be a worker. I was told that I was as yet too impure to serve God or the supreme personality, so that, by serving my immediate authority, Leo, I would acquire humility and transcend my false ego. Then and only then I could expect to approach Sir Supreme, the supreme personality of the WORKS. He was a pure being and the mediator between workers and King (God).

By yielding to the authority, we were yielding to King's representative. The objective was for us to make the logical transference on our own. But by the time this logic of surrendering through submission to authority became mandatory, we were already so engulfed in the flames that, instead of realizing we were being consumed by the fire, we accepted it as a life-line out of the consuming fire of the physical world.

"Surrender meant you had to fund-raise. In other words, you had to earn your keep," Mahlia offers. And then some. . .but I didn't know it then.

I questioned and questioned, and all my questions were answered until one day I no longer asked them. I could figure out the answers for myself, since I was becoming indoctrinated. Before long, I was quoting Malayo-Polynesian verses I had memorized. During the first week, I remained at the ashram while the other girls went out to the airport to fund-raise.

Saadya spontaneously asks, "Doing what?"

I spent my time cleaning up after the breakfast, sweeping and washing the floors, reading, reciting King phrases, and trying to get "extra rest." We never went to sleep, because that would be selfish. Rather, the agents only "rested up" for service to the spiritual monarch, Sir Supreme. Rest was only necessary so we could continue going out on soul-saving activity to further the mission.

AT ALL COSTS

JUST REMEMBER THAT, I THOUGHT, I was just checking things out. I was not thinking I would be making any type of commitment. For the first week, everything was new to me. I was bombarded by novel, exciting sounds, smells, and sights. I was made to feel comfortable in the midst of the other workers. I was made to feel accepted, that I belonged, so much so that there was no place else for me. That first week felt like summer camp. All the girls seemed so happy and carefree. It was fun sleeping on the bare wooden floor and rising at 3:00 a.m., and by 6:00 a.m. we had been dancing and singing and hearing Superior Text class all that time. I was being implanted with an intense affiliation solely with the World Organization for Righteous King Service. Being ingrained within the recesses of my mind was the WORKS' requirement of service to King, in order to make spiritual advancement. This placed me in the hands, and at the mercy, of the leadership of the Center. I was being trained to regard myself as a humble servant of God as an agent in the WORKS.

Initially, the overall excitement and the supercharged atmosphere infused my very being. This, along with the constant bombardment of persuasion, led me to such foolishness during that first week.

It was important to me to be able to make a statement and a difference in the world. Instead, at that point in my life, my aspiration for sincerity was exploited and violated. It manifested itself in a deviation—as defined by the dogma and ideology in the WORKS Barstow Center. Seeking truth instead morphed into obligation and dutiful affiliation. Along with the other group members whom I was in constant company with, my aspirations were supplanted with austerity. I was constantly reminded of the group's doctrine, and my compliance with it obligated me to its precepts of surrender, self-effacement, self-sacrifice, austerity, and cooperation with the hierarchical network of authority and rigid adherence to the rituals, routines, and rigor inherent in the lifestyle.

I was primed and armed with analogies and clichés that were initially used on me to align my faith, so that I would subscribe to the exclusiveness that the WORKS claimed on righteousness and real religiosity. Now that I was no longer ignorant to the truth, to reject it would be offensive to the spiritual monarch. Since affiliation to the WORKS somehow bonded me supernaturally with Sir Supreme, leaving would be slapping him in the face, and I would be destined to an ungodly existence in the physical world. It would be a huge mistake to separate myself from God. In King Service, I could affirm my true spiritual identity. If I ventured to deviate from any of the lifestyle programs, or withdrew from the leadership, even if they were self-proclaimed, it would be no different from disavowing the all-knowing supreme personality of God.

All the analogies and thought-terminating clichés were bantered around among the workers during times of doubt, to instill an affirmation of loyalty and faith in the process. What actually resulted was a deflation of my desire for distinctiveness. I was taught to desire conformity, and to develop humility and anonymity. My ability to be a questioning and critical thinker grew narrow as I accepted the group's activities and behaviors. I could accept the behaviors at the Center and on soul-saving because the infallibility of the group's doctrine justified them. The WORKS offered refuge from the physical world outside, distracting us from God. Simply put, the world outside the WORKS was a godless realm, with no exceptions. For this reason, it had to be shunned and avoided at all costs.

NO HOLDS BARRED

"SO WHAT WAS REALITY LIKE at the Center?" Mahlia asks.

Across the board, our day at the Center began with reciting Righteous King phrases. It went something like, "Praise the name of King, Let the name of King be praised, the name of King is praised." By reciting these King phrases repeatedly as part of our morning program, we were supposed to be focusing our minds on King. In reality, the process was short-circuiting my mind. The entire morning program also included a class based on the Superior Text, the old-world verse recited line for line and repeated by the workers. I sat through Superior Text class, which in itself was metaphysically stimulating. In each session, the worker read and repeated the verse, which was interpreted by one of the men teaching the class that morning. Each class was about the importance of our soul-saving activities and meant to imbue us with a sense of omniscience, feelings of superiority, and distinctiveness from the "regulars," saturating us with a sense of obligation.

Saadya picks up on this unfamiliar use of the word "regular." I explain that a regular was any person outside of the WORKS. Any person who did not recite King phrases was in spiritual darkness about who King was. Saadya simply states, "A regular was someone who had to give you money."

All in all, as a recipient, and participant in this elevated discourse, I was obliged to engage as many regulars as I could in the clandestine mission of spreading King Service and love of God on behalf of the beloved spiritual monarch, Sir Supreme.

Both my daughters questioningly glance up and off to the side. "When do we find out about Sir Supreme?" I promise I will tell you about Sir Supreme later.

There I remained, an individual, unbarred yet held captive by all I saw, heard, smelled, and everything else that engulfed me, overwhelming me with the suggestiveness of divinity it was intended to. No holds were barred when it came to what would keep me there. Everything was just so much fun, and wholesome fun at that, at first—sensations I could only appreciate the more I allowed myself to, as I continued to follow along with the routine.

Mahlia gasps, "24/7!" She's distracted by a call from her husband.

In other words, if I surrendered all my doubts of all that was dubious, I would be successful in making spiritual advancement. I was holding steadfast and thinking critically, yet I came to accept everything within weeks.

"How exactly did that happen?" Saadya asks.

One morning, Denise, one of the girls already in the WORKS for several years, suggested that I drop my defenses and give the program a chance for an entire week. By then, if I wasn't satisfied with the results,

I could leave. And I, right in the main room, in front of the carved figures, dropped to my knees, bowed my head, and offered my humility to Sir Supreme, the spiritual monarch.

"What in the world is 'offering humility'?" Saadya asks.

I hadn't immediately realized that these words would be foreign to her and would need an explanation. They were foreign to me also at first. However, I soon learned the lingo, and definitely understood that I was to prostrate myself by dropping to my knees, bowing my head, and uttering words of respect to my spiritual monarch. "Why the spiritual monarch?" asks Saadya. Without him, I wouldn't know about King and how service to him would guarantee me a place in his kingdom. Besides, he was the link that connected us to the higher things of King.

"I am starting to see a pattern here," Saadya tells me. She recognizes WORKS as a cult.

While Saadya is right, I didn't know it then. I also didn't know about group reform. When physically part of a group, yet emotionally and ideologically removed from it until I "changed" and adopted its standards, I would never be supported as an individual or accepted into the group. Once I identified as a member, I was incapacitated to resist the onslaught of thought reform. Instead, the group is the agent of thought reform and the conveyor of the message.[1]

SLEEP TIGHT

MY DILEMMA WAS THAT, in order to benefit, I would need to submit. Mahlia returns and says, "And as a result you actually succumbed."

Then Saadya summarizes, "You went to the Wednesday dinner, and what was being preached resonated with you."

Basically, it was a combination of the philosophy and the lifestyle.

---

1. Robert J. Lifton. (1986) *Thought Reform and the Psychology of Totalism.* Chapel Hill, NC: The University of North Carolina Press, p. 12.

When I first met the workers at the Barstow Center, I reconciled myself to taking one day at a time. Hence, I remained at the ashram, performing as a member of the Barstow Women's Soul-Saving Group or Book-Gifting Group, as we were known.

Saadya declares in no uncertain terms, "Mom, you were panhandling." Not if we had anything to say about it. We were missionaries, agents on a mission who fund-raised to collect money and pass out literature.

After a little over a year, the soul-saving group had grown from ten to twenty women, as girls came from Centers throughout the Organization, including Denver, Boulder, Sacramento, Canada, and New Zealand. For this reason, ladies' groups were beginning to form throughout WORKS, fashioned after the Barstow group, which was really an extension of Leo and his mentality. Due to the growing number of us, the Center had purchased a house only two doors down from the worship Center on Fredericks Street. We moved in at a time when the girls were getting physically sick, in growing numbers, one after another. This was because we were living in such close quarters.

We all slept in the same room and ate in one of the ashram apartments where half the girls "rested up." Viral infections were rampant in the ashram, and one after another, the women were falling ill with stomach and intestinal ailments. One group had returned from the Philippines one of the first weeks I was at the Center. Several girls remained in their sleeping bags on the floor for days on end, and it is possible they had Hepatitis A, because years later, antibodies showed up on my blood work indicating I had been exposed, although I never had symptoms.

A JELL-O MOLD MENTALITY

AFTER I TOOK DENISE'S ADVICE ABOUT DROPPING MY DEFENSES, I found shelter in the promise of peace of mind and comfort from the growing doubts that had plagued me previously. Once I had dropped to my knees, tears welled up in my eyes as my heart opened, and what I perceived as a river of pure love seemed to flow through me. "That's what you were led to believe would happen," Saadya asserts. Since I had never experienced that before, I began to accept that my staying was okay, and that I should trust in the spiritual monarch the way the others did. I had had no conception of a spiritual monarch before meeting the agents. At the Center, the importance of having Sir Supreme as a spiritual monarch was heavily preached. My loyalty to his mission would ensure my spiritual advancement. I needed him. Mahlia says, "More like he needed you."

As a matter of fact, that's not how he was portrayed. Sir Supreme was regarded with affection and reverence. Every word attributed to him was regarded as gospel and accepted on blind faith by the agents. That morning, bowed before the carved figures, I had my first experience of my mind shifting into the WORKS frame of mind. My heart softened, and from that time on I was convinced that I had had a spiritual experience. Hence, I understood why I needed to follow the dictates of my authority. I trusted in them. I would recall this experience whenever my allegiance began to waver.

"But, Mom," Mahlia says, "I am straining to grasp the events you're describing. I know the very central scripture in the Bible tells us—we are not to trust in man, but only in God."

Saadya begins reading aloud from Psalm 118:8: "'It is better to take refuge in the Lord than to trust in man.'"

"Trusting in the Center authority was equated with trusting in God," I reply.

I soon started identifying as a worker, actually on the very first day I was sent to the San Bernadino Airport to fund-raise. My identification as a worker was reinforced by simply telling people I approached that I was with King Service. I had the opportunity, that very first day, to preach about King Awareness just as it had been preached to me. I no longer felt doubtful or felt the intense need to question and judge the philosophy and the lifestyle. Going out on soul-saving was all part of the indoctrination to secure and reinforce all I had been hearing at the Center. Out on soul-saving, I viewed the regulars as leading a sub-standard existence, racing around trying to find some sense of satisfaction by indulging their senses. As fallen souls, they were to be pitied and needed to be saved by our soul-saving activities. If the regular gave a donation, it was considered service to King, and they would automatically make spiritual advancement even without knowing it.

Qualities to be admired and aspired to for spiritual advancement came under the heading of *surrender*. The entire process of surrender culminated in fervent reciting, acceptance of the mission, and a pledge of humility. There was no time to stop and consider the *effect* of total surrender. I just needed to keep surrendering. The benefits reaped through my painstaking efforts made remaining in the ashram a worthwhile endeavor.

"So you are using some type of a spiritual reward as an excuse for not leaving," notes Saadya. Kind of, but it goes deeper. I was not capable of leaving.

Remember what I told you about group reform? Mahlia replies, "It's like peer pressure, and you had to go along as part of the group." I couldn't think in any other way. My mind had been reconstructed, molded, and shaped according to the dogma.

Saadya quips, "Like into a Jell-O mold mentality."

FATAL ATTRACTION

ONE AFTERNOON AT THE SAN BERNADINO AIRPORT, I stopped at a newsstand to read an article in Newsweek about the CAUSE. I had heard about it, but only cursorily. Whatever I'd heard hadn't been favorable, except for one morning, when Leo gave us a lecture on how hard the members of the Church for All United Souls Eternal—*Causers,* they were known as—worked by going round the clock on marathon drives to get more recruits. The point of his harangue was to make us enthusiastic to work harder and try harder at our own soul-saving activities. We were made to feel we were competing with the CAUSE, and that we owed it to each regular we came in contact with not to be tricked into giving a donation to a Causer, which wouldn't really benefit them since they would be giving to a spiritual imposter. In contrast, we knew the WORKS was the real deal. It was the workers' moral obligation, therefore, to work as hard as we could to get a regular to give a donation to King.

The real message behind Leo's lecture that morning was that, if the members of the CAUSE were working so hard, how much harder should we work—we who were working for the true cause, the mission of our spiritual monarch, God's real representative. "Yikes!" Saadya exclaims.

I couldn't understand how and why the people involved in the CAUSE would allow themselves to be deceived. I didn't suspect in the least that the very same techniques that were used on the recruits in the CAUSE were being used on me in the WORKS. I actually thought that I was clever enough not to have gotten involved in anything like the CAUSE. However, I realize now, that I could've just as easily, if I had gone over to the CAUSE house in San Bernadino.

The initial attraction is what makes any person available to the cult's recruitment techniques. Then the potential recruit remains an outsider looking in until the person adapts to the lifestyle just for the experience, as I did. Taking all the whys and wherefores into consideration, on examination and with careful scrutiny I can understand that this is exactly what happened with me. No one can say with certainty that they would remain immune to the internal system within the confines of the cult's all-encompassing structure. The inherent features of the WORKS that attracted me were already imbued in my leanings. I had been learning about New Age spirituality while in college, and was a practicing vegetarian.

I wrote the following upon reflection of what transpired for me.

Daily the sun rises, daily it sets; this is one thing of which we can be sure and we endure. Each sunrise and setting marks another day, forewarning and foreboding what may be in store, revealing and exposing the unexpected. Disillusioned in my attempt to give meaning overt to the subtlety that surrounds me, never to relinquish my faith, all of which serves to whet my appetite. Reality created, emotions were labeled as if they really knew, unless I dared to face death in dark despair. Reach out to be touched, reach out to be loved all the while reaching out in His love, seeking Him is my new reality, now determined by my outlook, from an inner vision. Memories fade, replaced at intervals by remembering events that no longer exist; I cling to the hope that, just as we spoke, there will be more. The false reality, too, passes, yet, alighted from within, I find myself subject to His warmth and tenderness, leading me to conclude His reality is endless, eternal, with much more in store, so, fearless and in His presence, I persevere.

THE SIGNAL

NOW SAADYA WANTS TO KNOW, "How did this Leo get the girls moving in the morning? What was the signal? Did the alarm go off to Z-100 or your favorite classical music station?"

I couldn't say that exactly, couldn't even say it subtly. We didn't listen to the radio, and we didn't watch television. The signal at the ashram came at first as Leo started reciting Righteous King phrases and walked among us while we were still lying on the floor, asleep.

When it was time, Leo would walk between the two ashram rooms when we were in the apartment dwelling, reciting the King phrases aloud until all the girls got up and began rolling up their sleeping bags.

Saadya asks, "How did so many of you manage in such tight quarters?"

There were twelve of us at first, but there were no beds, and there was no furniture, only bodies lying horizontally in two rows on the floor in the front room in each of the adjoining apartments.

The apartments were actually one-bedroom apartments with a kitchen and bathroom and one big living room where we laid out our sleeping bags. I had one from my travels across country in the Volkswagen minibus. Months later, a down feather sleeping bag was purchased for me, which took up less space, and which most likely was Leo's motivation for getting it rather than for my comfort, because soon afterwards I was sent out on traveling soul-saving (TSS) in an Econoline van with five other girls.

Nevertheless, I was flattered that a good-quality sleeping bag had been bought for me. The sleeping bags did not touch, except when we were traveling in the van. Then we had no choice, but this did not bother anyone. We would be so tired and appreciative for the opportunity to "pop out."

Ordinarily when we woke up at the ashram—Saadya is quick to remind me, "You mean 'popped up'," remembering how I described the girls behavior the very first morning. Visibly touched, she says, "Oh, my. Go on." We rolled up the sleeping bags and piled them one on top of the other in the back room closet, first come first serve; whoever got there first would lay the sleeping bag on top of the ones already on the pile. Some of us would hitch our bag onto the top shelf if we could reach it.

NOT TOO POOPED TO POP

LEO MADE MENTION, ON ONE OCCASION when he was deriding all of us for not being sincere when we recited our Righteous King lines early in the morning, that he was particularly annoyed that we were giving into sleep, claiming that if we fell asleep it was from making a conscious decision to fall asleep. He said that some of us were falling asleep even as we darted back and forth. I thought he was alluding to me, and it embarrassed me. I felt he was turning the spotlight on me, and I didn't like it. I reasoned I was not the only one. But deep down I knew, and the embarrassment lingered uncomfortably. I decided, as I was supposed to due to the derision and the underlying purpose it was intended to serve, to be awake and alert during the morning routine.

The phrase "pop up" was being used formally, and before lying down, actually more like when I was rolling out my sleeping bag, I would resign myself to "pop up" once the signal was given. I was a morning person, so I was predisposed to do so. Once I heard the signal, I did exactly that.

"I get it," Saadya says. "You either popped up or popped out."

Mahlia chuckles, "That's my mom, not too pooped to pop!"

Besides that, I think I woke up quickly because I rationalized that I was going to have to get up, so just do it right away rather than lament over having to. And so, that is exactly what I began to do, which gained me recognition. It also earned me the responsibility of making sure the other girls were following through in a timely manner when the signal was given to begin the early-morning routine. All the girls congregated in the same room to recite the Righteous King phrases, individually yet together but not in unison. It created a humming sound, which was supposed to be the sound of heaven.

Mahlia wonders, "Is that when you would begin to pace?"

FLOUNDER

THAT WAS IN THE BEGINNING, when the objective was to stay awake while reciting. As time wore on, my system acclimated. However, whenever that still-small voice broke through and got my attention, on my own, it was virtually impossible to leave the Center. When it occurred to me that I might want to, I was encouraged to reveal my mind to another worker, usually one in charge. We were told, and we told each other, that if we were to leave, we would be like a fish out of water. I would flounder pathetically and, like the fish, could not survive. In this way, my integrity was mitigated, my judgment diluted, my desire dissipated. I became even more dependent on the WORKS. Our dependence on each other was based on us never wanting to deviate from Center regulations, and instead tolerating any mental and physical austerity for the sake of the communal obligation.

I was inextricably entangled.

"Without a doubt—and I'm amazed at how you were able to maintain yourself for so long!" Mahlia tells me.

It was very difficult for me in the beginning. I was attracted to the ideals and ideology, but I was not comfortable with the hierarchy of authority to which I had to yield. I learned from the other girls who served as role models for my behavior. I observed how they behaved in the morning, in the ashram and at the Center. I observed how they behaved around men at the Center. There was even a code of behavior for the way the girls behaved toward each other. To avoid familiarity, we often addressed each other with a title to hold each other in a place of esteem.

Saadya astutely surmises, "I bet you referred to each other as Sister." We understood that, in such close quarters, familiarity breeds contempt, as Leo said, so we remained respectful by referring to each other as Lady Suzanne, Sister Kaylah, or Leo Premier, using one of those titles with whomever we addressed, and were referred to in this way by whoever addressed us. The only exception was Leo, who also called us by our Center-given name. Mine was Chana, meaning "favored by God."

"Lady Chana," Mahlia announces.

I nod, lifting my eyebrows, and offer a half-smile.

In fact, I was told to watch the other girls in order to learn humility, and especially to see how I should behave towards Leo, whom I came to know as the man in charge.

SIR SUPREME

ASSUREDLY SKEPTICAL OF THIS WORLD of the WORKS I am revealing, Mahlia reminds me, "You were going to tell us about Sir Supreme."

I had at first only read about Sir Supreme at the book table when I went to the Wednesday event. But after a while I kept hearing his name. I had known my aunt and uncle on my father's side followed a spiritual master from India who had a following in Philadelphia, where my relatives lived and I went to college. Once, when I went to visit them, I heard him give a lecture, but I was not impressed. I couldn't understand why my relatives were. Somewhere along the line at the onset of my stay at the WORKS Center, I had made the analogy between them having a spiritual master and the WORKS having a spiritual monarch, named Sir Supreme, whom the agents in the WORKS followed. Sir Supreme said we should recite Righteous King phrases. We should work through a selfless service to prove dedication and loyalty. I was thus inculcated to feel guilty of ever having any private thoughts about resuming my life outside the WORKS. Any thoughts, doubts, or suspicions were considered to be an offense against the spiritual monarch.

We had to constantly be on guard against any thoughts that might jeopardize our spiritual advancement. This was how we should pursue purification. By remaining in the WORKS, I was bound to the spiritual monarch who would usher me into the realm of spiritual bliss. I aspired to a standard in which I had to function apart from the cultural norm. Thus, we were not subject to the same laws as people outside the WORKS. In other words, agents were not subject to laws of the land.

Saadya asks, "Such as?"

For instance, when driving, we could go as fast as we wanted to, as long as we didn't get caught. According to Leo, it was better to drive fast, so we would get out on soul-saving sooner. Clarke, the Center president, announced to the contrary on several occasions that we were ruining the vans by not allowing enough time for the engines to warm up. According to Clarke, in the long run, we would be saving Sir Supreme money, even if we get out on soul-saving a few minutes later.

Because we were workers, the same standards of conduct of society did not apply to us.

We were untouchable. Nothing could stop us. We executed all our activities with calculated deliberateness to carry out the mission of soul-saving. We were above the level of physical energy. We didn't sleep in excess. We didn't eat in excess, and in fact we did not eat a dinner meal at all. Our last meal was the afternoon meal, which we ate closer to 2:00 p.m. And the only purpose of sleep was to rest from the day's activities. I was told that we rarely dreamed because we didn't enter that level of sleep in which dreams occur. If any of us dreamed about Sir Supreme, soul-saving, or even King, it was supposed to have really happened in the spiritual realm. Some of the girls talked about having had a dream the night before, and it was considered as if she had actually had the experience.

Mahlia notes, "That's so awkward."

NO TURNING BACK

IT WAS A COMBINATION OF WHAT WAS ATTRACTIVE in the group and what was made unattractive for me outside the group. Life on the outside would have been one big disappointment and disillusionment. I heard only heartache, heartbreak, misery, and suffering existed in the world beyond the border of the WORKS. Yet inside the WORKS, I could expect to only recite, dance in ecstasy, pass out some books, and my life would be perfect. Whenever things became any more complicated than that, I would be reminded that Sir Supreme only wanted us to "recite and be happy." This was meant to ease the tension. What it did was influence me, initially, in making a psychological transition between these two worlds. Further on, reinforcement of this perspective emphasizing the positive aspect of the lifestyle downplayed its harshness.

Three years later, I wrote this about the lifestyle:

Say King phrases. Be happy and recite, Soul-saving, the ultimate! Follow the program, don't deviate. Just surrender. What else is there to do? Take meals, take rest. We are not this body, we are spirit soul. Go home, back to King. Don't feel your separation. Recite, surrender, and obey as your ticket back home. Follow the process of hearing and reciting; you are an impure soul. Surrender, obey, don't deviate, heard repeatedly each day, till hearer becomes speaker, becomes repeater each day. Worship King to break the inevitable cycle of birth and death. The flowers, incense, different tastes, and foreign scents, with no time to waste, an upset pineal gland, enthusiastic perpetuation of the process. We forget why we are there. Garbed in scarf and tunic, I stop asking, "What am I doing here?"

DESTINATION

LET ME FURTHER EXPLAIN, I tell Mahlia. I pause briefly, waiting for Saadya, who has just left the kitchen to take a quick phone call.

I can tell that Saadya cuts the call short to rejoin the conversation. The road map analogy I told you about was frequently used to cultivate our docility. That meant complying, cooperating, engaging, and participating in what the others were doing. I did so because it was the road map that would lead me to my final destination.

King Service was a process to provide practice of keeping my mind on God at all times, especially at the time of death. Mahlia chides, "So you wouldn't be reborn as an amoeba." Or anything else!

The process, in the WORKS, of simply reciting Righteous King phrases and following the instruction of the authority was guaranteed to take me on a spiritual journey right out of this miserable physical world. By taking one step at a time towards purification, I could keep my mind solely focused on reaching my final destination of King's utopian paradise.

"Solely or soulfully," Saadya says, giving me some much-needed credit.

I was not sure how this was going over with my two daughters. All I knew was that they were listening, asking questions, cutting their phone calls short, and commenting to gain a deeper understanding of the subject of mind control.

SERVANTHOOD

I WAS BEING TRAINED, in pure allegiance as a selfless servant, in preparation for my future in the spiritual world. I was being prepared through surrender, and austerity, to prove my loyalty and service to the spiritual monarch and the mission. We even served each other. Serving the other workers strengthened a deep affection of kinship for my god-brothers and god-sisters. I was taught to think of myself as a servant of a servant. This was another very important step along the road leading me to my final destination. "But it wasn't gonna be heaven," Mahlia informs me.

Saadya probes further. "So you thought you were being trained to be good enough to be with God."

Mahlia interrogates me. "How did you go from thinking about your life to trying not to think about it or question what was going on around you?" When I first encountered this group of people, I listened. All along, I believed that I was critically reasoning and constantly examining for myself the issues involved in my continuing to stay. Yet the pattern emerging was one in which all my arguments were being refuted and ultimately defeated.

Point for point, I accepted the explanations offered to me by Leo and the other girls in terms of the philosophy and practices. They were justifications for my trading my anti-establishment angst for the new fantasy offered in the Superior Texts about a kingdom in which I could ultimately be carefree in full enjoyment just as King is with his entourage of lesser gods in loving relationship. As all the explanations and justifications for the new complexities and new realities confronting me at the Center came to light, I understood more how important it was for me to remain steadfast in the ideology. How could I forfeit such an opportunity for just a few short fleeting years of physical comfort and enjoyment?

"That's what they told you?" queries Saadya.

In essence, the basic premise was that all knowledge in the physical world was ascertained through limited senses, as well as faulty and insufficient information, thereby making any conclusions unreliable, and the people who gather them untrustworthy sources.

GOING OVERBOARD

EVERYTHING THAT MATTERED was what we were supposed to abhor, things like family, anything to do with our background, and just about everything about our past. Everything separate from the Center, its activities, and its ideology were dismissed as frivolous and meaningless. We had to forfeit anything that had been attractive to us before joining the WORKS and recognize it as a distraction to our endeavors toward our spiritual enlightenment. I came to regard everything that had occurred to me before joining with disdain, abhorrence, and repulsion. We were even discouraged from pursuing any interests separate from our soul-saving activities. Instead, we were encouraged to regard everything else as a waste of time. For example, several of the girls at the Barstow Center had given up a professional career in music or dance and dedicated themselves to soul-saving—"soul-saving the ultimate!" we used to say. This phrase embodies the sentiment that there was no higher service or anything else worth doing.

The attractiveness we still felt towards other activities, such as swimming, skiing, listening to music, even sleeping, were signs of our ongoing desires for the things of the physical world. On our own, it would be impossible to maintain our King-mindedness without the company of the other workers. The WORKS was considered an umbrella that sheltered us from the onslaught of the rains of the physical world.

Mahlia exhales. "I get it. The physical energy was raining down on you, and you needed the WORKS to reign you in, as in being held on a tight rope."

My gaze into her eyes deepens, and she allows this look to linger a bit longer. In the first place, dependence on the group was cultivated for protection against falling prey to the physical energy because of our own spiritual weakness. In this way, the group gained control over the totality of my life and the lives of all the other agents.

THE SOUL-SAVING GROUP

"WHAT ELSE IS THERE to tell about the soul-saving group?" Mahlia asks.

Let me give you some background. The soul-saving group collected donations and distributed King Service books and literature in other forms, such as magazines. *The Knowing King* magazine was a favorite to hand out, especially to people who gave a quick donation. The books were reserved for people we were trying to finagle out of their change when they gave us a large bill, but more of that later.

Now I am going to give you the whole picture: who, what, why, and the wherefore. The soul-saving group lived together, ate together, recited together, and more importantly fund-raised together, and as importantly slept together in the same ashram. We were together at night, at meals, and in the morning. In other words, around the clock. In the morning, the women acted weird.

"And you didn't?" murmurs Mahlia.

"*Shush*," I tell her.

When we first rose, we were ourselves, but not for long. Some girls took a longer time to rise, but all were instructed to "pop up" out of their sleeping bags.

I know Mahlia loves to linger in her bed, especially in the mornings when she has nothing immediately to do. So I tell her, "I know you can't relate to why I would get up so early, and for what."

"You know me so well," Mahlia admits, and I confirm that for her with a wink and a smile. I go on to explain.

I remember thinking during those first weeks how weird this group of girls acted, but that they were also very *cool*, with one exception—on the first week, I was being reminded not to put my hands or fingers into my mouth, as I had gotten into the habit of biting off my fingernail cuticles. I objected to being told by Jayda, the girl who rode my bicycle back to the ashram, not to do this, because it was none of her business.

Saadya insists, "You were still maintaining your individuality." As an afterthought, she adds, "And your dignity." That's when Leo told Jayda not to say anything to me, while he explained to me that it was just unsanitary for anyone to put their fingers in their mouth.

Mahlia tells me, "He knew how to play his cards right."

And I had to deal with the hand being dealt. The first hand initially attracted me to the spiritual dogma and how genuinely these people related to each other. As the days wore on and turned into weeks, and the weeks turned into months, I would come to accept everything surrounding and included in the organization. I remember thinking, during those first few days, and even saying, I wished I had never met the agents and never gone to the Wednesday event. I really wanted to leave.

It *would* have been okay for me in the physical world, I told myself, had I not stumbled on this higher knowledge. I had been safe in my ignorance. But because I had come into contact with the agents, I would be taking a fatal step backward if I left. Eternity was guaranteed for me in King Service. The austerities were hard, but a worse fate awaited me if I left.

In fact, sometimes it was easier to acquiesce than at others. Leo had a knack of making it palatable to acquiesce. Yet there were isolated incidents that left me feeling terrorized—nightmarish episodes during which I felt even my soul-saving sisters wanted to harm me.

Mahlia hauntingly affirms, "But you were already one of them, so however distasteful, you would have to suck it up."

THE CHASE

THAT IS JUST WHAT TRANSPIRED late one Friday night (we always stayed out until past midnight on weekends) when three of us were fund-raising at Riley's at Los Rios Rancho, a popular tourist spot in the Glen Oak region. One of the girls, Belinda, was in charge. This evening, I was tired and timid, worn out and feeling exhausted. I complained of having stomach pains. Belinda and Kaylah alleged that I was having gas pains. I disagreed, telling them I knew what gas pains felt like, and that this was something else.

Neither would accept my explanation, and they would not tolerate my assertiveness. I was being denied the ability to discern something as personal as a stomach cramp and as tangible as a gas pain. It no longer was a matter of what was ailing me.

Mahlia says, "The issue became whether or not you would surrender to them."

I had been made to feel that my advancement in spiritual life hinged on this one point concerning the nature of my ailment. I suddenly realized how important it was for Belinda to exercise her authority over me. She needed to be right, and I needed to accept her appraisal of my symptoms. The need to submit that was instilled in me at the Center was intended to weaken me into docility. This would give anyone in charge power and influence over my own discernment. Yet that evening I saw through it as lies, and the illogic in the demand for me to surrender—over the etiology of my own stomach discomfort—was blatant.

It all came bubbling up for me. I had to get away. I had to escape from their clutches that dug deep. I had to flee to free myself from their stronghold. I bolted up the street, running away as fast as I could. I kept running as though nothing could stop me, and running away felt good.

But midway up the second block, I stopped. I froze, having no clear place to go. Belinda caught up with me. She spoke more personally and with more understanding. I finally surrendered to her. Both Mahlia and Saadya are aghast. Saadya breaks the silence, saying, "Oh, Mom, you were ensnared. You were shackled." She recites, *"When will you stop running. Will you stop panting after other gods? But you say, "Save your breath. I'm in love with these foreign gods, and I can't stop loving them now!"* It wasn't about love, it was about surrender, and where do you come up with this stuff anyway? Saadya answers, "Jeremiah 2:25 – college Bible classes, remember?"

Anyway, I surrendered to all Belinda represented to me in the WORKS. I was trapped. My spiritual life existed only within the confines of a WORKS Center, and my survival depended on the internal structure. The only thing that stopped me from running farther away was that I had been led to believe that there was no place else for me to go. Wherever I ran, I would take with me all the teachings from the WORKS. I knew too much and would be unable to escape from the apprehension of running away. I remained captive in this prison that needed no bars for eight more months. This solidified my trepidation that there was no way out.

"That explains the recurring dreams of entrapment," Mahlia confirms.

Undoubtedly, I was in a trap with no escape hatch. The next day after the chase, Leo spoke to me about the incident, saying that Belinda had no right to insist on what she thought was the matter with my stomach. His show of disapproval of her actions once again made it all right for me in the WORKS, just as it was intended to.

FAMILIARITY BREEDS CONTEMPT

WE WERE A CLOSE-KNIT GROUP. Leo made sure of that. He orchestrated and moderated our every activity as well as our goings and comings, which left no time or wiggle room for reflection. There was plenty of opportunity to interact and engage in social discourse, but it was always in the context of where we had come from and what the benefit of being King minded had for us. There were some girls I resonated with more than others. There were several I felt close to, but on the whole we functioned as a unit, one cohesive group of god-sisters wanting to make spiritual advancement. We admired each other and remained respectful toward each other. If we had an ill thought, felt resentful, or envious, or harbored some other negative thought or emotion, we were trained to quickly offer humility to the other girl.

Mahlia says, "I missed it. What is 'offering humility'?"

This term now requires explanation for Mahlia.

We dropped to our knees, bent at the waist with our forehead on the floor, our hands placed flat on the ground, and postured like this we recited words that glorified our spiritual monarch.

In this way we would humble ourselves to each other. Offering humility was an act of contrition, asking to be forgiven by the other sister who was left to draw her own conclusion as to why the one offering humility had needed to do so. However, we usually knew, because some offense had just occurred. Such humility was expressed even if it was an offense that had been committed in one of the sister's thoughts. Those were the times we didn't know for sure. But we accepted the offer of humility and moved on.

MIDDLE

TRANSFORMATION

"PLEASE APPOINT A NEW MAN as leader for the community. Transfer some of your authority to him so the whole community [of Israel] will obey him" (Numbers 27:15, 20).

Saadya notes, "Yet the girls bought into the system." We bought in because the dogma was perpetuated and we perpetuated it among ourselves. Pride was instilled in us by Leo for being in this elite group. As the Barstow Women's Soul-Saving Group, our reputation for doing everything together preceded us.

"You even got sick together, living in those apartments," Mahlia reminds me. Each day up to two and three girls had to stay back from fund-raising. That is exactly when it was decided that we shouldn't wait to move into the newly purchased house closer to the worship Center, but do so immediately.

However, when all the girls went out, daily collections were collectively more or less three thousand dollars a day. That didn't include the men's soul-saving collections, as there was also a group of men who fund-raised. The men's scores usually increased the Center scores by fifteen hundred dollars daily.

We were unquestionably being obedient to our authority and dedicated to soul-saving. Our group was a role model throughout the WORKS. So after I was at the Center for seven months, we moved from the ashram on Fredericks Street into the large two- story house, only one house away from the Center. About a year later, another house was purchased behind that one. They had connecting backyards. Some of the men built a footpath through the yards to be a shortcut to the worship Center.

The house was purchased as an investment, but the idea was to expand the children's school program to attract more married couples to the Barstow Center. One of the sisters was a teacher, and she was supposed to be in charge of the girls' school. Leo would have direct supervision of the entire project, with the idea of training all the children to eventually become dedicated soul-saving workers.

But when Sir Derek came to live at Barstow, the plans for this house changed. Instead, the house was transformed into his palace, with nothing but the best. Sir Derek was our newly appointed spiritual monarch, since Sir Supreme was getting too old, and like Sir Supreme, he was considered holy. He took the place of Sir Supreme and, eventually, Leo as well.

When Sir Derek came, something happened to the spirit of the group. The atmosphere in the ashram changed. Several of us noticed it, and I remember speaking to one of the girls, who also had. The essence of innocence was gone. The house was large. Some girls having so-called seniority were given their own rooms to share with one other girl. There were more doors for secrets to be hidden behind.

HOLY FOOD

I AM LOST IN MY THOUGHT. Mahlia calls out to me to get my attention, "So tell us more."

I have been thinking about the time when we didn't return for the Wednesday dinner. Leo thought that we would tolerate staying out later on Wednesdays, foregoing the entire Wednesday event involved with having guests at the Center. He soon learned that the Wednesday dinner program was not frivolous but actually served to enliven us. In its absence, our performance on soul-saving the ensuing week suffered. Our scores decreased, and we had a harder time out on soul-saving activity in general. Leo concluded the Wednesday dinner provided a mid-week respite that proved to yield a monetary benefit, so this much-needed reprieve was reinstated, albeit with a modification.

Leo informed us that we would be eating early in the afternoon, when we first returned to the ashram, instead of with the guests. In this way, we would be able to preach better to the guests or to preach "nicely," which meant that we could spend whatever time was necessary giving them the impression that we had all the time in the world, and that life as a Righteous King worker was low-key and kicked back.

"Which couldn't have been further from the truth," declares Mahlia. "The girls worked so hard all week long, it was a pity for you to miss out on the Wednesday dinner event."

It offered us a respite, but then Leo had to modify the enjoyment, and we had no choice but to wrap our minds around his rationale and embrace it. Saadya accentuates this point: "You were all for one and one for all!"

While we are on the topic of the Wednesday dinner, there was yet another modification that occurred during the time when we returned to the Center for the Wednesday dinner and the holy food was served from huge buckets that were kept along a corridor. The soul-saving agents, both men and women, would help themselves to the various buckets of holy food and eat immediately after the worship and singing known as the "offering," which was a time when the food was offered to the carved figures.

Mahlia, smirking, making eye contact with Saadya, bursts out laughing. She manages to speak the words, "Did the carved figures eat the food?"

That was not the purpose; the purpose of the offering was for the food to be *transformed* into holy food.

Mahlia regains her composure and apologizes, "I am really sorry, Mom. I know this is not easy for you to be telling us."

"Yeah," Saadya tells her playfully. "What is the *matter* with you?"

That's okay, I reassure them both. After all, they are my darling daughters.

BEING PROGRAMMED

"Mom," Saadya sums up, "this is really riveting. You had to remain loyal to Leo and all his decrees?"

Yes, and new programs were always being introduced. All they amounted to were varieties of the routine. Different ways of getting us to wake up were tried at various times. Sometimes we would rise to a tape of Sir Supreme reciting the Righteous King phrases over loud speakers in all the rooms in the ashram.

"I thought you said there was no furniture in the ashram," Mahlia reminds me. These speakers, along with the rest of the fifteen-hundred-dollar sound system, procured with funds collected on soul-saving that Leo withheld from the Center coffer, were an exception.

"Did the people who gave you donations know the money would be used to buy a sound system?" Mahlia asks.

Leo represented Sir Supreme and therefore exercised his autonomy with no one questioning any of his actions at the ashram.

A FAULTY SYSTEM

"Break it down for us, Mom," Saadya pleads. "We're really trying to understand."

The basic premise underlying the self-righteousness of the leadership was that all knowledge in the physical world was gathered by people with imperfect, limited senses and resources. Mankind drew its conclusions from faulty and insufficient information, thereby making it and its truths unreliable and untrustworthy. However, King's representative, namely Sir Supreme, had information about the spiritual world and the true nature of the universe both spiritual and physical.

We simply could not place our trust in the hands of the atheistic scientists who were cheating and misguiding the masses. In my earnest endeavor to learn about God and the world around me, I was offered an overall intertwining and meshing of the WORKS logic to refute every absurd scientific explanation for the wonders that encompass the world, that were devoid of the personality of the Godhead, missing the true purpose of life. In a similar way, how limited the concept now appears that, as a King worker, I had been led to believe that true worship of God meant being subjugated to personalities and acculturated to their narrow and limited yet fantastic projections of divinity, and that by doing so I too could achieve divinity.

Saadya says, "Sounds like their very own twelve-step program, or some kind of purification through works."

Mahlia adds, "Getting purified through the self-aggrandizement of the leaders at the expense of God."

I tell my two daughters that I am proud of them for hearing what I have wanted them to for so long, and how they are grasping the depth of this experience. Mahlia tells me, "In Ephesians 2:9, it says, 'Not by works but by GRACE you have been saved, lest no one should boast.'"

"You learned that in college?" I ask.

Mahlia responds, "It's a marvelous mystery and an extraordinary rescue."

With newfound confidence, I wrote the following, weeks after being rescued myself:

> Pure in flight is a dove with vision clear. Her heart aglow, choosing life's path, careful not to fall prey, seizing the opportunity to see as things are with the goal of dreaming and hope of the chance to rejoice in His dance.

BAIT AND SWITCH

THE RELATIONSHIP BETWEEN MEN and women, and the dynamics, were spoken about frequently and often within the WORKS. On soul-saving, I began to notice what was being preached. Women seemed controlling of men as they hurried through the airport terminal. I espied how people fashioned their time aspiring to attain the ultimate in physical comfort for selfish reasons. It seemed that people were so busy rushing around trying to satisfy their senses, too busy to take time for God.

Saadya asks, "Is that what they told you?" That's exactly what was talked about at the Center on a daily basis, and that is what I thought I was avoiding by being immersed in the service of soul-saving. Furthermore, this translated into exhaustive reciting of the King phrases. Therefore, the first part of my day was spent in intense recitation of the Righteous King phrases. The ensuing time was spent on soul-saving, the activity from the "Old World" literatures that defined agent service in the WORKS.

On the contrary and to be sure, however, the soul-saving of the WORKS agent differed drastically from the soul-saving explained in those early literatures.

In the early literature, the loyal servant was supposed to beg alms and take only what little he would need for sustenance. This was the model for us, since we, too, begged alms, as we also were totally dependent on the Center for providing any and all of our necessities. The Center provided us with food, clothing, and shelter, and beyond this, friends and camaraderie. In this way, my only considerations would be for spiritual advancement. I was driven each day to the point of exhaustion and collapse with the burden I bore from the labor of the mission.

In the evening we were worn out, but at the beginning of the day, it was different. It was exhilarating to be up and out before sunrise as we walked the short distance from the ashram to the Center for the morning program. There was a sense of camaraderie. These were people with whom I shared the exuberance of being up and active at odd hours of the day or night.

Although it is difficult to sleep while you are on the go, I would be so exhausted at the end of the day that, at night, I lay flat on my back, pinned against the floor. I could not move a muscle. I noticed that the other women would similarly collapse and, usually, fall off to sleep in a matter of seconds, only to awaken four hours later in the very same position they'd fallen in.

My psyche was bombarded by constant and awe-inspiring preaching about what my duty was—to please the spiritual monarch, to please the Center president, to please the authority, Leo and/or Sir Derek, whom I will tell you about later. That left little or no room for me. I was discouraged from entertaining any personal considerations. There was no room for any of this within the sphere of my participation. I had to surrender and accept. "That meant accepting everything beyond your initial attraction for wanting to know about God," Saadya sums it up. The secret of knowing the god of the WORKS was to commit myself to the rigorous routine, however it was prescribed. I also had to accept the lifestyle of austerity just as it unfolded and was being revealed, even if it was not what I had at first been led to believe about being in the Organization. Saadya says, "They call that a bait-and-switch."

ANYTHING GOES

LEO ORCHESTRATED EVENTS for soul-saving to also be fun. Curious, Mahlia asks, "Such as?"

Once, during the Christmas season, six of us, fully clad in Santa Claus outfits , went down to San Bernardino's red light district and stampeded our way into all the clubs along the strip.

"Is that supposed to be a pun?" Saadya asks. Mahlia is likewise amused.

My daughters are alert to the inadvertent pun, because these clubs featured live sex acts. Leo was driving us around the city that Christmas Eve. He mentioned to me that he wouldn't go in to one of those places because he had been plagued for a year by what he'd seen in one of those clubs years earlier when he was fund-raising.

As we were running across the street excitedly, one of the girls clumsily lost her footing, fell down, and couldn't get up, stuffed in her Santa outfit, just as you would expect—a roly-poly Santa wanna-be. I offered assistance after regaining my own composure from laughing hysterically at her awkwardness in not being able to get up on her own.

Another time, Leo took six of us to a drive-in movie to collect donations by approaching the people in parked cars. To avoid paying for each of us, three of the girls packed themselves under the deck built into the van to create a false bottom with the extra space underneath used to store cases of books to be passed out on soul-saving wherever we went. The space was about eighteen inches high.

Once inside the drive-in, the situation became complicated and grew hysterically funny when one of the girls wedged between several cases of books could not get out, she was so twisted and contorted. I had to maneuver each of her limbs out for her, while she relaxed each one in turn. I belly-laughed uncontrollably at this episode, which could only be described as a classic slapstick routine. I found it genuinely comical. Leo didn't think it was funny and reprimanded me for losing my self-control. I regained my composure and apologized. Leo then validated my reaction as a release from the pressure we were functioning under.

GOD SISTERS

THIS OCCURRED WHEN I WAS STILL FAIRLY NEW. I was initially attracted, and then I was trapped. I did not know that, without an opportunity for reflection, I would not be able to distinguish the new reality from my original intention of gaining spiritual enlightenment. The process had a disarming effect, taking its toll on me. I later learned, after my deprogramming, that the group relies on eliminating any opportunity for reality-testing by keeping us from having any time to ourselves beyond the confines of the Center and its sanctioned activities. Mahlia, quick as a wink, states, "Job had it right," and then quotes Job 34:3, "*The ear tests the words it hears just as the mouth distinguishes between foods.*" Job may have been able to, but we simply could not.

At first, I was witness to, and participant in, the days and nights of following the program along with the other girls, which, after Leo's modification, began at 2:00 a.m. so that we would have all our King phrases completed before the start of the early-morning program. This served two purposes. Firstly, it would establish us in King mentality for the day ahead, and, secondly, we could head out right after breakfast.

Saadya asks, "What was the morning program all about?"

The morning service was the offering of music, dance, and singing in front of the carved figures. It began at 4:15 a.m. After an hour or so of singing, dancing, and announcements, it was time for the Superior Text class. We used to stay at the Center with all the agents for the Superior Text class. After a while, upon Leo's recommendation, the women agreed for him to begin conducting a class exclusively for the soul-saving women. He geared class to promote our loyalty to him and to soul-saving activity. The moral lesson concluding every class signified, and elaborated on, the message of complete dedication for the purpose of spreading the King mindset. That meant remaining steadfast to fund-raising.

Leo led us to truly believe we were having a divine impact by going out to influence regulars to engage in service to King by giving a donation. Leo and the Center leaders were also aware they needed to keep us motivated to go out every day to collect, hopefully, large sums of money. And they knew that they had to keep us thinking it was our moral obligation to mankind. We really thought we were benefiting the people who gave a donation.

Saadya says, "Leo used the religious rhetoric to keep you motivated." This was not a cut-and-dried matter. Conducting Superior Text class for the women was his attempt to minimize the time we spent at the worship Center, so we wouldn't get ideas about doing some other service, which would interfere with his exclusive dominion over us, as individuals and as a group. He wanted us to remain loyal to him and steadfast in our service in the exclusive women's group that he alone had direct jurisdiction over.

Immediately following class we changed out of our tunics and into our regular clothes for fund-raising, and by 7:30 a.m., we were eating the breakfast meal prepared by several of the "sisters."

"Right," Mahlia says. "If the girls were referred to as sisters, they would not be thought of sexually." This is how the men were instructed to regard the women. There was very little interaction between the male and female agents. We basically had limited direct contact with each other. However, the women remained a very cohesive group. No outsider had any access to what went on within the ashram. The Center agents could only speculate over the reasons the group was so tight. We heard rumors about Leo and the sisters long before there was any validity to them. Leo told us that people couldn't believe that we weren't taking some kind of drug to keep us up and out on soul-saving with the zealousness with which we executed our service.

"That must have given him the idea!" Mahlia remarks.

MIXED EMOTIONS

"YOU BELIEVED SOMETHING *that was never true in the first place,*" Saadya quotes from 1 Corinthians 15:2.

I was attracted because I didn't want to live my life in time and space. I wanted to be in the here and now. I wanted to transcend the definitions of who I was, such as how old or young, or anything associated with the physical.

"There seems to be nothing to limit a man or woman in time and space," Saadya philosophizes, "if there is no mind to get in the way. All limitations and barriers disappear with the disappearance of the mind."

Ultimately, it was more my intuition and reasoning that were forfeited as I blindly followed this course. The more I surrendered, the more I would be rewarded. This was the recipe for success in the WORKS and especially at fund-raising. The results baffled us. We knew that, if we persevered, we would have results—and I mean big results. We would "do big," as Leo liked to say. It just got to the point that I stopped trying to figure out how and why it worked. I knew I had to completely absorb myself in this activity of approaching everyone I saw, wherever I happened to be.

"It does sound like hard work," Mahlia realizes. Soul-saving was by no means all fun and games. It could also be anxiety-producing at times. There was strength in numbers, so starting at 8:00 a.m., when we all piled into one van or another, depending on the location we had been assigned, we were in the company of our soul-saving sisters. We spent the entire morning prepping, and revving up, for hitting the turf. We were pretty much okay up to then. But when we piled out of the van, we were on our own. That's when we could be met with mixed emotions.

HOT PURSUIT

THERE WERE SEVERAL VANS—women's and men's. They went variously to the San Bernadino Airport, San Bernadino County Museum, Fullerton Museum of Art, San Manuel Stadium, or Deep Creek Hot Springs, just to name a few. Then there were the cars that were loaded with cases of books for gifting to whoever would accept one and, better yet, leave a large donation in exchange.

The *Knowing God* magazine was also for gifting. It was popular and always had a colorful front cover, usually of Sir Supreme or a depiction of King in his kingdom. The regulars thought it was fantasy, but we in the WORKS thought otherwise. These pictures were a reality for us. We were happy to be passing them out and happier when a regular appeared somewhat interested, but the bottom line was the magazines and books were used to get the Ora, the money.

The training for collecting donations consisted of accompanying another girl as she hit up regulars, or her sharing her rap with you. The training included when to introduce the book to the regular, how to leaf through the pages to get their attention, and how to impress them with the beautiful pictures. Then there was the aspect of making it seem like the regular had just won a prize. *"I'm only allowed to give away five of these books today, but you have to promise you will take care of it. You have a book shelf at home, don't you? Okay, then I can let you take it with you—but everyone is giving a little donation to help."*

There was the time when, at the San Bernadino Airport terminal, I recognized a man who had, once before, signed over two hundred dollars in travelers checks to me. But on that particular morning, I was not at all in the limelight, or anywhere near it. I was tired and easily distracted.

Therefore, I alerted two of the other girls, who did very well as a rule. They got this guy to write two checks each for two thousand dollars. After he wrote the first check and made it payable to the worker, she asked him to make out another check payable to the Center, and he never asked for the first check back. Both checks were collected on.

Mahlia wonders, "How did you ever let him go?" Well, we didn't.

Later on, this guy was invited to come to the Center and meet with Leo and those two girls for a special meal and tour.

Mahlia asks, accentuating the question, "What, all for the purpose of him turning over more Ora?"

"Obviously," says Saadya. "Did he?" Leo was not able to get any more money out of him. "So that was the end of him?" During that visit, he was smart enough to retreat from the hot pursuit.

THE LIMELIGHT

THE POINT REMAINS that a worker knew when she was in the limelight of dutiful service. At those times, it never mattered if a regular turned me down. I would just walk right on over to the next person. At the end of the day, the results were there. One such day, I got a hundred-dollar donation, and later on in the evening a young man interested in King Service gave me one for fifty dollars. People were also leaving twenty-dollar donations. Those were very exciting times. I knew I was in the limelight. I knew I was surrendered.

But just as exciting as those times were, there was for the worker the possibility of rejection. Those moments of being turned down by the regulars brought every negative emotion, and there was no escaping them. We just had to continue to get people to stop by picking up our pace and not thinking in between regulars. If we got our mojo on, we could get past the negative emotions. If we didn't, we suffered through-out the day. We knew no one would want to give money to someone who was not psyched up. If we rebelled even subtly, the mere thought of approaching a stranger and asking for a donation was dreadful, so we tried not to think about it. Instead, we would recite the King phrases and approach one regular after another for the duration.

We knew that the more people we approached, the greater the chances of getting into the limelight. "So you had to keep on keeping on," Saadya realizes. This is why we had to begin each day with a strong resolve for collecting. We were told it all belonged to King anyway. We were just reclaiming what was rightfully his.

DOLLARS AND NO SENSE

"In their greed they will make up clever lies to get hold of your money." (2 Peter 2:30)

THE FUNDS WE COLLECTED in soul-saving activities were, for the most part, used for the reasons we said. I told people we were missionary students raising funds to print books. There were several workable variations of this, but the bottom line was that we were printing books with universal knowledge that would benefit all of mankind.

I was told it cost the WORKS about ten cents to print each book. However, the sums of money we collected far exceeded the cost of the number of books that were actually passed out. We rationalized expenditures to be used for other reasons than what we said they were to be used for. In the three years that I was at the Barstow Center, I saw the purchase of two large houses, the complete renovation and remodeling of the worship Center with materials such as granite imported from a supplier in Denver, Colorado, but originally imported from Mexico; elaborately carved wooden doors handcrafted and shipped from the Philippines; decorations; and cloths and silks to stock the Center's store, which sold exclusively Philippine imports.

In addition, five hundred acres were purchased in western Nevada, and the Center leaders joked about hoping to drive down the value of the adjoining four hundred acres because no one would want to buy the land next to a WORKS Center. Then they would purchase it at the depreciated value. Additionally, the Center purchased six new Econoline vans and several new cars, not counting all the cars that were rented over the years. Other expenses that came out of the money collected in soul-saving activity included food, clothing, shelter, and travel expenses for the new spiritual monarchs and their entourage to go wherever there was a WORKS Center.

Shocked, Saadya says, "And there are Centers all over the world?"

Sir Derek, the newly appointed spiritual monarch at Barstow, made several trips, taking along with him several male agents. Travel expenses were also paid for all the agents who, each year, went to the Philippines for the festival in Cebu.

Saadya, who likes to travel and spent a semester her junior year studying in South Africa, inquires, "Mom, did you ever get to travel?"

Mahlia says, "Tell us about the Philippines later. I want to hear more about your soul-saving activity."

With a slight nod, Saadya signals me that she is willing to defer to her older sister.

SPARE CHANGE

AFTER RECEIVING SAADYA'S APPROVAL, I begin to speak about the spare change technique and the manner in which it was orchestrated. Specifically, when someone was about to give a donation, just as they reached into their pocket, I would ask if they had a large bill that I could give them change for. I had accumulated so many small bills since I had been out since early that morning, and I would actually show the person a handful of smaller bills. All the while, I was constantly talking and engaging the person in conversation to divert their attention from the money they gave. As soon as I had their twenty-dollar bill, or a larger denomination, in my possession, I would fumble around with the smaller bills, straightening them out and all the while talking.

"I know," says Mahlia. "Possession is nine-tenths of the law."

"Mom," Saadya is now less than happy to say, "I'm really trying to give you the benefit of the doubt, but listening to you talk about etiquette and special techniques is stretching the *spirituality* aspect of this group."

Mahlia offers, "That is exactly the point. They were manipulated under the guise of spirituality."

"Exactly," I say. "We were on a mission," I emphasize, as it was stressed to us at the Center.

And so the rap went something like this: *You know what? I get to give out promotional copies of the book we are printing to ten of the most sincere people I meet. You look pretty sincere. But you have to promise to take care of the book and take it home with you. You have a book shelf at home, right? You look like a pretty intelligent person.* Beforehand, we had practiced with each other until we perfected our timing. It was very important, when you put the book in the person's hand, to begin to leaf through the pages, pointing out details in several of the pictures.

Savvy Mahlia recognizes this technique. "The ploy was to visually distract the person from realizing they were being seduced into giving a larger donation."

So once the book was in the regular's hands, we would run the rap of how we wanted to raise enough funds to print a thousand books and were trying to get everyone to give the most they could. *I wouldn't normally ask,* I'd go on, *but just this once could you make a sacrifice and leave the whole thing,* referring to the larger denomination.

Usually by this time, they had forgotten the twenty-dollar bill and just wanted to leave, so, more often than not, they would say, "Okay," and walk off with a book tucked under their arm. If they said they could not leave the whole bill, I'd quickly say, *"Of course you can't. It's too much."* Then I'd count out two or three one-dollar bills and ask, *"Would that be alright? Could you leave it at that?"* Or I would give back a five-dollar bill to alleviate their worry and then begin to ask if they could leave it like that, since it was a worthwhile cause. If the regular persisted in wanting more money back, I'd then count out one-dollar bills until they were satisfied, and thank them as they walked away.

"Unfortunately," Mahlia remarks, "just walking away from the WORKS was not that easy for you." That was never a possibility.

Although, most times when we walked away, it was with more of a donation than the regular would have given had we left the amount up to them. This usually went smoothly, without irritating the person.

Mahlia role plays: *"Oh by the way, do you have a large bill that I can give you change for? I've been here all day, and I have a lot of one-dollar bills I want to get rid of. Everyone is trying to do the best that they can. We do this only one time a year. Ordinarily, I would never ask, but since it's so special and for such a good cause, could you leave the whole twenty? Is that all right? Really, I would never ask in a hundred million years, but it is only just this once. Would that be alright?"*

Mahlia can work a roomful of people, and understands this was a manipulative ploy. It was all for the mission, our higher calling, and service to King.

We were coy, cunning, and flirty, and we were irresistible, some more than others, and some of us more at certain times, not losing sight of what our objective was. "Show me the *money!*" Mahlia says, quoting a line from the movie *Jerry Maguire.*

When we were enthusiastic in soul-saving, a worker could collect large sums of money, which of course we referred to as "Ora." Soul-saving collections usually ranged from two hundred to a thousand dollars daily. Several of the girls did well, collecting almost consistently on the high end.

Using the spare-change technique, soul-saving collections almost tripled, to the point of getting people to leave several large bills without ever giving any change back. We were trained to be fast talkers, stay in control, and manipulate the situation by being sensitive to the person we were talking to. Of course, throughout the transaction, we were focused on getting the largest donation possible. But as soon as we saw any indication that the regular was getting agitated, we started handing back money one dollar at a time to appease them.

Undoubtedly, the amount of our collections depended on the totality of relinquishing our desire to be doing anything else. Results in soul-saving never ceased to baffle us. We knew, if we persevered, then the results would be there. At the end of the day, we marveled at how King had rewarded us for our loyalty and dedication.

"But you never personally got any of that money, right, Mom?" Saadya asks.

Not a penny for ourselves. Everything was turned into the Center coffers, though there were times when we could use the money to buy a soda, like a Seven-Up. We weren't supposed to have Coca-Cola or Pepsi because they contained caffeine, a stimulant, but there was a time when that rule grew lax and some of the girls were buying Pepsi or Coke to drink. That puzzled me because caffeine was initially presented as being a drug. Drinking caffeine was another deviation from the restriction against taking drugs. But then again, a lot of practices started cropping up in violation of our vows.

SPEAKING IN TONGUES

MAHLIA PURSUES ANOTHER LINE OF QUESTIONING. "So you fund-raised at busy airports. But what if you were somewhere else?"

Besides the airport, we could be assigned to a mall or strip mall. We were concerned that, if we were assigned to collect at a strip mall, there wouldn't be enough people frequenting the stores for us to hit up. However, we were not allowed to use this as an excuse. Instead, we were encouraged to keep our minds in the limelight, and as a result King would send along the regulars to compensate us for our faith, duty, loyalty, allegiance, and unerring self-sacrifice.

While San Bernadino is a huge tourist city, we usually went to those places that tourists would frequent—the Fullerton Museum of Art, the County Museum, the San Manuel Stadium, Deep Creek Hot Springs, or Glen Helen Regional Park. These tourists came from Japan, Germany, Switzerland, Brazil, really all over the world. We learned and practiced just enough lines in their languages to be able to communicate with them. Usually the thread of the conversation was that we were teachers with schools all over the world. We told people we had schools in the capital of whatever country they were from. We would always try to personalize the conversation by asking where they were from and telling them how beautiful it was in their country. Saadya says, "You didn't miss a trick in the book," and now quotes from Acts 2:7-8, *"They were completely amazed! How can this be?" they exclaimed. These people are all from Galilee, and yet we hear them speaking in our own native languages!"*

Clearly, the trick worked. Tourists were so happy to be able to speak to someone in their native language as part of their experience on this leg of their journey. Whenever we spoke English to them, we pronounced words in what sounded like their particular accent. This usually won their favor, especially the part when we said we had relatives in their country. It seemed to bond us in some way.

One year, several of the girls in the Organization the longest spent time in Japan on traveling soul-saving. There, they learned bits of the language and were able to convey them to the rest of us. When we started using these lines, we saw that they were effective in getting donations, and large ones. We started getting them whenever we encountered Japanese tourists. Also, huge sums could be collected from the Japanese simply because of the inflated value of their currency compared to the American dollar. A hundred yen was the equivalent to one American dollar, so when we asked for a hundred dollars, it would not seem outlandish to the hurried Japanese visitors passing through the airport terminal. They thought they were leaving the equivalent of a hundred yen.

"Yikes, Mom, so they thought they were donating a dollar!" Saadya calculates.

In fact, once we saw how effective it was just to know a few simple sentences in Japanese, we asked those who knew a different language to teach some expressions to the rest of us. We even asked people we met on soul-saving activity from another country to translate a few simple lines from their language for our own use. I once had a boy from Portugal translating for me into Portuguese, and a young woman from the Philippines translating into Tagalog.

THE LEGAL SYSTEM

"I WONDER IF ALL OF THIS WAS LEGAL," Mahlia challenges.

Saadya responds, "It may have been legal, but I can tell you that it certainly was ruthless." We were trained to be absolutely ruthless. Saadya adds, "And you all felt like you were above the law." We were oblivious to any fear of apprehension by the police. We felt the laws were part of a culture we felt completely alien to and therefore did not feel subject to. Yet we had frequent brushes with the law concerning our methods. For example, now and again, one of the agents would have to appear in court to comply with a summons. One common claim against us concerned obstructing the sidewalks. The agents were always getting smacked with a summons of that nature, and I was no exception.

This had occurred on the sidewalk approaching the Glen Helen Regional Park, where I was gifting books daily one year during the summer months. The police were always trying to find ways to keep us out of the park. At the airport, claims were made against the agents by passengers and travelers who claimed to have been harassed by the workers. And the agents often got speeding tickets for exceeding the speed limit: It was not unusual for a vanload of girls to be traveling at speeds over eighty miles per hour in a fifty-five-mile-per-hour speed zone.

Mahlia asks, "Did you ever get involved with the police?"

If she didn't flat out ask whether I'd had "brushes with the law," I might have not volunteered this information. Since she has, and as our eyes lock, I can tell she is not backing down but waiting for me to begin. My first encounter with the police came only a few weeks after I started going to the San Bernadino Airport. We approached people in any section of it; even on our way to the restroom, we would approach them. There were no official restrictions at that time. So we had been trained, "If it moves, hit it up."

One morning the police were looking for me, so as soon as I arrived with the vanload of girls and was dropped off at the terminal, I was met by an officer and escorted in the police car to the domestic flights terminal, where the police office was.

An experienced soul-saving sister, Denise, reputed to be firmly set in the King Service mindset, arrived on foot, shortly after me, to monitor what was going on. I was allowed to make one phone call. I naturally called the ashram to find out exactly what I should do. I recalled an incident that had occurred the day before involving a young man who donated a few dollars. Right after he left his donation, his companion, another man a bit older, had come up to me, irate that I had taken money from his friend. I'd asked if he would like me to return the money. My offer had been declined, and we'd parted.

Since I was allowed to make one phone call in the police station, I called Leo and told him that I had an idea why I was there. When I hung up the receiver, I was immediately instructed by the officer to tell him why I thought I been brought in for questioning.

I described the complaint against me, but there was nothing that the police could do. I was admonished that I would be watched closely. I was sufficiently warned and equally intimidated. I no longer felt like engaging in soul-saving activity that day. All my strength and focus had been zapped by this encounter, any justification and motivation to fund-raise drained out of me. As we were walking back to the terminal, Denise began preaching that nothing could stop our mission. She explained that the incident had been a test of my sincerity; that, in actuality, there was nothing the police could do to stop us. King was too strong for them. I had nothing to worry about, because I was properly situated in King Service, and because I was soul-saving, King would always protect me. I should just ignore the episode and continue to endeavor on soul-saving activity. In spite of the distraction, I should start hitting people up and not stop, even for a second, and then I would soon be back in the limelight. The mission was too important. After all, I owed it to the regulars.

SHORT CIRCUIT

THIS EPISODE CATAPULTED ME into the reality that I was required to persevere against any and all opposition to our endeavors as agents of the WORKS. I was systematically to be calculating on soul-saving.

Saadya says, "But, Mom, you wanted to be spiritual, and you wanted to know more about God." Yes, that is the truth. She continues, "How does wanting to have a spiritual mind wind up leaving you without one?"

Mahlia alleges, "You had a mind, but it was a criminal mind."

I need to make the following distinction. On the one hand, we didn't set out to break the law, and we were careful not to. On the other hand, we would not allow anything to stop us. My objective was to collect as much money, and pass out as many books, as I could at certain times, yet to spend as little time as possible with each regular, so as to approach as many people as possible. There were times I was instructed to pass out books indiscriminately to anyone who would take one. At other times, I was to use my discretion and give a book only to someone who was interested. I was admonished to speak briefly to people who seemed willing to listen. My ideas, like those of every other worker, were shaped by the King Service dogma.

I was being programmed in a repetitive and simplistic manner. Any one of us could parrot back the philosophy. I was trained in the art of hearing and reciting. This method of learning short-circuited my mind. We didn't need to think about or question our activities, just *do* them. I learned Old World verses and their English translations during classes simply by hearing them and parroting them back over and over again. We also repeated the verses first sung by one of the male agents leading worship in front of the carved figures. We sang in unison as a congregation, and very soon we were all dancing to the beat of the drum and the clanging of cymbals. Our other behavior and activities were marked by ritualistic adherence to the routine. The routine kept us in line, so that we were aligned to the WORKS' etiquette expected of us. In other words, I was aware at all times of how odd my behavior might seem to an objective observer. But I understood proper WORKS etiquette as purposeful and to be held in the highest regard, to guarantee favor with King, as well as with Leo. "Mom, haven't you ever heard that we are saved by grace? It is a gift from God. Being saved is not a reward for the good things we do," Saadya says, paraphrasing from Ephesians 2:8-9. Well, I was not hearing that, and grace was nowhere to be found in the WORKS.

IDENTITY CRISIS

MAHLIA CONTINUES HER LINE OF QUESTIONING with an astute observation. "So you got a strong dose of the King dogma, huh, Mom?" Yes, that is how it morphed. The real issue for me was my identity, and how, day by day, I was molded into identifying as a worker, growing increasingly alienated from the culture and society I had been hearing so much preaching against. I had three different identities. Firstly, I was me. Secondly, I was an agent, accepted by the other workers. Thirdly, to the police, I was someone representative of the entire WORKS Organization, while to the less tolerable regulars and passersby, who would not stop to engage, I was also that WORKS persona, not a person.

Mahlia has been listening, but also texting, and then she asks, "Why? What happened when passersby *didn't* engage?" They usually just kept walking by, ignoring me, or they would accept the ribbon we pinned to their lapel and then decline to give a donation. There was frequently the regular who dug into their pocket and gave whatever change they had, emptying their clenched fist into my open palm. After a quick thank-you, the loose change got deposited into a front compartment of my book bag kept exclusively for that purpose.

Saadya says, "Well, that doesn't sound so bad."

Except once, walking past a couple on the sidewalk at the San Bernadino Airport, I heard the grumbling of the neatly dressed man who was standing next to a woman, probably his wife. I'd never seen him before, and he'd never seen me. His grumbling was audible.

He was saying something about how we should get jobs, *real* jobs at that. I had to walk past this couple, and when I did, he bopped me over the head with his folding metal-framed suitcase roller. It sent chills up my spine, because he'd assaulted me from behind. I hadn't seen it coming, but I could sense something was about to happen.

Mahlia confirms my suspicions. "You should have known." I did not heed the warning signs or my own intuition. She snidely remarks, "Well, that certainly wasn't the first time."

Saadya is perplexed. "Whoa—what did you do about it?" Well, it wasn't about what I could do, because it quickly got turned into "What *could* I do?" as it was presented to me by one of the other girls who had witnessed the assault.

Saadya concludes, "If you went to the police, you would fall into the physical energy." Besides, the police would be glad I got walloped.

Mahlia notes, "Something they wished *they* could've done." That is exactly the rationale I was offered for why I had to just chalk it up to experience as a worker out on soul-saving. I had a higher purpose, and I could not allow this small-minded regular to hamper my service to King. This episode further served to reinforce my identity as a King worker.

Now that I think about it, there was a fourth identity. To the Center leaders, I was some fresh young naïf and very green worker, still subject to attacks by the physical energy, that force that could tempt and trick me out of service to King. Therefore, we were admonished against entertaining any doubt about the entire application of the philosophy that could swindle us out of being able to actually live it.

Mahlia exclaims, finally getting it out of her system, "I know this is very heavy, but stop making excuses. You fell for all of this." I see this warrants further explanation.

I thought I was a sincere do-gooder not out to harm anyone but to bring some goodness into the world. I identified with the group because of what it stood for. I thought I was acting on my own volition for a cause I believed in strongly enough to make a few simple sacrifices. The way Leo spoke, we could leave at any time; yet in the same breath, he solidified what we would be forfeiting with nothing to gain but eons of suffering. This kept me at the Center, amid these people I admired for doing something for something they believed in, with integrity.

Saadya is quick to balk. "What *integrity?*"

Despite our compulsively driven, unconventional methods, our motivation, kept in the forefront, was the ordained mission. This is what I identified with, while still being me, as much as was possible.

That first encounter with the police at the airport, when Denise had to talk me back into my worker identity, illustrates the conflict and confusion I had to confront every day out on soul-saving.

The confusion both perpetuated the fervent reciting and was perpetuated by the reciting. The most important thing was to recite the phrases, to empty the mind—to "squeeze the mind like a sponge," we were told. This expression was attributed to Sir Supreme.

Total surrender and dedication to the mission were firmly established and fixed in the fervent prayer to meet the challenge that each day held. In this way, our inalienable rights were denied us, and we learned to feel guilty for wanting our freedom of choice, to choose whatever might be different from the WORKS lifestyle.

"What would have happened if you went to the police after getting walloped over the head?" Mahlia off-handedly asks, glancing at her phone. I pause until she looks up and puts the phone down. The police would have questioned my actions solely based on me being a member of the WORKS. They would consider me only in that regard. They would view me only as a worker in the World Organization for Righteous King Service. The other girl who witnessed the assault, and I, were sure the police would sympathize with my attacker. So my identification as a worker became ever more strengthened, as I felt I belonged nowhere else. Consequently, I put my group affiliation before family, friends, and who I had been before I joined. This encounter with the stranger on the sidewalk only reinforced what I had become.

MY RIGHT TO LEAVE WAS WRONG

MAHLIA GENTLY ASKS, "Was there ever a time when you really wanted to leave?" There was the time at the San Bernadino Airport when I seriously entertained the idea of chucking all the preaching and teaching. I felt a strong pull to leave, and the appeal of leaving the WORKS grew increasingly, as I played out how I would board a United Airlines flight and head to Connecticut. I entertained this notion, embracing the feasibility of actually leaving. I allowed myself to feel this but only so far. When the idea became real, to the extent I might act on it, something happened inside me. Something took over. A force pulled and tugged at me. I cried and heaved, and I hid inside the phone booth in the lobby near the United Airlines terminal. The inner conflict was so compelling.

And then something happened.

I triggered the WORKS' preaching and teaching, and I knew I would never be able to make it in the outside world alone. I would be out there in an ocean filled with monsters and evil tidings, and would be virtually on my own with no one to turn to, because whoever I would turn to would be someone outside the WORKS, and there would be no way they could possibly understand my King mentality. Whoever I would turn to would only be a regular I couldn't trust.

Saadya validates this. "You mean someone not versed in King Service, and that ruled everyone out." More conclusively, that ruled out the idea, even though I was trying to come up with someone I would be able to turn to. In the teachings of the Center, all regulars were alike, so even some of my former friends I knew did not grasp the divine nature of King Service. I ruled out everyone, including my parents. I was forced to conclude that I had to stay. "The thinking you were and were not doing was no longer your own thoughts, but those of what your mind had been contorted into thinking," states Saadya.

Mahlia tops it off by saying, "That is why it is known as mind-control."

"How would you have gotten out of San Bernadino?" asks Saadya. "Would you have gone to your cousin's apartment?" No, no, I would not have—we had not established that kind of relationship between us in the few days before I went to the Wednesday dinner. My mother had told me, so I knew and remembered my parents had reserved an open ticket for me with United Airlines that I could use at any time. That day, I was out alone on soul-saving activity in front of the United Airlines terminal at the San Bernadino Airport. I was nervous, tired, and over-anxious. I just wanted to get the day over with. It was not turning out to be an okay day.

I was approaching regulars, expecting to be turned down. I was transparent. People were looking right through me, or so I thought, which made me vulnerable and insecure about my endeavors to fundraise. They could see my insincerity, my lack of commitment. At other times, I tried too hard, over-compensating each time I approached a passerby. I was in the wrong mindset. It was torture. I was under the influence of the physical energy.

Mahlia embraces my predicament. "You weren't in the King mindset, whatever that was. Sounds like a disaster."

Worse than that, I was feeling miserable and cold. I went inside and sat inside the telephone booth, the kind that is situated in the center of the lobby and open on one side. All along, I was thinking about picking up that airline ticket. I just wanted to get away from my misery. I was in escape mode.

Mahlia continues, "Who can blame you?" I was so close to getting that open ticket, yet I was still so far away.

I was thinking about my home and my parents. That is when, *wham*, all that had been instilled in me at the Barstow Center kicked in and began to reverse my thinking. I concluded that there was no mental escape from WORKS. By physically removing myself from the Center, I would be plagued by all the same miserable feelings I was feeling then.

"The only way for you to feel good was to be a good little worker," Mahlia suggests.

Saadya adds, "You thought the reason you were in such a state of confusion was because of your lack of sincerity." Now you are getting it, I tell them.

This was a cold, harsh reality that I had been programmed into. I began to pray and cry helplessly to the picture I kept in my book bag of Sir Derek, our new spiritual monarch. Mahlia grasps this inconsistency: "Either you are a spiritual monarch, or you are not. If Sir Supreme was the spiritual monarch, how did Sir Derek get to be one?" Sir Supreme was old and needed help, as the WORKS grew internationally, so he supposedly appointed ten of the younger male agents closest to him to carry on the mission.

Now Saadya wants to know, "So what happened when you walked out of the telephone booth?" When I emerged, I resumed my soul-saving activity with renewed enthusiasm.

The result of people responding more positively toward me reinforced my choice of having turned back to King. The group was my link to God, or so I had been led to believe. At that time, I vowed never to use that airplane ticket back to Connecticut. "Big mistake, Mom," Mahlia says, shaking her head in annoyance, not with me, but with the power exerted over me.

This incident removed any future possibility of me taking advantage of my parents' sincere efforts to keep the doors open for me to leave when, in fact, they had been tightly shut while I wasn't looking. "So, in other words, your right to leave was wrong," Saadya concludes.

MORE BRUSHES WITH THE LAW

AFTER A PREGNANT PAUSE, I recall another incident involving the police. After thoughtful consideration, I ask my daughters whether they want to hear about yet another episode with the law. "Tell us everything," they tell me.

There was the day on traveling soul-saving when we spent the day at the Binghamton University campus in New York State. The campus police were alerted to our presence early in the day. We knew we had to keep on the move, so as not to get caught or detained. That would put an end to our soul-saving for the rest of the day. Even if the police knew we were there, if we didn't stay in one place for too long, we wouldn't be tracked down so easily. We would be on campus for only the one day. So we had better not get caught, caught off guard, or fall under the influence of the physical energy.

It seemed that, when any of us had difficulty on soul-saving, it was because our mental state had fallen into the clutches of the physical energy. If we were unfocused and unmotivated, we would more likely be the ones to get caught. Consequently, we would be physically detained and, even worse, lose a day of collecting money. On traveling soul-saving activity, it would be a waste, since time was money. Mahlia tells me, "You were greedy." We knew there was so much Ora out there waiting for the asking, waiting to be retrieved from the regulars, to engage them in service to King.

Saadya offers, "Yeah, and I bet the Center authorities would have no trouble figuring out how to use that money." Mahlia shushes her in deference to me to continue.

At one point, I worked my way to the front of the university library. I dodged inside the building to hide when I saw the campus police coming towards me. They had not yet recognized me as a worker. I knew my position at the front of the library was threatened when several of the students I approached questioned me about whether I had proper authorization to be there.

Once inside the library, I sat down in a roomful of students. I chose a book off one of the shelves, sat down in a comfortable chair, and pretended to be engrossed in the book. I was spotted when two officers came into the room and one of them eyed my book bag on the floor. They walked over to me, and I was then escorted out of the library and cautioned to discontinue my activities.

Saadya points out, "That was all you had to do." That's correct, but instead I kept on soliciting donations, asking students for money for our missionary organization, as I roamed about on campus, indoors and out.

Towards the late afternoon, I entered the Student Union building as the campus police were once again closing in. I saw one of the officers only a short distance away, walking directly towards me. I turned and headed for the restroom. I was hoping he would not follow me in. Once inside, I further retreated into one of the bathroom stalls and took advantage of the opportunity to relieve myself since I was already there and wanted to kill time. I had hoped he would give up if I didn't come out right away. This was not to be. A girl entered the restroom and told me a friend of mine was outside and wanted to talk to me. I knew the police officer had sent her in with this message. I thought, at the time, how ridiculous was the officer's observance of the restriction not to enter the girls' restroom. I mean, there I was, and he knew it, and he knew it was me he was looking for, and I knew it was me he was looking for. He knew that I was in there. I was hoping that, the longer I stayed in the restroom, the more likely it would be that he'd just give up the chase. It turned out not to be so.

When I finally emerged, I played dumb. I acted as if I did not know anyone was waiting for me, especially the police, or that I was doing anything I was not supposed to be doing. I pretended that I had been caught by surprise.

I was secure in the knowledge that being a worker for Righteous King, I was in the right, doing what I was supposed to be doing. Since my activities were sanctioned by God himself, I could not be doing anything wrong. This applied to any and all of our activities.

"So you got snagged," concludes Mahlia. Then realizing what she's said, she adds, "In more ways than one. What happened?"

This time the police brought me down to the campus police office. They checked my WORKS fund-raising identification card, which had my real name. They ran a computer check and came up with my Connecticut address and even my parents' names. I was impressed, but moreover, I realized I was vulnerable to being found out. I felt exposed by them knowing something about my identity outside the WORKS. I really felt like a school girl being caught doing something and threatened that the principal would call my parents.

Looking back, I realize how little people know about the cult phenomenon. I realize how much parents would welcome and embrace being notified where their son or daughter was, and be given the opportunity to regain communication with their child, a cult member, even if it was against the will of the cult. Mahlia says in realization, "You *were* in a cult."

I didn't know it then, and when I found out, I didn't want to believe it, but more of that later.

Mahlia murmurs, "I can hardly wait." At this remark, I am not sure whether she is becoming less or more facetious. Nevertheless, when she encourages me to go on, I am certain of the fact that she is in this conversation for the duration.

I tell her and Saadya, "The officer asked me how many others there were on the campus, which only revealed how little he knew of what was really going on." I told him that there was one other girl I knew of. This was not the truth. I was just protecting my god-sisters, the other agents, so as not to alert the police about them. "Didn't you feel you were lying?" The truth had no meaning for me when relating to people outside of the WORKS. I was responsible only to the Center authority, other agents, and ultimately the spiritual monarch.

I was again escorted, but this time to the police car and seated in the back, and we began to cruise down the streets throughout the campus. When I spotted another worker, Sherine, I pretended not to see her. However, she was very visible because she was acting just like a worker. She was spotted because she was carrying a book bag, wearing a jacket like mine, and it was obvious from the movement of her lips that she was reciting the King phrases. The officer stopped the car and called her over. She slid into the back seat next to me. We were happy to see each other.

Back at police headquarters, we were not very upset about being detained since it was already late afternoon and we'd both had a good day, meaning we had already collected our share of money for a day out on fund-raising activity. The police officer in charge informed us after detaining us only a half an hour that we were lucky it was late in the day on a Friday and he wanted to go home. We were allowed to leave. We made it back to the van on time to meet the others. This was not an unusual day for us. We were used to dealing with the police. They were just not used to dealing with us. And of course, that was before there was street surveillance, so the only way of finding us was by having to.

Saadya comments, "So you really weren't worried about the police."

It never bothered us to be threatened with the prospect of being arrested. We were anesthetized to the prospect of incarceration. If we were ever incarcerated, we were to recite Righteous King phrases oblivious to our surroundings, letting others know they were spiritual beings and teaching them the phrases to recite, so they too could get purified.

So the police never posed a real threat. Nothing could stop our mission to save hopelessly lost souls. However, the only drawback in going to jail was that it would be time lost. Mahlia interrupts sarcastically, "Yeah, from being able to collect donations."

I may have been wrong after all about Mahlia's possible change in attitude. Or perhaps this is her way of protecting me. Yet she was right. Losing time from collecting really disturbed us. There was so much unrealized potential. So while in jail, we would have to preach to anyone who was willing to listen.

LOCK AND KEY

THE PROSPECT OF INCARCERATION DID NOT AFFECT US, nor did it serve to assuage our activities. The threat of spending time in jail posed no real danger or challenge to our King Service either, because it reinforced our identity as a WORKS agent and our reliance on the routine that maintained our distorted perception of the world. "Mom, being in the WORKS was similar to being in jail, because you were already under a mental lock and key," Mahlia proposes.

To which I reply, "There was no key."

And furthermore, none of us ever stayed in jail more than overnight. This wasn't enough time for us to get out of the mental state we were in, since we were still reciting even more fervently behind actual bars. We were taught to keep track on our fingers of the number of times we recited the phrases, just in case our recitation abacus was taken away from us with the rest of our belongings. This was a valuable skill for any worker if we were ever prevented from being in the company of other workers or physically removed, somehow, from the WORKS.

Thus, no one could hold us prisoner because we could mentally escape any compromising situation by completely spacing out and removing ourselves from it. We were prisoners of our own device, completely inaccessible to outside influence.

Mahlia points out, "That's a line from 'Hotel California', the Eagles song."

"I know," I tell her, because when I first heard it, I knew exactly that the lyrics were about deception, similar to what I encountered in the WORKS.

Saadya hums a few bars. "*Did* you ever?" she asks. Ever what?

"Spend time in jail." She squints and shudders at the thought.

Indeed. The first time I was in jail, although the charges were dropped, I spent the time reciting the King phrases. I had no books to read, and I was alone in the cell. Now that I was locked up, I had an excuse for not having to be out on soul-saving. The thought of having some privacy was quite nice, and from what we were told by Leo, this would be the time to take the opportunity to rest up. Since the only King Service input I could receive would be reciting phrases, I recited almost constantly. When I was in a common area, I found one interested person I began telling the King book stories to. She swore she had been set up for prostitution, and then arrested by the police. We were also in adjacent cells, and I gave her my lunch of franks and beans—not exactly what a vegetarian would have difficulty relinquishing, no matter how hungry they might be.

I may have remained isolated in a small prison cell, but I was able to have my own time of worship, singing, and dancing right there in the cell. I ripped up pieces of toilet paper to form the letters that spelled *King*, and I laid them on the mattress where I could see them. I remained spellbound and mystically manipulated.

Another time I spent in jail—

Mahlia exclaims, "*There was another time!*"

I break into a huge smile at her candor, knowing that she gets it from me. The police liked to trump up charges, claiming we were obstructing the sidewalk just to get us off the street they were patrolling. We knew the charges would be dropped by the judge the following morning. This time, I was in a common area filled with young girls, all of whom had been arrested the night before for prostitution. I held one of my ears closed with my finger, so I could recite softly and still hear my voice through bone conduction. I didn't want to recite too loudly because I was already drawing attention to myself by pacing the floor along the edge of the wall. One of the girls was intolerant and told me to shut up, just before throwing an ash tray, filled with cigarette butts and ashes, at me. Another girl told her to leave me alone.

I was later approached by the girl who had come to my defense. She was quite shy and timid, yet curious about what I was doing and why. I explained I was calling upon God for strength.

We were both being held captive by an external entity, and I found an audience in her. I also listened to her story as she explained that she found strength in God as well. I seized this opportunity to preach to her, and this reassured the fact, for me, that, although I was not collecting and would not have anything to show for my efforts, I could still engage in dutiful service by preaching. "Mom," Mahlia says, "did you know that Peter preached the word of God, I mean the gospel, sang songs of worship, and praised God while in prison (Acts 12:5–17)? An earthquake occurred, freeing him and releasing him from the physical chains that bound him." A Bible story, no doubt.

The only difference is that the chains that bound me were not physical. "Mom, that is not the only difference here," Mahlia insists.

I certainly took advantage of this time in jail to catch up on my sleep. I was able to relax because I was not overly concerned with what the judge would do or say, since I expected the charges to be dropped with only a warning.

In this instance, I was falsely accused of obstructing a sidewalk. I called the Center and spoke to Leo. He told me it would be more practical for me to spend the night in jail than post bail, since the charges would likely be dropped the following day, and he was right.

Mahlia maintains, sipping from a cup of green tea, "No, Mom, he just didn't want to be bothered." Nevertheless, he told me to call the ashram when I was released, and said that someone would come for me and bring me to the airport to continue collecting the following day. Mahlia sets two cups on the kitchen counter in order to pour Saadya and me our own tea.

FREEDOM

THE FOLLOWING DAY, just as Leo had said and as I expected, I was released from jail. I was met outside by some boy who was at the Center and happened to have his own car.

"So," Mahlia says, "you got into a car with a perfect stranger?"

I guess I did, but I did it for the holy food. I had not eaten for twenty-four hours, and I would have liked a cup of tea.

I take my first sip from the cup Mahlia has poured for me. "How is it?" she asks. I smile and wink as the warmth from my daughter partners with the warmth of the brew.

He brought me a plate of food prepared for me at the Center. It consisted of various curried vegetable dishes and lots of sweets.

Just as I had expected, I was driven to the airport to resume soul-saving and engage in fund-raising. When the other girls saw me, they offered humility by bowing their heads, quietly reciting phrases of respect for Sir Supreme.

"They couldn't just say hi and give you a hug. No, Sir Supreme had to get the credit!" Saadya thus describes the girls' behavior. But although the phrases did bespeak the worthiness of the spiritual monarch, the girls were showing me respect by humbling themselves as they bowed their heads. Mahlia and Saadya are befuddled. "This is how we did things," I tell them.

PRISON WITHOUT BARS

UNRELENTING GROUP PRESSURE, along with being inculcated with the need to conform, produced the same result as imprisonment. As a potential convert, I placed my allegiance in the hands of those who desired to control me. "To earn your keep, you would have to be controlled—otherwise, you wouldn't want to turn in all the donations you collected," explains Saadya. "And you might question what the money was being used for." Collecting money was presented as a privilege, and, anyway, I didn't need the money. My spiritual life was far more important. Almost as if on cue, Mahlia and Saadya look at each other with big grins on their faces; finally, Saadya breaks the silence and says, "With that sentiment we would have to agree."

As a new worker, I received a heavy dose of peer approval along with a large amount of attention. Under these very structured conditions, this emotional diet had the effect of securing the group as the means of my connection to God. I was getting to know the girls and what they believed in, and was led to conclude that I belonged there in no uncertain terms.

Compliance and cooperation consistently contributed to a sense of being removed and distanced from ordinary life on the outside, as my perception of it had morphed. As a recruit, I was isolated, having limited and very controlled contact with the outside world. Instead, I was being taught and encouraged to recite aloud or to myself, and when I wasn't reciting, I was receiving some other form of input about the philosophy from within the hierarchical system. "I don't understand why reciting would be so bad. Don't people sing under their breath—you know, how when a song gets stuck in your head?" Mahlia asks.

Yet there is a strong distinction.

Reciting those phrases altered my state of mind. It made it easy to implant new ideas, new realities, and to control my thoughts, so everything happening around me was perceived according to the WORKS doctrine. Living in the ashram, and being absorbed in the lifestyle, consumed every moment, and there were always other workers around, which left little or no time for reflection. Our conversation centered on something to do with being King-minded, how we wound up at a Center, and why it was fortuitous for us to be there. Under these circumstances, I did not understand how the group's hierarchical structure and "mind-hacking," as it is now sometimes called, worked and would have such an effect on me.

Everything was interpreted for me. Everything involved in the lifestyle was explained as being spiritual in nature. My affiliation was with other agents who were on a path according to the WORKS doctrine for spiritual advancement. And so was I.

At that time, I didn't know anything about these controlling techniques, so I didn't recognize them for what they were, and what power they had, or the effect they were having on me. I just knew that I had to stay from one Superior Text class to another, from one holy food meal to another, and I had to do what I was told to do for the purpose of making spiritual advancement. My obedience would be for my benefit and for that of the regulars I came in contact with. They too, would make spiritual advancement, if only they would give a donation.

DOOMED

MAHLIA SAYS, "SOUNDS LIKE YOU were very sincere." All the girls were. Our sincerity and ardent service were reflected in the mirror of soul-saving activity. Any deviation, however minor it may have been, would be sure to cause difficulty when asking for a donation. We all needed to be sincere, so that we would be convincing to the regular. Therefore, we were super-careful and diligent not to make any offense against each other, and especially not against an authority.

This included any deviation from following, to the letter, any detail of the morning program. It also included anything to do with the routine throughout the day. Doing anything different, or differently, was considered a deviation. We were not to deviate unless we had explicit permission.

"So you did everything the way you were instructed!" observes Saadya. Exactly the way we were instructed. She says, half smiling—but it wasn't funny—"Making a decision for yourself was a no-no." We had to be one hundred percent committed. The regulars we encountered might perceive any hint of insincerity. Rather than seeing the worker as an integrated part of the mission and giving a donation, the regulars would see our lack of sincerity. That's when we would have a hellish day on fund-raising, and none of us could risk that.

"Whoa, Mom, that is so intense," Saadya reflects. "It wasn't worth taking a chance because you had to be out there all day anyway. I know I'm right because of what you were telling us about the day you hid in the telephone booth."

For sure you are right. This created an enormous amount of anxiety for each of us in the soul-saving group. We had to constantly exemplify loyalty, duty, and sincerity in this privileged service.

In this way, I was trapped into thinking I needed the WORKS for purification, and because I was constantly confronted with my impurity, I needed the WORKS to save me from a fate worse than death. Separation from the WORKS would mean millions and millions of deaths, in which I knew the suffering I would have to experience, even due to the particular sin of so much as stepping on an ant, not to speak of being attached to my senses. I would be doomed to an endless loop of having to repeat the cycle of birth and death for all of eternity.

"As if this cult held the key to salvation," Mahlia says.

"That's another reason it was a cult," adds Saadya. My daughters are validating what I have been reporting to them.

I learned about the far-reaching scope that strict adherence had when I made a purchase without first getting explicit permission to do so. I was rebuked for using some money to buy a summer skirt for soul-saving that I could wear during the warm weather. The infraction, as Leo explained it, was that I had not first asked permission to buy the skirt. I'd bought it one afternoon on a day I had stayed back at the ashram. Saadya remarks, "So even though buying a skirt was a benign act with noble intentions, it was construed as dangerously independent."

Any form of independence needed to be eradicated at its very roots. And not getting permission from anyone in authority, such as Leo or his right-hand girl Camila, whom I will tell you more about, would not be tolerated. Mahlia shouts, "Mom, it also suppressed your *autonomy!*"

It was meant to.

MIRROR ON THE WALL

CONVERSELY, IT SEEMED THAT Leo and Camila could act in any way they wanted to. It surprised me when Camila bought, even with Leo's knowledge, panels of mirrors for the girls' bathroom, in the house that was now the women's soul-saving ashram. This was an episode which I felt was totally inconsistent with the philosophy of not being "bodily conscious."

Mirrors just didn't fit in with how we were supposed to be unconcerned with our physical bodies.

Camila explained that the agents should have nice things, so they would be happy in the WORKS. And furthermore, anything for a worker was sanctioned, because we weren't doing or using it for our own personal enjoyment or gratification. By contrast, regulars were exploiting their material possessions by using them selfishly. Since we were using everything in King's service, it was okay to have mirrors. Saadya notes, "So buying mirrors with donations for poor starving teachers, and for books, was sanctioned."

"And it was up to Mommy to ask them to give," Mahlia says with obvious annoyance.

KEEPING SCORE

COLLECTING WAS A PRIORITY. We even kept track of our soul-saving scores. The scores were the amounts of money we had collected the day before. Our score was a direct reflection of the amount of our selflessness the previous day.

In fact, we referred to the amounts as "collections," and the scores were announced, aloud, in front of the assembly of all the Center agents, male and female, each morning, at the end of the morning program, resulting in everyone hearing each other's scores from the previous day. We didn't want to be embarrassed by a low score, for all to know that we hadn't been psyched up. Mahlia says, "That reminds me of when my second-grade teacher would have everyone stand and then each student sit down when she called off the names of whoever had done the homework. If we hadn't done the homework the night before, the others would know it, because we would be left standing." It was the same principle, and it worked. Mahlia adds, "And it made you work." That it did.

To avoid displaying our lack of faith in the process, or our having succumbed to our selfish desires, we encouraged each other and kept doing what was expected of us. Saadya takes this one step further, asking, "What if you stayed back from fund-raising the day before?"

That too would be announced, along the lines of, "Chana had the day off."

For a time, it was my responsibility to compile the scores. I would then hand them over to the Center president, who, as I said, would read them aloud, along with announcing any other messages, as part of the morning program, to all the agents living at the Center. Participating as a group, worshiping in front of carved figures, and hearing the same messages, created a sense of cohesiveness for us on our mission to save souls, especially our own. It became common practice for the girls to increase their total or their score by manipulating the "add-on."

THE ADD-ON

MOST OF THE GIRLS HELD ONTO a certain amount, referred to as an add-on, sometimes up to twenty-five dollars, maybe more, in order to have money first thing the following morning when we started fund-raising, so we could commence with the spare-change technique.

Mahlia notes, "It was all planned out and premeditated instead of really having been collecting small bills all morning."

Indeed, we already had the add-on to use for the spare-change technique, right off the bat, to finagle people out of an amount above what they would have given.

We would hold onto the add-on but still calculate it into the sum total at the end of the day. However, when our score was low, we would turn in the add-on and count it toward our score for that day as well. Saadya chuckles, "So the money was counted twice." When this was called to Leo's attention, he did not object. It was a better reflection on him and the job he was doing overseeing the operation of the ashram.

Saadya remarks, "I bet he *liked* getting the credit for all the work the girls were doing."

SUPER BOWL ESCAPADE

ONE DAY LEO HAD US REPORT a hundred dollars more than we collected. That was the day of the Super Bowl in New Orleans. Agents from various other WORKS Centers were also there collecting. We were told it was going to be huge. Saadya, a football aficionado, says, "Of course. The Super Bowl's a huge event every year." No, I mean huge for fund-raising collections. We knew the scores from all the different Centers would be compared, and Leo wanted to come out on top. All the Barstow Center women were in New Orleans, having driven there in several vans for the big event. We knew exactly how we were going to get in. Saadya is amazed because she would love to go to a Super Bowl game but has not yet done so.

Realizing I am telling her we didn't have tickets, she asks, "How exactly did you pull that off?" Many times in the past we had flashed our ID cards and said we were the student teachers. This time we went *en masse* as a group of fifteen or more. We had one chance and knew we needed to keep walking no matter what. We had to be enthusiastic, self-assured, and proceed with an authoritative entitlement. There could be no room for hesitation. We had to demonstrate to the person at the gate that we were authorized.

This was a time before there was security like there is now. No cameras, no videos, no metal detectors. Mahlia observes, "You could never pull that off now."

We did then.

We found an entrance where there was one person manning the gate with no one else around. It was after kick-off, so the throngs of spectators and fans had already dispersed into the stadium.

Saadya says, "That must have been Super Bowl XII, at the Super Dome in 1978, when the Dallas Cowboys played against the Denver Broncos." We were in fact oblivious to anything that had to do with the actual football game. All we were concerned with was getting in and collecting. Our pace was quick and resolute as we announced, "We brought the ribbons!" We had accomplished exactly what we'd set out to—to get in.

Mahlia draws the analogy: "*Enter through the narrow gate, for the gate is wide and the way is broad that leads to destruction.*" Is that in the Bible also? "Matthew 7:4," I am told. I was only talking about the Super Bowl.

Anyway, we got in announcing we had the ribbons for halftime. It always seemed official enough the way we were trained to carry it off. Since Leo figured we would have had to pay the hundred dollars to get into the game, he just had us tack that amount on to inflate our scores, making him look better in the eyes of the other Center leaders. There was so much competition fostered among the various Centers to keep the agents enlivened, in what was referred to as 'Sublime Rivalry'.

Saadya, who almost went to law school in New Orleans, is now asking me with practicality, "I want to hear more about the rivalry, but tell me first how you all got to New Orleans." We traveled in a van. There were usually six girls in one van, so the sleeping bags were laid out side by side. We had to adjust ourselves to ensure there was enough room. The driver of the van slept on the two front seats, supported by extra baggage in the space between the passenger and driver's seats. Mahlia quips, "It sounds like she wasn't the only one with baggage." Aren't we all? "That's why the truth will set you free," Mahlia reasons. I strategically steer the conversation back to traveling soul-saving and forget about Sublime Rivalry for now.

SATURDAY NIGHT EXPLOIT

TRAVELING SOUL-SAVING ACTIVITY was a marathon. We collected wherever we were, wherever we went, and wherever we happened to be passing through. We traveled across the United States, and whichever town or city we wound up in, we would collect money and, just as on a marathon, it would be all day and late into the evening.

On late nights, usually Fridays and Saturdays, we stayed out on the streets or went to late-night places or special events, anyplace where there would be throngs of people at that late hour. It never really mattered how much money we already collected during the day or how tired we were. There was nothing else for us to do, so we stayed out. We always hoped to get that large donation we had been praying for the entire day.

So when we would get a series of twenties or fifties or hundred-dollar donations, we concluded that King was answering our prayer.

We could never give up. We had to remain focused on our dutiful service, and once we were rewarded, we would immediately begin to pray for another large donation. Our minds were in a loop. Mahlia says, "More like you were a mouse in a metal cage going in circles on one of those exercise wheels."

Saadya offers, "Going nowhere fast." Realizing what I said, she asks, "You actually prayed to God for money?"

The prayer usually went something like this: *King, I am so impure, I am the most impure. I know I don't deserve anything but please send me a big donation. Please let me do big for my spiritual monarch.* Likewise, it was not satisfactory to collect for only a few hours and then stop for the day. We were conditioned to never be satisfied. Saadya indicates, "That's called greed." Mahlia points out, "That is what I call exploitation." We were led to believe that, no matter how much was collected, we could have done better, and had to try to improve the following day. Soul-saving was our eternal service. We never took vacations. Instead, we would stay back at the ashram to read, usually only one day at a time but didn't entirely relax. Staying back at the ashram only provided a reprieve from the demands of high performance that had been building up on our already overloaded nervous system.

I pause, wide-eyed, and, holding my breath, I realize Mahlia is right. We were being exploited.

CALLING ALL CARS

ONE YEAR, TWO GROUPS OF WOMEN were on the road, engaging in traveling soul-saving. We had to keep in contact, so the only way was to involve an answering service. "That is so funny, Mom, no cell phones!" chimes in Mahlia as her own phone is ringing. She glances down and dismisses the call. "Couldn't be better than this," she concludes.

I tell her it was even before beepers. Saadya asks, "What is a *beeper?*" Mahlia glances at her incredulously.

Saadya assures us, "I know what a beeper is."

Mahlia breathes a sigh of relief. "Don't you remember we used beepers in middle school?"

Saadya recalls, "Mommy would signal me to call her after soccer practice, but I remember she always came to my games."

In this case, messages were taken from one girl or group of girls and relayed to the second group, or messages were relayed or received between Leo and the girl in charge. Despite being on the road, we needed to be in contact for various reasons. For example, in the morning, arrangements were made between Leo and the girl in charge, who was also the designated van driver. Instructions were given about where we were to be dropped off. We then made arrangements among ourselves for when we should call into the answering service and leave the message to inform the girl in charge, where we would be so we could be picked up, either for lunch or at the end of the day. We specified the location or we received information about where we were to be and when, so we could be picked up at the designated time and place.

We moved around and covered a lot of ground, so to speak. We would not stay in the same location we had been dropped off at because it increased the likelihood of being asked to leave the premises if people complained about our solicitations. It was always impossible to predict, in the morning, where any of us would be six hours later for lunch, or by the end of the day, so we needed to communicate our whereabouts. We could go wherever King directed us and we had enough soul-saving experience to know that wherever there was people, there was the potential for doing well. Therefore, we typically went wherever there were crowds.

People in crowds didn't have time to question what we were collecting for and usually felt that it was their obligation to pay for being part of the crowd, especially if they were at a special event. In all that time, not one of us was ever late or lost. The van was our means of transportation, as well as our only shelter. "What a pity!" declares Saadya. I glance at her questioningly. She clarifies by paraphrasing from Psalm 91: "It was a pity you didn't know about the shelter that the Lord Almighty provides." Yikes, she has a scripture for everything. I am wondering if I should continue.

THE GAG ORDER

MAHLIA ASSURES ME, "Saadya is only trying to help." When I glance at Saadya, she nods ever so slightly, perceptibly enough to reestablish our line of communication. On special occasions we traveled for a few days at a time. We had a destination in mind, and would stop along the way to collect. One such time, we traveled north to Stockton. Two vans were rented and the odometers were promptly disconnected, so as not to register the actual mileage. We were on our way in a van, with six to eight girls, each with her own book bag filled with the add-on for immediate use when we made our first stop en route to Stockton. We were on our way to the Stockton Center to see Sir Supreme. He was visiting from the Philippines. This was to be a rare opportunity for agents from nearby WORKS Centers to hear the spiritual monarch preach in person. I was to appear that Friday in court for a summons I received for possibly obstructing a sidewalk during one afternoon when I was at the Glen Helen Regional Park.

I called the court telephone number when I learned that I was supposed to be traveling. The date was changed, so my court appearance was postponed for a different day. However, the court followed procedure and notified the Center about my impending scheduled appearance for that Friday of the weekend we drove to see Sir Supreme. The two vans had already left the Barstow Center when Clarke, the Center president received a phone call from the court secretary who told him that if I did not appear on the scheduled date and time, a warrant would be issued for my arrest. Clarke called the Stockton Center and left a message for Leo.

After we arrived in Stockton, Leo told me I had to fly back to San Bernadino, and that there was nothing I could say to change this. He did not give me an opportunity to explain that I had been in contact with the court and that I had postponed my court appearance. When I opened my mouth to speak, I was given a gag order. It is not possible to speak to someone who refuses to listen, let alone Leo. Any attempt to explain further would only serve to incur Leo's wrath. He simply would not tolerate any insubordination. I knew that if I tried any more to get him to listen it would have put him over the edge. For a moment, I considered that, although I had taken measures not to be guilty of contumacy, I might have needed to appear in court, after all. So just as Leo insisted, I flew out of Stockton.

Upon arriving at the San Bernadino Airport, I was met by a male worker who I did not know. We drove straight to the court and when my name was not called from the agenda, I inquired and was told that the date had been changed upon my request, just as I tried telling Leo. The boy who picked me up this day, interestingly enough, left the Center permanently only days later. I actually thought he left because he had my company and had fallen down from spiritual life, just as I had been led to believe would happen to the male agents if they associated with a female. I felt I was to blame but had not spoken a word of this to anyone and had no corroboration. Mahlia infers, "He left because his eyes were open to the authoritarian hierarchy and totalitarian rule at the Center."

Saadya says," It's just too bad leaving was out of reach for Mom."

I was then driven back to the Barstow Center, where the Center president inquired about the outcome of my court appearance. I related the incident to Clarke, and he instructed me to go to the smaller Barstow-Daggett Airport and fly back up to Stockton and take a bus from the airport to the Stockton Center on South Union Street, which I did. "You did this all in one day, just because Leo wouldn't listen to you?" announces Saadya as a declaration of the absurdity. I had to obey Leo, and that was that. He could not get past giving an instruction and having his authority challenged. When Leo saw me, he questioned what I was doing there. This time he had to listen to me, as I then explained the fiasco caused by him not listening to me, to begin with. He made absolutely no comment and just walked away.

DICTATIONS FROM ABOVE

THIS POEM WAS WRITTEN less than a year after my three years in the WORKS, and captures the essence of life for me as a worker. I wrote it during the time I was beginning to grasp the enormity of what had happened to me.

> *It's easiest for me to write when searching for your love. I have not stopped asking why we are here, thirsting for answers. At those moments when all else seems insignificant, my experience I recant. We spoke of King repeatedly and no longer had to wonder, we spoke as if we really knew, as all else wished they could. We believed as we did, in a way no one else could, without King's names vibrated, producing, for our souls, a place to be consecrated.*
>
> *We were dedicated for King's glories to be told, amidst a climate in which our methods stood berated. This philosophy, I internalized to know right from wrong within my heart, as dictated from above, when the workings of my mind was the object that impeded. So shelter I sought, while dutifully I fought protection*

from myself. Not one moment was wasted on some frivolous thought or any thought, for that matter, nor whimsical act ill-motivated, as they all were viewed to be. Every instruction, command we executed as though our life everlasting depended. King's mercy and kindness we prayed for and worked for. We had no rest or peace within, separate from our obligation, to satisfy King's desire and those to whom we answered. In my search, I sought the answers, yet now it seems my life and search has really just begun.

FEAST OR FAMINE

"LEO WAS A SCOUNDREL AND A TYRANT," observes Mahlia. The gag order was not the only time I had experienced Leo's tyranny. One afternoon while designated as a driver of one of the vans, I had backed the van into the side of another vehicle in the Center parking lot. I was made to fast for two days. As further retribution, I was required to go out on soul-saving to collect the sum of money to pay for the auto body repairs to the van. The Center was planning to sell the van I had damaged, so it had to be in good condition.

This occurred during the time when I was not going out on soul-saving on a regular basis because I was putting all my energies towards editing for a few of the WORKS' publications. I, in fact, collected, in those two days, more than it would cost to repair the damages to the van. In conversation with Lilly, the Center president's wife, I disclosed that I was required to fast for two days. This came to Lilly as a huge surprise. Neither she nor anyone else at the Center had any idea that Leo required this of me, either as a consequence or a punishment. I remember the pained expression on Lilly's face as being one that clearly and unmistakably showed she thought my fasting was unwarranted.

Outraged, Saadya proclaims, "What about unreasonable!" She then notes, "It is so ironic that you first went there for a free dinner and then food was being denied you."

Food played a big part for everyone. That first Wednesday, I was even offered a second plate of food. "Mom, they were dishing out a plate full of baloney," quips Mahlia in true form.

To be sure, the Wednesday event was a big deal for us. We went out on soul-saving every day of the week. We followed the same routine every day. However, on Wednesdays, we would return to the Center, in the early afternoon, to participate in the entire program held at the Center. On Wednesdays, the Center cooks prepared different dishes, consisting of potatoes, rice, peas, and beans, along with various vegetable dishes and a variety of desserts. Of course there was no meat.

These foods were so different from what I was used to eating on other days. The Wednesday dinner was a real treat. We all and we always looked forward to it. At one point, the women would eat the dinner in a separate room. Plates of food would have already been prepared for each of the women. There was a little more than enough for a taste of each different dish.

It came full circle because when I first met the soul-saving group, I was introduced to them in the same fashion, right in this room where the women were eating their allotted portions. That first Wednesday dinner, I became aware that the women were asking Leo if they could have second helpings. When I questioned him about this practice, he explained that this was to help the women control their appetites so they would not be eating out of lust. Saadya says, "Now, you were also asking if you could have seconds."

When I had already joined, having any seconds of the Wednesday dinner was a no-no. Leo determined that if any of us soul-saving girls ate too much that late in the day, we would have difficulty rising as early as we did the following morning. Mahlia considers, "Things really changed and took a turn." Not before too long. "Didn't you realize what was happening?" By that time, it was too late. I too had changed! Mahlia caps the exchange and says, "You became one of them." I was entrenched. When I first agreed to stay overnight, I had no idea this *could* happen, or that the phenomenon even existed.

Saadya looks up and says, "But Leo knew this would happen."

THE FAST TRACK

FASTING WAS NOT ENTIRELY UNHEARD OF as a WORKS practice. The Center workers, as a whole would fast on certain days of celebration, such as King's birthday, any of the carved figures' birthday, Sir Supreme's birthday or Mardi Gras. The cooks were occupied the entire day with preparing food for the special occasion. There would be an extravagant meal and everyone would break the fast at midnight. Guests would come to partake in the special holy day festivity. Their presence and participation confirmed that King Awareness was, indeed, a bona fide religion.

Moreover, the way Leo always presented it, fasting was an opportunity for us to make spiritual advancement. Therefore, fasting was integrated on a regular basis as part of the women's program. It started out as a weekly one-day fast, but then for about two months, we fasted on Mondays and Tuesdays. Our fast consisted of two cups of juice on these days. On yet another fast, in the morning, hot milk was served for our breakfast meal. On occasion, Leo arranged for us to drink cups of heavily sweetened and thickly flavored hot chocolate and malted milk just before laying out our sleeping bags to get rest. Saadya observes, "I think this was because Leo didn't want to get in trouble for starving the girls." We would drink lots of milk, wake up satisfied and not complain when the next fast rolled around. However, on the nights we didn't get the hot milk, I can remember the intense feelings of emptiness and thinking I would never make it through the night on such an empty stomach.

Some of the girls were so hungry from not eating all day they would have two cups of the hot chocolate malted milk. After about two months of doing this, Leo could see that some of the girls, myself included, were putting on weight. Leo reasoned that after two consecutive days of not eating, we were driven to overeat on the other days of the week. Petulantly, Mahlia remarks, "Overeating and over-drinking." We were on survival mode.

Saadya asks, "Didn't you want to raid the refrigerator?" Truly, one evening while desperately trying to fall asleep to escape my hunger pangs, I actually had the sudden urge to do just that, raid the refrigerator. I fought off the impulse generated by my survival instinct of needing to fill the pit in my stomach. Fortunately, I was successful in not acting on that impulse. Somehow, I made it through to morning, holding off until the breakfast meal was provided at the designated time, for us all, after the morning program.

Confused which fast I am referring to, Saadya says, "But I thought you said you drank chocolate milk before going to sleep—I mean rested up." The fast when I wanted to raid the refrigerator was after a day when we fasted, for the entire day, on water only. That night I found myself lying awake in my sleeping bag, and seriously had to fight, with every fiber of my being, not to get up to go to the kitchen and get something to eat. When I did finally eat, it was an attempt to fill the empty bottomless pit in my stomach.

Mahlia conveys the sentiment in Isaiah 58:6, "*Is this not the fast I have chosen? To untie the bands of wickedness, to undo the heavy burden, and to let the oppressed go free, and that ye break every yoke?*" My bands were yet to be broken, and yes I was burdened. Mahlia alleges, "You forgot the part about being oppressed."

THE ICING ON THE CAKE

THEN MAHLIA OFFERS, "IT SEEMS LIKE so much emphasis was placed on eating." Simply put, it was an acceptable satisfying sensory activity. I recall there was a period of time when the buckets of food were left in the corridor for us before the guests arrived for the Wednesday event, and we were told we would be eating before the guests, so that we would not be hungry while they were at the Center. This would give us more time to preach to them and be available without the distraction of having to eat. Helping ourselves to those buckets of food applied to both male and female agents. We took as much as we wanted; however, this system of having all that food at our disposal was too much to handle. The agents, especially the men, would spoon heaps and heaps of food onto their plates and return for seconds.

Mahlia says, "They were ravenous." Even the women acted like they hadn't eaten in days. "That's because they hadn't," she adds.

Saadya giggles. "What bizarre behavior over food." Wait until I tell you this. We loved finding a piece of food stuck in our teeth and chomped on that for a bit longer. Then I tell them about the time, after my rescue out of the WORKS, when I was visited by a former WORKS agent named Toetje, and Gregory, whom you will find out about later. Toetje was from Holland but had joined a WORKS Center on the East Coast while traveling in the United States. He was rescued out of the WORKS several months after me. Gregory had been instrumental in helping him understand the cult aspects of the WORKS as he had been less than a year earlier with me. Gregory and Toetje stayed over at my apartment, also on the East Coast, so they would not incur the expense of a motel room. They camped out on the floor until the date they needed to catch their flight to Amsterdam. Gregory was going to accompany Toetje, so he would not slip back into the King mindset if left on his own, since Toetje had only so recently been rescued.

One morning, I found all the icing eaten off a cake. The bakery box with the remaining cake lay on the floor under my dining room table. I knew any explanation was going to be peculiar, and the culprit had to be Toetje. Even more peculiar was that he would stash it under the dining room table, as if his deed would go unnoticed. I planned to ask him when I saw him later in the day.

Although Toetje initially denied any culpability for stashing the left over cake under the dining room table, he later shamefully admitted to it. He was more embarrassed over being lascivious than at first having lied to me and Gregory.

This boy, after six weeks out of the WORKS, was still in the habit of licking his plate clean. Watching him do that reminded me that it was a common practice of the WORKS agents. By licking the plate clean, we would be getting the full blessing from the holy food. Holy food was supposed to embody the essence of King himself.

This practice was accepted at the Center and the ashram, even among the women. However, during Wednesday dinner events, we were admonished not to lick our plates in front of the guests because they would not understand that, in the King mentality, licking your plate clean was proper etiquette.

Anyway, we began overeating at the Wednesday dinner. The next day we would be back to our regimented diet of bean soup, rice, and a biscuit. Mahlia says, "No wonder the Wednesday dinner was so special."

In spite of the Wednesday dinners being so extravagant throughout the Organization, when Sir Derek came to Barstow, he put a halt to that. Instead, the cooks were instructed to make only rice or potato, some vegetable dish, and some combination of tropical fruit juices. Under Sir Derek's edict, the regulars were to be served minimal portions, just enough for a taste, rather than a bellyful. This was intended to discourage people who were merely down-and-out, and not genuinely interested in the philosophy, from coming just to get a free meal. Saadya offers, "But in your case, it was too late for just a free meal. They owned you."

Mahlia says, "Eating a vegetarian meal was not the problem here. The problem was that you swallowed everything else being shoved down your throat."

INCONSPICUOUS

Saadya picks up on the conversation, coming to my defense. "Mom, you thought this was the real deal spiritually?" I thought it was all that and more. In essence, my existence was merely a moment in time, actually in an eternity, yet at the same time it was no accident that I was at a Righteous King Center. My energies would be meaningless if not expended in the service of King. I would have significance only as a King worker in the World Organization for Righteous King Service.

Conversely, I was encouraged, and trained, to be inconspicuous within the group of women. This meant that I would have to ignore and deny myself of myself. At the Center, by keeping my body draped from head to toe in the tunic and scarf, I was not calling attention to myself. The only aspect of the lifestyle that tolerated any degree of ego was that which involved being a model worker. This was my existence, or rather non-existence, and self-sacrifice would blossom into the attractive quality of humility necessary for being successful in King Service. I would be successful if all I did was carry out my duties of going out on soul-saving activity to collect a lot of Ora. Saadya professes, "When you don't think you're leaving anything behind, it's easy to leave everything behind."

FORSAKE NOT YOUR MOTHER

I learned to equally hate the world of politicians, news reporters, scientists, and mothers and fathers. My utopian ideals were channeled into a belief system that demanded complete subjection to totalitarian rule over its adherents. Mahlia adds, "Namely, you."

Saadya, who navigated through her teenage years struggling socially and feeling she could not communicate with her parents, wants to know the part about hating mothers and fathers, bluntly asking, "Did you harbor hatred for Grandpa and Grandma?"

Mahlia affirms, "It's hard to believe. You and Grandma get along so well and spend so much time together."

Nonetheless, I'll tell you about when my mother came to visit me at the Center six months after I joined. She flew into the San Bernadino Airport. I was expecting her arrival. Since I was already at the airport on soul-saving activity, I met her at the United Airlines terminal somewhere before 1:00 p.m., which is significant because all the girls would be taking a break to eat the afternoon meal shortly thereafter. I stayed with my mother while she waited at the baggage carousel to claim her suitcase. We exchanged niceties about the flight and how we were both doing.

"How did Grandma and Grandpa learn about you being at the Center?" asks Mahlia. I first told my mother over the phone, point blank, that I had joined a Righteous King Center in Barstow. Her response clinched it for me when she said that she recalled, one day when she, my father, and I were in downtown Hartford on a Saturday afternoon—seeing WORKS agents in tunics performing an amusing skit in the street, followed by a dervish dance set to music. Her response communicated something to me that I am sure was never her intention. It actually validated my decision because she had witnessed the ecstasy the Hartford agents were in. Now she could understand my experience at the Center, and the joy I was having during the singing and dancing in worship to King.

Mahlia intently asks, "What could she have done or said differently that would have dissuaded you?" Without an opportunity of testing the reality created at the Center, there would have been nothing she could say or do. To reality-test meant I would have had to mull over what I was learning about and then come to a well thought-out decision. However, the likelihood of me leaving to think things over grew slimmer with each passing day.

I was genuinely happy to see my mother and thought I would be able to tolerate the visit, just as long as we made small talk. I dreaded a confrontation because I was convinced she wasn't on a high enough spiritual level to understand anything about King Service and I never expected her to comprehend or sanction my involvement.

Our initial exchange in the airport terminal and baggage claim area went relatively smoothly. Nothing at first shocked her. I was dressed in green slacks and a tailored blouse.

I invited my mom to have lunch with us out in the van. We always met at the van in the parking lot for Superior Text class while we ate lunch. She agreed to join us. I remember that lunch consisted of salad with raisins and peanuts with a curry dressing. She accompanied me into the parking lot where the other girls were gathered alongside the van. They offered her a Righteous King greeting, to which she replied, "*Shalom.*" This would have been an appropriate enough salutation except that it came out as flat-out nasty. I had never heard my mother greet anyone like that before, or even use the expression.

Leo was in the driver's seat while the other girls sat cross-legged on the platform built in the van to allow for storage space beneath for books, sleeping bags, or other possessions when we traveled. I sat in the front passenger seat. My mother did too, wedged between me and the passenger door. The girls introduced themselves individually, and Superior Text class began. My mother sat motionless at first.

But as Leo read from a passage and began to offer interpretation and commentary, she exploded. He was reading from a passage explaining God as King, enjoying his world while looking down on Earth with disdain.

Mahlia points out, "That had to be very difficult for Grandma, even though she's not very religious. As a Jew she would know that God loves and longs for His creation." Mahlia, you hit the nail on the head. My mother was getting increasingly agitated.

There she was, fresh off the flight from Connecticut, sitting in a WORKS van, listening to her daughter recite verses out of the Superior Text in a foreign language, learning about a foreign god. She listened to the lecture, which went against every fiber of her being. Finally, she exploded, bolted out of the van, grabbing her suitcase. I remained exactly where I was without blinking an eyelash or moving a muscle. I watched her lug that suitcase across the parking lot and into the terminal. I remained glued to my seat, and stayed in the van just as a little worker was supposed to. Leo even praised me for not going after her.

THE VISIT

SAADYA NOW ASKS, "When did you see Grandma next, and what happened?" I didn't know when and where, or if at all, I would see her again. For all I knew, she might even have taken a flight back to Connecticut. However, that evening when I returned to the Center, I received a message from her. She'd left the telephone number of the motel where she was staying. I called, and we made plans for the following day. She was going to pick me up in a rental car. I would be able to get her to engage in King Service during her visit, since it was important to me that she reap some spiritual benefit. We agreed for her to take me shopping, so I could get some new clothes for soul-saving activity. On soul-saving we had to blend in, so we didn't wear a tunic as we did back at the ashram.

At the store, while trying on different outfits, I was caught between wanting to keep my mother's expenditure to a minimum and wanting her to reap a spiritual benefit. "So the more money Grandma spent, the greater her spiritual reward?" Mahlia asks.

That was what I thought. She wanted to buy me personal things that she thought I needed. Yet as far as I was concerned, my needs were minimal.

All the while, I felt my anger surfacing. I was furious with her. But I didn't take the time to recognize why or understand it then. Now, looking back, I realized I blamed her for not investing in me. My mother felt financially pinched by the time I was old enough to want to participate in after-school activities. I cajoled her unsuccessfully to let me take dance lessons, piano lessons, guitar lessons, and finally Hebrew classes, so I could have a *bat mitzvah*. I was told I didn't need dance lessons, she didn't have enough money to buy a piano, and when I counter-offered to take guitar lessons, she said I was not musically inclined. I didn't need to have a *bat mitzvah* either, since "Girls don't have to do that." A form of self-expression was denied me, so I embraced the opportunity of doing something; the way it was presented in the WORKS, I thought, was extraordinary.

Although, as a consolation, I was able to join the Girl Scouts. I excelled in school work, was voted into office in the student government, and even elected president of the student body one year. I was also sent to summer sleep-away camp two summers in a row, at which I was selected as color war captain both years, and then the experience of summer camp came to an end. "Because it cost too much money?" asks Saadya. More than my mother wanted to pay. Instead, I felt deprived and was miserable most of the time during subsequent summers. I hope that makes some sense to you, because when I was growing up it was devastating for me. Saadya remarks, "Sounds like you still had some growing up to do."

With this inner turmoil I was feeling in my mother's company, I could only imagine what was going through *her* mind. Yet we spent the whole day together. While she ate in a restaurant near the San Manuel Amphitheater, I remained outside. I tried remaining with her in the restaurant at first, but once the menu was presented, being surrounded by people engaged in sense gratification, with no outlet for engaging as an agent, I could bear it no longer. I simply got up and walked out, telling my mother I would wait for her outside.

Sitting there with her was purposeless in the scheme of things. Saadya asks, "What things? The scheme of the King mindset?" That was the only way I could think. Thereupon, I saw exactly what I was programmed to perceive, a scene that evoked purposelessness as the regulars were mindlessly indulging their senses.

Mahlia surmises, "Also, you couldn't hit up the regulars as they were eating lunch in a restaurant." Thus, I could not actively engage in the mission, although the restaurant was filled with regulars. My frustration was manifesting on a visceral level. "So before you flipped out, you walked out," she adds. I waited outside, reading a WORKS magazine.

When my mother later joined me on the sidewalk, she told me what she had eaten, and I really felt happy for her that she'd had a bit of a good time. I was well aware that I was experiencing dissonance, as well as creating a disturbance for her, just by being the way I was. Saadya assures me, "No matter how hard the Center was training you to hate your own mother, by taking her feelings into consideration you were indeed having Godly love for her."

Mahlia concurs: "You were not a lost cause." But I was.

My main concern was that I considered myself happily situated in the WORKS and wanted my mother to realize this. I was cognizant that she wanted her little girl back, but I wanted not to be pressured to abandon my newfound identity in the WORKS. I thought my King Service was much bigger than either of us and more important than both of us. I recognized her powerlessness. Telling me what she had eaten further highlighted the incongruity between us and drove me further away from her and deeper into the WORKS. There was no mistaking that I viewed my mother as a regular.

Later in the afternoon, I surprisingly considered staying at the motel with her. Leo was not at the Center for me to get his permission. When I called, I wound up speaking to Clarke, who advised me against it. He told me not to think of her as my mother. He reinforced the WORKS mentality telling me that she was just another regular. He also fore-warned me that, if I was removed from the company of workers, I might lose my affections for the Center and Center life.

When Leo returned later that evening and saw me, he evidently had been notified by Clarke that we'd had this conversation, and he rebuked me for even considering the idea of sleeping over at the motel to stay with my mother. He accused me of being attached to the mother-daugh-ter illusion. When I saw truth in what Leo was saying, I felt really bad about having entertained the notion. I still had a natural affinity with, and feeling for, my mother. But I decided I would prove that I was more spiritual than *that* and was an agent first and foremost, dedicated to the mission of saving souls.

THE PROMISE

ON WEDNESDAY, MY MOTHER CAME to the Center for the Wednesday dinner event. The plan was for her to first come to the women's ashram where I slept, and we would walk to the worship Center together. I stepped out of the apartment and joined her at the top of the staircase landing. It was the first time she had seen me wrapped in a tunic and scarf. Her reaction, as I met her on the front porch, was one of horror and disbelief. She clasped her hands together and exclaimed, "Oh, my God." It wasn't what she said that struck me, but the look in her eyes. She was mortified. I pitied her for not being able to see beyond the clothes I wore or the fact that I slept in a sleeping bag on the floor. I pitied her because she was not able or willing to appreciate the need for austerity in making spiritual advancement.

Mahlia says, "I don't think Grandma was interested in your spiritual advancement."

Actually, she had something else on her mind. As she and I walked the two blocks from the ashram to the Center, she asked me to promise her that I would not get married to someone there. I was able to do that easily, because as a soul-saving sister, I felt married to Leo. In fact, I had just turned down a marriage proposal.

MY FIRST PROPOSAL

LEO HAD TOLD ME one of the men, whom I'd never met, wanted to marry me. I was aware of him only because he was the only African American agent at the Center. Leo wanted me to tell him that the decision to decline the offer was mine alone. Leo told me what to say when I spoke to my secret admirer over the phone. I told the young man that not getting married had nothing to do with him, but that I did not want to get married at all. I told him that I was a soul-saving worker and did not want to live out my King Service tied down to a husband and children.

Before either of my daughters could say anything, I explained that it was an either-or situation. With Leo, it was either I went out on soul-saving or not. Getting married would ultimately prevent me from fundraising, as I would get pregnant, which would require me to remain at the Center to take care of a baby. Saadya says, "I think you were just being loyal to Leo and doing what was expected of you."

Then Mahlia breaks out with her jingle, "Chana and her husband sitting in a tree, k-i-s-s-i-n-g. First comes King, then comes marriage, then comes Chana with a baby carriage."

We're all stunned at this comic relief. But Mahlia is right. Leo didn't want to jeopardize losing me as a soul-saving agent, loyal to him and to collecting Ora.

A BOWL OF CHERRIES

OF COURSE, I DIDN'T GO INTO DETAIL as I walked with my mother down the street towards the Center. After escorting her into the worship room—a rather large space—I left her at the rear when the offering to the carved figures began, and went up front to join my god-sisters. I was proud of my surroundings and wanted my mother to see how happy I was.

Mahlia says, "It sounds like you were trying to impress Grandma." I *wanted* her to be impressed. I thought if she could see me dancing for joy, she would be convinced that I was truly happy. Proving that I could be happy in life was ingrained in me; I can remember her saying often enough, "Life is not a bowl of cherries." It annoyed me, and I didn't want this philosophy prescribed for me. The agents' display of exuberance amid the singing and the beat of the drums, I was certain, would disprove her distorted philosophy of life.

Mahlia nods her head from side to side. Rhetorically, she asks, "Did you actually expect her to condone this lifestyle?" Why not? is how I thought at the time. Afterward, I found her in a designated area where guests were seated and served—not on the floor as I had been that first time, but at tables. She was at a table, talking with Leo. I asked her if she had eaten—not so much to see if she liked the food, but thinking she might be hungry by then. She told me she had tasted some of the food and didn't like it: Everything was either too sweet or too pungent. She was right. That night most of the preparations, including the vegetable dishes, were smothered in sweet or pungent sauces.

Mahlia says, "Don't feel so bad. Grandma probably didn't have an appetite."

"Even if she did, she probably lost it," adds Saadya. Probably, and she was clearly ready to leave after what seemed like a polite conversation with Leo.

I asked Leo's permission to accompany my mother to where her rental car was parked. Out on the street, once we were alone, she objected to my having to ask Leo's permission. After all the other things she had witnessed—the fervent singing, dancing, and offering flowers and incense to plants and carved figures—I was surprised that this would be the issue she would question me about. After six months at the Center, I was already accustomed to asking Leo's permission for everything. I thought nothing of it, yet she had picked up on the odd behavior. Saadya remembers that this was what I had questioned Leo on that first time I encountered the policy, when Jayda had had to ask if she could ride my bicycle.

I explained it to my mother, but not exactly the way it had been explained to me. Instead, I told her that Leo was responsible for so many of us, it was reasonable for us to let him know our whereabouts. She must have seen right through this lie. She was still disquieted by my show of submission. Saadya comments, "You couldn't tell Grandma that you were submitting yourself to make spiritual advancement because Leo was King's representative on Earth."

No, I couldn't.

We kissed on the cheek, said good night, and my mother drove off. She was supposed to be leaving the following day, and we both assumed I would see her off at the airport.

That morning, however, Leo told me he was sending me to the Silverwood Lake area for soul-saving activity. I told him I felt badly because I had made plans to have my mother page me when she got to the airport, so I could see her off. He gave me the same rap about not being attached and, even more importantly, not taking any chance of being kidnapped.

I ALREADY GAVE

WHEN I DIDN'T ANSWER my mother's page at the airport, she called the Center and was told I was not at the airport that day. When I returned from Silverwood Lake at the end of the day, I saw Paula back at the ashram; she told me that she'd seen my mother at the airport and approached her for a donation.

Mahlia says, "That is flat-out *hutzpa*!" Paula told me my mother was crying, and that, when Paula asked her for a donation, she'd said, "I already gave my daughter!"

The only communication I had with my mother after this was confined to a few letters and phone calls. Each time I heard from her, she tried to talk me out of King Service. She and my father began sending me newspaper articles about the CAUSE, all of which I thought had nothing to do with the WORKS. My mother continued to challenge why I had to ask permission from Leo. Mahlia says, "Well, with all those miles between you, her approach was the only one she could have taken."

Actually, my advice would be to tell the cult member something like, *I know you view me as a fallen soul and you cannot associate with me. I know you think I'm not up to your level. I know you think this group has all the answers. I know you think this group is the only place you can receive favor from God. I know you think you are on a special mission, and that that is what makes you special to God. I know you have to submit to your authority because they represent God.*

"Just call them out on whatever it is they are being led to think, to show them their thinking is not such a special secret after all, but common knowledge that this is what they are being led to believe."

As the months wore on, I was increasingly entrenched in the WORKS philosophy. Why shouldn't I have to ask permission or submit to authority?

Mahlia stresses, "More like you were incapable of any *other* perspective." Every justification for submission continually thrown at us was the rationale for this peculiar lifestyle, our activities, rituals, and practices.

Mahlia then notes, "I can tell you thought you were making spiritual advancement."

I glance into her eyes to get an accurate read. She further explains, "Your mother's arguments fell on deaf ears, as well as an unquestioning mind." All the while, I was confined by boundaries set by Center leadership, impenetrable by anything anyone could say or try to otherwise convince me of. The other agents were likewise entrenched. I was a prisoner in a prison without bars, and no holds were barred.

My mother realized this. After an additional two and a half years, it was this visit that set in motion what would culminate in a deprogramming. "A *what?*" both my daughters exclaim. I will tell you later.

Isaiah 46:4: "*Even in your old age and gray hairs I am he, I am he who will sustain you. I have made you, and I will carry you; I will sustain you and I will rescue you.*" Mahlia attributes this to the fortitude my mother, her grandmother, had in the circumstances surrounding her visit with me in the WORKS.

In an effort to redeem myself with my daughters, I tell them what I wrote months later after my rescue from the cult, upon consideration of the extraordinary experience my mother endured:

> *Dear Mom, Mommy Dearest, you are, as the relation implies, to be one is to know to be one in our relation, none other as unique. I watched you trying to understand and reach out through the chasm of distance and time. I've watched your face change in an instant, consistent with a grimace, a glaze, I will never forget. When the sight you were to behold, no words ever foretold, having watched me turn from diaper to dapper, from tunic to sweet savoir-faire. You left the scene emboldened. Now my attempt to tell you: It's more than being my dearest of moms. It's you who to me are so dear.*

NAÏVETÉ

ONE MORNING, SIR DEREK, the supreme spiritual monarch for our region, was encouraging us to ask him questions. We had been told that Sir Supreme, and now Sir Derek, were so much more advanced and elevated than us, and that they knew King intimately. Since King always reveals himself to the supreme spiritual monarch and even speaks to him, I wanted to know what exactly that is like.

Sir Derek answered that King was revealing himself to all living creatures, but it depended on their sincerity how much they could actually perceive. He did not exactly answer my question, which was reminiscent of the first question I had asked the first night I ever went to a King Center. I had asked Leo the same thing—after hearing him speak of God so knowingly, my curiosity was piqued that someone could actually know who God was and what he looked like; I had already believed in God, and it was perplexing that he would maintain anonymity, since it wasn't at all difficult for me to accept that God existed and was very much alive sustaining creation.

So it was not outlandish for me to pose the question of what it sounded like when King spoke. After all, the pure spiritual agent of King, Sir Supreme, and now Sir Derek, were supposed to have first-hand experience with the spiritual world and the knowledge of the nature of the universe. I could tell Sir Derek was amused by my naïveté.

SCHOOL WORKS

"'GO TO HILKIAH THE HIGH PRIEST and have him count the money the gate keepers have collected from the people at the Lord's Temple. Entrust this money to the man assigned to supervise the restoration of the Lord's Temple. Then they can use it to pay workers to repair the Temple,'" recites Saadya from 2 Kings 22:4-5.

Well, I don't know of any of us workers getting paid. Instead, we turned in the money we collected to the Center authority. They could use it at their discretion. We just wanted to get as much as we could, and we even competed to do so. It was referred to as Sublime Rivalry.

"Are you going to tell us about it?" asks Mahlia matter-of-factly.

Not yet. First you have to understand that all monies were turned over to the Center leadership, who had complete jurisdiction over their appropriation. The entire WORKS had been divided into geographical units worldwide when Sir Supreme realized he was getting too old. Each of the ten newly appointed leaders was in charge of his own region. He, and he alone, had jurisdiction over the funds collected by workers in his region. At one point, the Barstow Center had the intention of purchasing an old convent in western Nevada for a million dollars, to be used as a children's school. It was Sir Derek's dream to establish a WORKS school close to San Bernadino and Sacramento, to attract more married couples in the Organization to settle in his region.

In August 1978, the women went on traveling soul-saving activity for three months, from October through December. Sixteen of us went across country in three different Econoline vans, stopping to collect in any city we drove through. We were unscrupulous. We would burn out a city, because we knew we wouldn't be there for any length of time. We would listen intently to Sir Derek on audio tape, on which we could hear him lecture about the importance for the children in the WORKS to be properly trained to always think about King. Sir Derek understood that the children were the next generation to engage in King Service. It was up to the adults to train them, so they could carry on the mission.

We, in the WORKS, held strong to the notion that we were the only people on the face of the Earth who had the absolute truth and were merely living out the requirements of spreading knowledge of God. It was thought to be no accident that these children were born into the Righteous King Organization. They were thought to be pure souls, not yet marred by the physical energy, having been born into the King Organization. It was our responsibility to see to it that they were properly educated in the King mindset. Eventually, when the children grew up, they would have to carry on the mission.

Mahlia comments, "Money is what makes a man act funny."

PSYCHED UP

ON TRAVELING SOUL-SAVING, we listened to these audio tapes of sermons recorded by Sir Derek.

"What were the tapes about?" Mahlia asks.

Saadya explains, "They were tapes about saving people's souls by making them give money to King." That statement is not far from the truth. In order to get the regulars to give a donation, it helped every morning to get psyched up by listening to tapes of Sir Derek talking about a children's school, as if it already existed. He spoke about the World Organization for Righteous King Service spreading rapidly all over the world. His voice and message instilled feelings of invincibility. Thereupon, we would get so enlivened from listening to the tapes. We referred to it as being psyched up.

We would go out on soul-saving feeling no one or nothing could stop us or the mission. Sir Derek's dream became our dream. There was nothing any of us girls wouldn't have done for Sir Derek. We were all enamored with him and believed that, if we followed his instructions, we would rapidly advance in spiritual life. It was our responsibility to help him fulfill his vision.

Since the vans were not stocked with books, it was impossible for us to hand out literature on traveling soul-saving. Sometimes, it was draining not to have books to pass out that could open the door to explain the philosophy. It always helped us to remember that, by collecting so much money, we could pass out literature when we returned to Barstow, or when we were back out at the San Bernadino Airport, or any of the other usual soul-saving locations in the area.

Saadya remembers, "Whatever happened with the school?" The school was never acquired because Sir Derek was criticized by the leaders of the other regions. They did not appreciate the importance of establishing a worldwide WORKS school, at least not in the Southwest United States. Instead, they advocated leaving the education of the children up to the individual Centers. So once again, the focus became one of collecting money and passing out books, with the objective of spreading King Awareness.

When all of us returned to Barstow after the months of traveling, some new soul-saving techniques were being developed. Sir Derek had us gather in the Center for a meeting. It was explained to us that we would be able to distribute incense, perfume, and various other Philippine imports, so that it would be easier to get even larger donations than we were getting for pinning a ribbon to someone's lapel. We were also to begin wearing lipstick to be more alluring, so as not to be turned down.

Sir Derek was always trying to be innovative to increase the Ora score for his region. All the Center leaders tried to instill a sense of competition among the workers. Each morning the "sublime" soul-saving scores would've been compiled from throughout the Organization. Firstly, the centers were categorized by size—large centers, which had over a hundred workers; medium-sized ones, which had over fifty; and smaller centers, which had less than fifty workers. It was crucial to place either first, second, or third in your center's respective category. The Barstow Center's leadership was so effective in keeping us motivated that we often placed first.

Secondly, knowing how much money was being collected by WORKS throughout the Organization empowered us. We were bombarded with the notion that WORKS had all this money at its fingertips. The women would comment on how hard the regulars worked for two hundred dollars a week, while we were collecting more than that in a day simply by asking for it. The workers knew that money meant power. So the more money that was collected, the more power and prestige it would bring to the Center and its leader. Saadya mumbles under her breath, "'Whoever loves money, never has money enough,'" quoting Ecclesiastes 5:10.

That's so true. So each day, the workers going out on soul-saving were given little incentives to keep collecting relentlessly. Sometimes, the girl who collected the most would receive a special photograph of Sir Derek. Sometimes girls were promised the next day off if they collected a certain amount. Most of us had been going out on soul-saving for over a year. We knew various strategies to keep ourselves psyched up to help us persevere. Typically, we were with several other god-sisters, so we would remind ourselves and each other of why we were out there, why we *had* to be out there, and even more importantly, why we would have to *stay* out there. Mahlia declares, "You had to endure this painstaking ritualism. But, Mom, with God, it's all joy, not work!"

HIGHER GROUND

Whenever we were feeling overwhelmed, it was helpful to remind ourselves that King Service was a universal organization, and although most people we came in contact with were not spiritually influenced, there were other living beings on the upper planetary systems who were King minded. So we were actually in the majority, considering all entities in the universe. It was the regulars who were in the minority on a universal scale. This understanding of the universal scheme of things empowered us to persevere, and to persevere with enthusiasm.

Saadya documents my journey thus far, "What a far cry you came from those first weeks." I remember thinking during those weeks how I was initially attracted to the spiritual belief system and how genuine the people were because of all their activity, how they executed everything they did, and even how they related to each other. As the days wore on and turned into months, I embraced the doctrine as being centered on God. It was truly inspirational!

I would have to accept everything involving what was becoming made known to me even as it stretched way beyond anything I could have imagined possible.

"Mom, you initially thought you were in an atmosphere of spirituality and in a place where you could learn more about God," Mahlia says, surprisingly supportive. This even sounds ridiculous to me, now that I am describing the way it unfolded. "Mom," Saadya says, "you have to realize that it was meant to make sense to you simply because everything was unfolding without you having any idea what was happening." I hadn't done any prior research on the WORKS.

Mahlia assures me, "It's not like you could have done a Google search!"

I actually recall having thought to myself that I wished I had never met the workers. But I dared not leave.

It would have been okay for me in the physical world had I not stumbled onto this higher ground. "Didn't the poster you saw on the college campus attract you by promising, 'Easy Going on Higher Ground'?" asks Mahlia. That is exactly what it said, and that is exactly what initially attracted me to the Wednesday dinner. I kept that in mind and filtered the lifestyle practices within that context. "That made it more palatable, and you were able to accept it," Mahlia says reassuringly, and adds, "So you felt the end justified the means." I did, because I was continually reminded that the end justified the means as a matter of fact. In essence, among ourselves, we spoke of soul-saving as being fun.

I would have been safe in my ignorance. However, because I came into contact with the workers and the truth about King and his kingdom, it would, I thought, be a fatal mistake for me to leave—would in fact be taking a fatal step backward. Even contemplating leaving caused perturbation. Eternity was guaranteed for me in King Service, as well as for generations of family members past, present, and future. I felt so responsible.

TRANSCENDENT ARMOR

ON SOUL-SAVING, WE HAD TO RECONCILE the contradictions inherent in meeting so many nice people yet having to dismiss them as fallen souls.

First of all, soul-saving was the front line of the war we were fighting for Sir Supreme. Sometimes it was hard to be callous, hard-hearted, or distant on soul-saving, yet that was what was called for. My path crossed with so many nice people who were not choosing to join the King Centers. They were supposed to be functioning on the level of kindness. Their kindness was deceptive, though, I had learned to believe, because they were trapped by the laws of the physical energy. These laws did not apply to us in the WORKS, so the regulars could be nice, yet we needed to transcend mere sentiment. We kept our feelings in check. We had to *remember* they were regulars.

Our intuition told us not to take the risk of sentimentality. If we did, we confided in each other, so as not to get seduced by it. For example, I was the same age as Howie Ronell. I'd had a crush on him when he was a childhood star. I still had a crush on him when he starred in a popular television show in the '70s. So when I saw him in the lobby of the San Bernadino Airport, I was caught between two worlds. I went up to him and asked him for a donation. Mahlia recognizes the name and confirms, "He went on to be a Hollywood movie mogul."

He did not see me as an admiring fan, only as an agent in the WORKS. He told me he didn't have any money on him, and I believed him. He rummaged through his pockets as proof. I even felt sorry for him—until my gaze followed him as he went over to the newspaper and candy kiosk. I watched him dig into his pants pocket and clearly pay for whatever it was he was buying. I was devastated that he would lie, or even that he could. I would much rather have preferred he tell me he didn't want to give a donation. How could Howie lie? I was immobilized until I was approached by Jayda. When I told her what'd happened, she acknowledged that she understood that I had had a crush on Howie Ronell. Her empathy solidified my identity as a worker. It strengthened my commitment to the WORKS and the mission of soul-saving. After all, if Howie Ronell could enigmatically lie to me, think of all the other unspiritual activities the regulars were engaging in, and how important it was for them to come in contact with us as their only hope to make spiritual advancement, even if they didn't know it. Maybe saving them a few dozen lower birth forms in the perpetual cycle of birth and death was worth me sacrificing the few short years of my own life.

Being transcendent armed us with a mentality that made us impervious to any attacks either internal or external. As soldiers for Sir Supreme, we were trained how to separate ourselves from sentiment, insult, or even injury. This enabled us to be thick-skinned, not easily offended. We were trained in thinking that nothing on soul-saving could possibly happen to us that could stop us. No matter how much we could be seduced by the illusion of the world, no matter how much inner turmoil we experienced, we would never have reason enough to abandon the mission and leave a King Center.

DAYDREAM BELIEVER

WE WERE TRAINED NOT TO let any police threat stop us. We answered to a higher authority so as not to let anything stand in our way. After all, our mission to save souls was sanctioned by God. We believed that King regarded us as special and would grant us special favors because we were working and sacrificing to spread knowledge of him. King protected us, and so did the spiritual monarch. The more we surrendered, the more protection we could count on. The more austerities we performed, the more assurance we had that King would reciprocate with large donations. "The more Ora you collected, the more you pleased Leo or Sir Somebody," Mahlia says, poking fun, but it cuts to the core.

One of those added austerities to our already austere lifestyle occurred when we began to fast two days out of the week. Those were days designated for drinking only juice. Other added austerities included eating very little, sleeping very little, and staying out on soul-saving longer hours.

We all did everything the same on the same days. This practice was supposed to encourage and strengthen us because we acted as a unit. Mahlia confirms, "So to speak, there was strength in numbers." Actually, any individuality was routinely nipped in the bud. Leo told us to even have worship by singing in the van driving back from soul-saving, so there would be no down time. Understanding the actual motive, Saadya says, "So none of you would have any time to get lost in your thoughts and find your right mind." In fact, one night after driving back from the airport, Leo told me not to gaze out the back window of the van, because I was daydreaming.

LEO CALLS THE SHOTS

EVERYTHING LEO TOLD US, we had to heed and adhere to. The program was always subject to change according to his whim. We had been attending Superior Text class at the Center; our menu of hot cereal, a few segments of apples, slices of bananas, and yogurt changed to our having rice, biscuits, and thick bean soup with fried cheese, and Leo began to conduct Superior Text class just for us back at the ashram. However, we always rose early enough to finish reciting all the King phrases in time for the morning worship and offering to the carved figures between 4:15 a.m. and 4:30 a.m. Then we went out on soul-saving and at night rushed to get into our sleeping bags so we could rest up. After a few months, four hours of sleep was considered a full night's rest. Otherwise there would not be enough time in the day, given the busy morning routine. We were told that Sir Supreme slept only four hours a night. That is how he had enough time to translate the Superior Texts from Polynesian into English.

Then Saadya says, "So Leo called the shots, and no one complained." So I thought.

When Leo took "single-man" status just after his sexual activities were investigated, I learned that it was one of the girls who first went to the Center president with several complaints against Leo and, in general, to inform the Center president about the issue of Leo having begun sleeping with the women, but more on this later. In her exposé, this girl included reports of the fasts that Leo was implementing. She told them about being made to fast one day a week, being limited to two glasses of juice with unlimited quantities of water. This type of fasting had been going on for several weeks, when it was announced to us that we would begin fasting on juice for two *consecutive* days because, as Leo explained, by the second day of fasting we would really be psyched up and in the limelight. Based on the way Leo explained the fasts, we accepted them for the most part, because in order to be a "pure worker," we had to entirely transcend physical considerations.

Saadya quips, "Such as eating! What about the part of eating for nourishment?"

Then Mahlia throws a jab: "Eating *is* a physical consideration, but denying the girls proper nourishment was exploitive and abusive." We heeded his whims because Leo contended, and had us believe, that King would reciprocate our austerity with large donations.

EXEMPTION BY DEFAULT

SAADYA EXCITEDLY SPECULATES, "You must have lost some serious weight." No one was losing weight, and soul-saving scores were not increasing, so the program was discontinued. Instead, we began fasting one day per week on just water. This lasted for several weeks. It seemed to be all well and good, except that Leo was exempt, as I learned one evening after a day of fasting, when he asked me to discard the empty bottle of bitter lemon soda he had been drinking, so that the other girls wouldn't see it when they returned to the ashram after a day of fund-raising. Mahlia comments, "What a deceptive snake."

Denise, one of the agents in the Organization the longest, who was remaining behind at the ashram then, was also exempt. Another thing they both were exempt from was abstaining from sexual activity, as I later learned that Denise became pregnant, for which Leo blamed her for walking around the ashram in tight jeans. Denise was made to pack up and was sent elsewhere—I was told, to live at the WORKS Center in Milwaukee. She was very pretty and very smart. Everyone looked up to her. When I later questioned Camila, whom I will tell you about later, I was told that Denise had a miscarriage. We never knew if this was true or not. I never saw Denise again, and no further mention was ever made of her.

On days we drank only juice, Suzanne, one of the girls who would later expose Leo, gulped down her two cans to fill her stomach, as if she were having a huge, satisfying breakfast. Then Saadya says, "It's like the emaciated fashion model who, when asked, 'What is your favorite food?' replied, 'Juice.'" We never got emaciated, and the program of fasting on juice was eventually abandoned. In fact, the women were gaining weight by overeating on the other days of the week.

Mahlia reasons, "They were compensating for the feelings of starvation. Mom, you eat every two hours, so how did you make it through just drinking juice?" I diluted my drinks and made them last throughout the day, so as to be able to take sips now and then. I couldn't bear the thought of my blood sugar dropping and not being able to ingest anything except water.

Although we were fasting, our activity was not curtailed in the least. So the only way to keep our minds off food was to keep hitting up the regulars. Mahlia's annoyance returns. She notes, "The calories you got from the juice must have been used up within a few hours." I am sure it was, because we were on our feet, covering miles in a day, to say nothing of all the energy being expended to sustain our mental stamina required in asking for donations. We had no option, however, but to persevere. This was our lot in life. Mahlia says, "You mean in the cult."

Then Saadya softens the blow, offering, "In the WORKS."

But Mahlia snaps back, "Same thing." This message is coming across to my daughters loud and clear.

FAMINE OR FEAST

I HAD TO PERSEVERE THROUGH A FAST when fasting was part of the routine and also when it was a punishment. The first time I experienced a fast as a punishment, it was because I had gotten up to use the bathroom after all the girls were already lying down for the night. This episode occurred when we were still in the two adjoining apartments on Shelby Street, a few blocks away from the Center. The night in question, I scurried into my sleeping bag when I heard Leo coming in to check on us. I was already supposed to be in it. I was panic-stricken, also, because I still had my clothes on. Some of the girls started to squeal, and I thought it was all in fun. After Leo cracked open the door, peered in, and quickly disappeared, closing the door behind him, another girl and I got up to undress and use the bathroom. Somehow, he must've heard us or someone told him, because he knew.

The following morning both of us were told we had to fast that day. Leo never explained what lesson I was supposed to learn, just reprimanded me for getting up when I was supposed to be lying down. Mahlia jests, "You were supposed to be down for the count. . . . It seems to me that a far more valuable lesson would have been that you were trying to deceive him." Yet I learned no lesson from this. I justified my eating fruit at the airport later on in the afternoon on the grounds that I was still a relatively new worker. Mahlia contorts her face and mutters under her breath, "It would've been better if you'd left."

Nevertheless, the second time I was made to fast was for two days, and I did. I didn't mind, because it was at the time when I basically on a self-imposed liquid diet, when I was not required to go out on soul-saving because I was engaged in editing some of the King publications, so there was less demand on me to sustain my energy that fund-raising required.

Saadya logically asks, "What brought on this two-day fast?" It was a punishment for backing the van I was driving into another one in the Center parking lot just when they decided to put it up for sale. Not only did I fast, but I was required to go out on soul-saving to fund-raise for as long as it would take for me to raise the ninety-dollar repair charge. Since I was busy until late afternoon, I went out to fund-raise later in the day. I drove the van to a body shop in downtown San Bernadino, had the damage appraised, and went out on soul-saving two evenings that week, after I had completed my editorial responsibilities. I raised the money. The van was repaired, came out looking better than it had before, and was, shortly thereafter, sold at an even higher price than would have been paid before the repairs were made. Mahlia says, "You already told us that the van was repaired."

There is a bit more to the story.

Camila told me that this incident with the van had been brought up before the Board of Authority (BOA) at the Center, and that my punishment was much more lenient than the Board had advised. I see that questioning look come over Saadya's face, and before she can ask, I tell my daughters that Camila was the girl closest to Leo. In other words, she was Leo's girl Friday, and there's more to tell about her later. For now, I will say only that I was infuriated Leo had told her about the incident. I urged her to tell me what the Center authorities on the BOA had suggested, but it was evident that she was not going to.

Mahlia is fit to be tied with this story. "Camila just made up this story," she insists. Lilly, the Center president's wife, knew I had gone out on soul-saving activity to raise the repair money, but she and everyone else was unaware that I had also been made to fast. When I told her, I could tell by the look of shock on her face that the BOA was never involved. If they were, she would have known. I knew then, for sure, that Camila had made up the story. Mahlia confirms my suspicion. "Obviously, so you wouldn't complain about having to raise the money *and* to fast, as well as be grateful that that was all you had to do. Camila wanted you to be beholden to Leo for being more lenient with you."

Saadya adds, "You bet. She wanted to intimidate you."

I never felt intimidated, though. I just felt angst for the mission.

GOOSE AND GANDER

NOW I HAVE TO TELL YOU about the time *Leo* busted up the side of a van about a year later in an accident he was responsible for causing. I remember asking him if he would be fasting for two days. I knew how dubious that was, and he grasped the innuendo; I had after all set a precedent. He knew I was referring to it. We both smiled as we shared the recollection, with me demonstrating that I had taken it in stride, with good humor, and been a good sport about it. Mahlia says, "What's good for the goose is good for the gander."

Saadya acknowledges, "That's good you didn't hold a grudge." No, but I definitely wanted to make a point.

SPEED

SEVERAL MONTHS LATER, Leo was again involved in a car accident. This time it almost cost him his life. He fell asleep behind the wheel of one of the cars while driving eighty-five miles per hour, and slammed into the rear of a truck. He received stitches in his scalp, spent a few days in the hospital, and returned to the ashram to recuperate. He continued taking his codeine medication for the rest of the time he was in charge. After Leo's car crash, the Barstow Center president formally instructed all the workers to drive within the speed limit. Clarke made no mention of the codeine because he didn't yet know about it.

One morning, Leo had to go up in front of all the agents sitting cross-legged on the floor during morning announcements, and admitted his wrongdoing. He gave a testimony about the dangers of speeding, vowing that he would never exceed the speed limit again. But that display of contrition, and his very statement, turned out to be a farce. He resumed his speeding and reckless driving immediately after his recovery.

I had first encountered this when driving back from the airport in one of the cars with him and several other girls. He told us it was a good test of our King mindset, because if anything happened to us, we had better be thinking of King. Jokingly, Mahlia asks, "Is that so you wouldn't come back as a grasshopper or something worse?" Yes.

Leo would proceed to change lanes incessantly, cutting off cars, weaving and speeding along the highway as well as local streets. This started getting him into trouble when Lilly reported his recklessness to her husband. She'd had endured only one of Leo's speeding episodes, yet that had been enough. The soul-saving girls were passengers on innumerable occasions while Leo drove at record-breaking speeds.

AN AVID READER

With Leo behind the wheel, several of us drove to Pasadena to fundraise at the Rose Bowl football game. We were en route from Barstow, having departed the night before, and were instructed to start reciting the King phrases on our abacus beads. We were having difficulty staying awake and alert after an already long day of fund-raising. Our fatigue was not the only thing we had to contend with in the attempt to stave off sleep. The challenge of remaining awake was compounded by the lulling effect the rocking motion of the moving van was having on us. Even with the van windows wide open, with bursts of ice-cold air streaming in, two of the girls were having a particularly difficult time staying awake. Leo concluded that they wanted to fall asleep. So he threatened them with a fast if they did. Leo saw their lack of inner drive as an indication of their willingness to give in, and their craving for sleep as disregard for the importance of staying awake to recite Righteous King phrases. Most times we slept in the van while Leo drove, but not this time.

Then Saadya laments, "Those poor girls—and I am referring to all of them, but in particular the two who were falling asleep." We all knew a fate awaited them, but none of us was sure what it would be, though we had a pretty good idea. With the memory of fasting for two days still fresh in my mind, I was able to force myself to stay awake; however, not these two. One of them, Suzanne, was from New Zealand and had come to the Barstow Center as a top fund-raiser. For this reason, she was nicknamed "Mary Gold."

She had already been living in Barstow for a year, collecting, usually, no less than three hundred dollars a day. Suzanne's reputation for always being enthusiastic in soul-saving preceded her—we had been told about her before she arrived at the Barstow Center. We'd heard that she was always psyched-up for book-gifting and fund-raising. She was portrayed as a model worker. Because everyone knew this about her, she had the added pressure of having to live up to her reputation. She was an avid reader of the Superior Text books. She often had a story to relate about something she'd read in one of them.

Saadya announces, as a delayed reaction, "She got her nickname from the marigold plant!" And we believed she was being granted special favor in fund-raising from the goddess Ora.

En route to the Rose Bowl, the rest of us in the van used the deck space to prop ourselves up on our knees, shake our heads, and sway our shoulders from side to side, to keep from falling asleep. But not Belinda and Suzanne. These two big collectors received only breakfast the next day. When Suzanne asked for seconds on cereal, I could see her flush as her face turned bright red when her request was denied. Saadya sympathetically understands Suzanne's embarrassment.

Mahlia acknowledges that "whatever emotion Suzanne was experiencing, it was intense enough to get her blood pumping, causing the flush."

Plucking a pocket bible I didn't know she carried, from her purse, Mahlia cites Luke 22:44: *"And being in agony He was praying very fervently; and His sweat became like drops of blood, falling down upon the ground."* Suzanne didn't sweat drops of blood, but she realized the reality of the impending fast, in which she would have nothing to eat until the next morning. Later that day, as it turned out, none of us had an afternoon meal. However, we did receive a gift of a blueberry cheesecake from the Sacramento Center, which was divided up between us, excluding Belinda and Suzanne. Mahlia says, "All because they weren't able to stay awake the night before!" Instead of eating a hefty slice of blueberry cheesecake, Belinda and Suzanne read in silence from a Superior Text book.

Several weeks later, Suzanne told me she realized, at the time she had been made to fast, that reading for her was as satisfying as eating. While we were eating the cheesecake, Belinda and Suzanne situated themselves in the rear of the van. Both had collected all day, as was expected. Suzanne had collected the most.

STAR WARS

SAADYA DECLARES, "SUZANNE WAS a real stalwart!" She embraced the austerity of the fast as a personal challenge and an opportunity to make spiritual advancement. We all did. One night, after a day of fasting, we were rewarded with hot chocolate malted milk. I had two cups.

"It's no wonder the girls gained weight even after a day of fasting," notes Saadya. Also, that night, I was among a group of girls Leo took to the movies. We went to the 11:00 p.m. showing of the 1977 movie *Star Wars*. While the Rebel Alliance battled to save the galaxy from the tyranny of the Galactic Empire, I battled with the urge to fall asleep. Leo bought large buckets of popcorn for us to share, and large cups of Seven-Up for each of us. I was positioned comfortably in my seat and continually had to shake off the urge. "Didn't you watch the movie?" Saadya asks emphatically. "It seems like it was such a novelty!"

I ate popcorn, sipped soda, and watched. I got into the different species interacting with each other in the galaxy, but my physical exhaustion and mental fatigue grew. The theater was dark, I made myself comfortable in the seat, no one could see me, and so, as a willing partner in my very own alliance with the prospect of slumber, I succumbed. I remember how sweet it was giving in. My eyelids were heavy; they drooped, my breathing slowed, my eyes closed, and then I fell into deep repose.

When I awoke at the end of the movie and I was leaving the theater, walking through the lobby with the other women and a throng of regulars, I was disoriented. I didn't know if I was in the physical world or the spiritual world created by the Center. Mahlia asks, "Did you think you were part of the world created in *Star Wars*?" Both were fantasy, but one had become real for me. In the movie, the *Star Wars* fantasy became just as real as the fantasy created by the WORKS about King's luscious green pastures, where he frolicked with his maidens. I accepted the movie as reality and could not distinguish between it and the milieu of the WORKS.

We drove back to the ashram, reciting on our portable abacus beads to get a head start on the morning program. When we reached the ashram, Leo had us complete our eighteen rods, or lines, as we called them, before the morning service and offering to the carved figures. After the service, we laid out our sleeping bags and rested up for about an hour. "You finally got some sleep after being awake for twenty-four hours!" Saadya calculates. The morning service ended at 6:30 a.m., so we popped out until we were awakened one hour later to eat breakfast, in order to go out on soul-saving at the regularly scheduled 8:00 a.m. However, despite lying down in my sleeping bag with my eyes closed, I was too over-stimulated to actually fall asleep.

The following day, I still felt like I was part of the world created in *Star Wars*, especially since Leo corroborated George Lucas' rendition of creatures on other planets and their never-ending battle between good and evil. Leo referred to their plight, drawing an analogy to our dilemma on Earth, between godliness and ungodliness, and of course illuminating the distinction between workers in King Service and regulars under the influence of the physical world.

BEET RED TO JOY

SAADYA WAS RIGHT ABOUT DRINKING hot chocolate malted milk when she said it was no wonder the girls gained weight after a so-called fast day, and now asks, "What about the days you fasted on water?"

The water fast was one day per week for a time. On that day, Leo had the women who stayed back from soul-saving activity steam vegetables; the girls returning from soul-saving were served the broth upon their return to the ashram in the evening. The vegetables were thrown away. Since beets were steamed in the water, making the liquid beet red, everyone was peeing red for days.

For a *period* of time, and before I can say another word, catching the inadvertent pun, Saadya asks, "Is that supposed to be funny?" Oh, dear! I pause reflectively. Some of it was fun, some of it was funny, but a lot of times it was neither. As I have told you, I remained back at the Center to proofread and edit some publications. In the late afternoons, I would prepare sweet treats using sweetened condensed milk and mixing in shredded coconut and carob chips. I topped each coconut patty with two whole almonds.

Mahlia says, "Sounds like an Almond Joy." I intentionally made the patties especially large, so the girls could have their fill. Needless to say, the returning sisters thanked me profusely.

FIGHTING OFF THE URGE

ONE NIGHT, I LAY AWAKE, sprawled out in my sleeping bag. In this state of rest, I was doing all I could to stave off the urge for an orgasm. As I lay on the floor, I was feeling calm, tranquil, and relaxed. I felt all the blood rushing to the central core of my physical being. It wasn't often that I battled with an overwhelming sensation such as on that occasion. I was struggling with the urge to give in to the demand. Yet I drew as much strength as I needed not to give in. At some point as I lay awake I remembered the sensual feeling from sexual release before I had joined the World Organization for Righteous King Service.

Regardless, in an effort to deny myself, I kept reminding myself how much I had suffered one day at the San Bernadino Airport, where I was fundraising after being with the group for only one week. I was in the bathroom stall, and it was the only privacy I'd had in all that time, the only place I had been left alone since arriving at the Center. This evening, I started thinking that King was testing me to see if I'd learned my lesson, because the very next day, I had a miserable time at fund-raising. I couldn't get into it. Not until three years later did I realize that I had a miserable time many days on soul-saving from the strain of having to engage in unending selfless service. As a WORKS agent, I was supposed to embrace the notion that soul-saving activity was a privilege, not a burden as at times it proved to be.

I brought myself just to the point of orgasm, withdrawing from its fulfillment. I thought I had escaped blemishing my record with King. I thought I would be justly rewarded for this formality.

"And *then* you finally fell asleep, or rested up?" Mahlia jeers. "And finally you got put out of your misery!"

Saadya affirms, "Yeah, from lack of food, lack of sleep, and lack of sex." Although sleep was a commodity, there were times when the program called for it in excess. There was a stretch of up to fourteen hours at one time. Mahlia upholds the implausibility of this, exclaiming questioningly, "When?"

NO REST FOR THE WEARY

WHILE ON TRAVELING SOUL-SAVING, on one occasion all of us had been collecting money in one small town. We burnt the place out. We had been collecting there for several days. We got to the point where everyone we approached had already been approached in some other part of town. People started getting irritated because they'd already given and didn't want to be asked again. Hitting up regulars we had already collected from was turning out to be a waste of time. We didn't recognize them, but they recognized us.

As a result, our instruction was to sleep all day, literally. We were told, not merely to stay out of sight and remain indoors, but to sleep instead at the motel room—all fifteen of us, three vanloads in one motel room with nothing else to do. We were to do some traveling to another town later in the afternoon in order to start collecting later that evening. The motel room had been rented just for the purpose of sleeping, and so we rolled out our sleeping bags, camped on the floor, and crashed.

I situated myself in the walk-in closet trying to get some privacy, though I left the sliding doors open, hoping to have some relief from the other girls' snoring, which was often a serious annoyance.

Mahlia is quick to offer, "That doesn't sound so bad. At least you got a break from soul-saving." Except that we hadn't eaten breakfast that day, nor had any plans been made for an afternoon meal. The arrangement was that we would rise at 5:00 p.m. and, en route to the other town, stop for one pint of Baskin-Robbins ice-cream each. Then off we would go to fund-raise until 10:00 p.m.

WHO MOVED MY CHEESE?

SAADYA ASKS, "*DID YOU* catch up on your sleep that day?" I kept waking up. It was a beautiful day outside. The motel room was getting stuffy. Most of the girls had kicked off the top cover of their sleeping bag, not even using the top sheet to cover themselves with. I was the only one, to my knowledge, who remained awake, and because I hadn't eaten anything since 3:00 p.m. the afternoon before, I was now battling with hunger pangs. At one point, I climbed into the soul-saving van I traveled in and was about to take a bite out of a piece of cheese when Belinda, who was one of the girls in charge, came driving up in another van. I knew beforehand that I would be deviating from the program and would have to suffer for my deviation, had I actually eaten the morsel of cheese.

Knowing there would be a repercussion for this action or any deviation from the program we were supposed to follow was so ingrained in me. I was trained to be able to expect the worst difficulty if I deviated. I contemplated the likelihood and, for this reason, had been reluctant to begin with. I hesitated once I had gotten to the point of holding the cheese in my hand and breaking off a piece of it to eat. That is when Belinda pulled up. I replaced the chunk of cheese in its container and turned away from the temptation, grateful that I would be spared the inevitable suffering I would have had to incur on soul-saving for deviating from the program.

FRACTURED

MAHLIA WANTS TO KNOW about something she heard me speak of in the past. She recalls me having reported that I had been to the Philippines with a group of people in the 1970s. "Mom, undoubtedly this is the group you went to the Philippines with."

To be sure, 1978 was the year I went with a group of fifteen women and ten men from the Barstow Center. We spent three weeks traveling to various WORKS centers throughout the Phillipines. For the most part, we slept in large, bare rooms with no furniture. Of course, the men were in separate quarters, and we did not interact with them.

By this time, the girls in the soul-saving group had all declined marriage as their lifestyle, so we were wearing white tunics, head scarves, and sashes. We were married to soul-saving and wanted to dress as simply as possible. In the past we had been wearing tunics of vibrant colors, with lace and embroidery. When we moved, we walked as a unit, and because we were clad in all white, it was said of us that we looked like a moving cloud.

While in the Philippines, I, like many of the other girls who made the trip in the past, grew ill. Besides suffering from the typical dysentery, I had a very painful hairline fracture on my right shin bone. Walking was an agony. Standing, or applying any weight-bearing pressure on my leg, was excruciatingly intolerable. The fracture was not diagnosed until after I returned to the United States. I was confined to a wheelchair for three weeks, from which I continued soul-saving activities without interruption of my duties of fund-raising.

Mahlia says drily, "The only break you caught in that group was the one in your leg." I exhale and smile at this humor, but it was true. Out on soul-saving, I remained stationary, positioned near a pillar in the lobby of the smaller Barstow-Dagett Airport. From there, I summoned unsuspecting people over to my side as I sat in a wheelchair and explained to them that I was collecting funds to print books for students. They dipped into their pockets thinking they were helping handicapped students. I recognized this immediately when I noticed their obvious sympathy and compassion. People were embarrassed to inquire further of me about the purpose of the collections. I collected close to three hundred dollars daily, an increase from my usual two hundred.

"The police let you do this?" asks Saadya. I had some difficulty with the airport authorities, since they previously knew me to be in sound health. I had to present copies of my x-rays for their own physician to confirm the diagnosis. Saadya presses. "They thought that you were working out of a wheelchair to deceive people into thinking that you were handicapped." Although this was not the intention, it yielded the same results, as if I were *feigning* a hairline fracture of my tibia as a ploy, merely for the effect of garnering sympathy from the regulars.

In my case, my claim was legitimate. However, the year before, one of the girls had sprained her ankle and resorted to using a wheelchair from the hospital, which was never returned. Just as I was now doing, other girls used this wheelchair on subsequent occasions. The sister with the sprained ankle did so well on fund-raising that she continued to use the wheelchair even after her ankle healed. When Leo told me this, I could tell he was amused. Whoever used the wheelchair did well on fund-raising, for the same reason that I had an increase in the amount of money I collected. Mahlia, now nodding her head from side to side, concludes, "People naturally assumed you were fund-raising for a group of handicapped students in the area."

LAME DUCK

2 SAMUEL 6:14: *"And David danced before the Lord with all his might, . . ."*

On the flight over to the Philippines, I recognized that I had a problem with my right leg. It was when all the girls were dancing in the airplane aisles to the beat of the drum and the clanging of cymbals, during the frenzied singing and dancing, that I realized I was incapacitated and had to remain an observer. I felt shooting pains down the front of my right leg. I could not lift myself off the ground, as I was accustomed to doing on other such occasions. My feet propelling me off the floor, driven by the music, had always been an automatic response of mine throughout the previous two years. I was truly concerned but said nothing. I ignored the possibilities, hoping that the symptoms would go away. They did not; instead, the pain grew more severe.

It was exacerbated by the constant walking that I had to do to keep up with the other girls. I experienced feelings of solitude while lagging behind, which I actually welcomed. I had trouble walking the entire time and on occasion was sent back early in the evening from an expedition we took into one of the local towns.

Keeping up was turning out to be increasingly more difficult each day. My stamina was negatively impacted by the pain. It was a challenge for me to scurry to the next location, as the other girls were walking quickly and taking long strides in order to cover a lot of ground. One evening, a rickshaw was summoned for me and another girl, who had other reasons for needing one. I felt both relief and gratitude to King for taking care of me. But I also felt sorry for the skinny man who was peddling the rickshaw. Yet I felt we had something in common. We were both making the best of a bad situation.

PAYING THE DOCTOR A VISIT

I ALSO SOUGHT RELIEF from the local doctor. He was a thin young man with a delicate, good-looking wife and a fragile-looking baby who remained with him on each of the five visits I made to his office. The office was more like an outdoor kiosk in an open-air market. This young Philippine doctor was practicing Ayurvedic medicine. The theory of Ayurvedic medicine, the way he explained it to me, is that air circulates throughout the body through various mapped-out channels of energy. Supposedly, I was experiencing pain because of blockages preventing the air from circulating through my bones.

I was given very large, brown-speckled, misshapen spherical pills that I was to take three times daily with warm and only warm water, in order for the pills to be of any benefit. The only problem with that was that hot or warm water were nowhere to be found on the premises where we were staying.

Without having any idea where I was going to find warm water, I paid the doctor in pesos that had been given to me by Kaylah, the girl designated by Leo to be a go-to in his place. I made some inquiries among girls from several other WORKS Centers to see if they had anything I could use to heat some water. These women had come to the Philippines for the festival to celebrate the birthday of one of King's incarnations.

Mahlia jabs, "Are you telling us that the god you worshiped so you would not have to be born into the world celebrated *being* born?"

I had never thought of that. "A lot of things seem to have slipped your mind," she says.

I found an English-speaking woman with a small child who offered to allow me to use the electric coil she used to warm water for tea. I felt momentary relief, entertaining the notion that, with warm water, the pills I was given might offer some relief from the pain I was in. However, neither the coil nor the pills worked, and I received no relief from the ache in my leg the entire three weeks of the trip.

When I returned to the United States, I went to the hospital as a charity case, and the hairline fracture turned up on the x-ray. The doctor ordered me to stay off my leg for six to eight weeks. This, of course, would have been reasonable had I been living a normal life. However, as a WORKS soul-saving fund-raising agent, I knew the doctor's orders would have to be circumvented.

Back at the Center, Leo advised me that singing was okay, which I could do seated on the floor. Needless to say, I was also instructed to remain off my feet during the offerings and dancing to King, as well as other activities, to rest my leg for all but one activity.

Mahlia accurately surmises, "You were supposed to save your strength for fund-raising."

Saadya recalls an adage, quoting Gretel Ehrlich: "*Walking is also an ambulation of the mind.*" Not in my case.

ONCE UPON A TIME

NOW MAHLIA INQUIRES, "WHAT ELSE happened with that lunatic Leo in the Philippines?" Not just in the Philippines, but in general, Leo was in the habit of asking questions about the King book stories he read to us almost nightly. He made it his habit not to call on anyone who demonstrated that they knew the answer until he had sufficiently embarrassed one or several of us who had not picked up on the minor details he was asking about.

One late afternoon in the Philippines, the fifteen of us and Leo had gathered on the lawn facing the front porch of the hotel we were staying at (an exception to our other austere accommodations). Our unusual appearance had attracted some others who may have been European— two girls and a boy—but I couldn't be sure because they didn't speak to us and I never heard them speak to each other. I conjectured that they were tuned in to some form of spirituality and had an interest in hearing a King story, since they were in the land of his supposed birthplace. Joining us, and listening in on the story, was to be a memorable part of their sojourn to the Philippines.

They seemed to enjoy the story well enough, but when the questioning began, Leo grew particularly demeaning. He announced that Camila, his right-hand girl, could recall minor details of the story because she was so intelligent, implying that the other girls could not provide the correct answer because of lesser intelligence. He repeatedly embarrassed the sister who did not know an answer by keeping her on the spot for just a little too much time before calling on someone else.

The visitors, who seemed to be enjoying the story before this question-and-answer session, grew disgusted with what they were observing. Before the story had been completed, they stood up and left. None of us was able to do that. Every time Leo made a cutting remark to any of us, I wanted to voice my objection aloud. It was frustrating being a part of that faceless and hooded group of women. It was downright demeaning. When the European visitors left, I secretly hoped that Leo would be insulted and offended by their leaving. I wanted him to understand why they'd left, and to learn the lesson that I was unable to teach him.

Listening to a King story in anticipation of some question, the harder I strained to absorb trivia through audio infusion and retain it for future reference requiring me to store it in my short-term memory, the more difficult it was for me to listen, and the less I actually remembered. This process undermined my ability to listen to the sequencing of the story or to enjoy the story at all.

"Horrible," says Saadya, while Mahlia is visibly annoyed. At first, when I listened to someone else read, I tuned into what I thought was the important and salient features of the story. But I quickly realized that questions were being asked about the most unimportant details and trivialities just to check our memory. I was surprised when someone was able to recall a minute detail. I'm pretty sure Leo referred to us as stupid and told us we needed to pray to King. Mahlia establishes the need for prayer, but for a different reason. "You needed to pray to get away from him."

LABOR PAINS

SAADYA UNDERSCORES THIS, saying, "This seems like a nightmare." Vivid recollections today are nightmarish, but I saw them, at the time of their occurrence, as service in the WORKS enjoining me, and having a call on my life. Any austerity, however intolerable, any measure of discipline, was exerted to make us less attached to our physical bodies and more attached and dependent on Center life. Austerity was explained as an opportunity for advancing in the spiritual realm. In general, sleep deprivation kept us in a state of arousal. This type of stimulation left us unable to think clearly about the myriad demands being placed on us as they were continually being exacted.

There were times I felt that it really didn't matter whether I was asleep or awake and just tired. I viewed myself as more and more surrendered in preparation for yet even more surrender to whatever it would take to stay committed to yield positive results in fund-raising. My only responsibility and concern were to follow my instructions. By my act of total surrender and submission, King would, thus, duly reward me on soul-saving.

I would do anything, so that I would be able to function effectively on soul-saving. I was manipulated with dogma, rhetoric, and propaganda to sufficiently cajole me to continue in the prescribed manner, day in and day out, in this pseudo-religious organization.

Mahlia, somewhat disturbed, asks, "Why didn't any of the girls revolt?" No one would dare to be an insurgent. You were simply outnumbered and could never hope to win an argument. If anyone was having difficulty, they were isolated from the rest. We were not encouraged to discuss our difficulty with just *anyone*. There was usually only one designated girl we should speak with if we were experiencing difficulty. After I spoke to a god-sister to enliven *her*, I would feel enlivened. We helped each other stay focused, but we couldn't let ourselves get distracted for too long; otherwise, we would both lose our focus. We needed to impress each other with what we believed in, but sometimes we realized it was rhetoric. "It's because you were role-playing, saying what you were supposed to," says Mahlia.

There *was* no reflecting on the matters at hand. Any difficulty in soul-saving was viewed as an attack by outside forces or regarded as a lack of sincerity. Both of these challenges were enough for us to endeavor even more, so we would have fewer reservations, and gain renewed drive to turn away from any alternatives and back to the mission. Any reluctance to engage the regulars was attributed to having a lower nature and predisposition, which needed to be overcome and superseded by engaging in our dutiful service, which would restore our focus and mental stamina. Mahlia is peeved. "You labored in pain, and you labored in vain." Nevertheless, we would go out on soul-saving, because we were on a mission.

ABSOLUTE POWER CORRUPTS

WE THOUGHT LEO was being totally dedicated to Sir Supreme and his mission of collecting money to enable us to hand out books about King to the sincere regulars we encountered on soul-saving. However, as time went on Leo became more and more autonomous. By him conducting his own Superior Text classes in the ashram, the only input we received came from him.

He slept in the same dwelling as we did, ate with us, recited phrases with us at first, sent us out on soul-saving activity, met us at the airport during the day to preach, arranged meals, prepared lunch, read to us during lunch break, drove us back from the airport, read us a story from a King book before resting up, and made himself available when we had questions. He asked us to promise him that, if we wanted to leave, we would first speak to him. Mahlia concludes, "He didn't want to lose any one of the girls." He thought we belonged to him.

Leo also became more absolute in his authority, demanding our loyalty and devotion to him as the conduit for our spiritual advancement. We were reminded, time and again, that he was Sir Supreme's representative to us in the WORKS, with authority emanating directly from King, our God. Leo was father, husband, disciplinarian, friend to each one of the girls, and lover to some, if not all, of us. That is one subject we did not speak to each other about. But once we realized that a sister was not in her sleeping bag, we knew whose sleeping bag she *was* in. At one point, there were over twenty girls in the soul-saving group under Leo's jurisdiction.

Just before becoming so possessive, Leo was sent to the Philippines to get some of Sir Supreme's company to "enliven" him. Leo was absent from the ashram while he spent two weeks in the Philippines with Sir Supreme; at least that was what we were told. Leo came back with stories about how Sir Supreme always asked for us, wanting to know all about the soul-saving group since we were collecting so much Ora and passing out so many books. His mission was, foremost, to get the Superior Text books into the hands of the regulars we met on soul-saving. Then more regulars would opt to join the WORKS. So we thought.

This was Sir Supreme's mission, and his mission was our mission. We were helping Sir Supreme spread King-mindedness by engaging in eternal service to the god of the WORKS. This made us feel all very connected, intimate, and protected by the almighty spiritual monarch. Saadya provocatively says, "There's something about works that *keeps* us from a relationship with God. We don't have to work to get God's grace. This is something He bestows upon us as a gift, not by our own attainment." Clearly, we were not getting any free gifts or free rides.

Meanwhile, Sir Supreme supposedly implanted some other wild idea into Leo's head about a practice foreign in American society and the culture we lived in. Leo thought he had received Sir Supreme's sanction to have more than one wife. About this time, he also started taking license by sleeping with the girls, feeling that this was somehow part of his service. He began preaching that it was his duty to do whatever it took to keep the women going out on soul-saving activity. Leo was deluded by thinking anything done in King's service would automatically guarantee him an elevated place in the spiritual world.

Leo told us how Sir Supreme had reacted to hearing some of the outrageous soul-saving activities we engaged in. We were led to believe that

Leo had told Sir Supreme about going on "strike," being stuffed in the van to sneak into drive-in movies, the spare-change technique, even dressing as Santa Claus. Leo also sent soul-saving groups out on the road for weeks at a time. Those stretches of time for traveling soul-saving (TSS) with five or six girls to a van, stopping only to eat, and sleeping for four hours a night, was no exception to what Sir Supreme had been told about us—but more about that later.

UTMOST LOYALTY

LEO'S TRIP TO THE PHILIPPINES only reinforced his tight reign and strict discipline, code of loyalty, and demand for obedience to his every instruction. We were like loyal puppies. He enjoined us not to call any attention to ourselves. He instilled in each of us the feeling that we must remain chaste by keeping our heads completely covered at all times, fix our eye-gaze on the floor to avoid making eye contact with any of the male workers, even inadvertently, and never allow ourselves to be heard speaking in public when there were other male workers within hearing.

This caused many of us conflict because, on soul-saving, we were supposed to be the complete opposite. This was explained to us with a cliché, one of many that began with the often-heard preamble "Sir Supreme says." For example, Sir Supreme says, "You should be like a kitten at home and a tiger at fund-raising." This sanctioned the duplicitous extremes assumed by our contradictory behavior in the two very different contexts.

We were literally trained how to behave at the Center and how to behave when soul-saving, leaving little or no time in between to be ourselves. We had no private life. We even boasted to regulars on soul-saving activity that, as missionaries, we had none. We portrayed ourselves as selfless servants in order to convince the regulars that they were donating to a worthwhile cause.

I never considered that what I was giving up was better than what I was gaining. I was led to believe I was giving up all the things in life that were ugly, gross, ungodly, and deplorable. Insightfully, Mahlia says, "You had no indication of the ramifications—in your eagerness to better yourself, you were naïve to the sophisticated manner in which you were being indoctrinated."

BREAKING THE VOW

WE LIVED IN BARE ROOMS and only rolled out our sleeping bags to rest up for those few hours after fund-raising.

One night Leo summoned me into his bedroom while the other girls were already in their sleeping bags. Mahlia tells Saadya, "Oh, no, here it comes. I'm not sure I want to hear this." I didn't know why I was being summoned, but I welcomed the opportunity to get individual attention. Earlier that evening, Leo had demonstrated the new sound system to me, allowing me to listen to King worship music with ear phones. I had loved listening to music as a teenager, pressing my ears against the large speakers situated in the console in the living room and listening to The Beatles or any other music of the Sixties and Seventies. I continued to be an *aficionado* of listening to music on the stereo system throughout college, in my dorm room, and in my apartment my senior year of college.

So that night, just as we were supposed to be getting ready to rest up, I was in Leo's room listening to music on the ear phones.

Mahlia alleges, "That must have given him some ideas." We had taken vows to live a celibate life, with no sex outside of marriage.

Saadya asks, "That's a good thing, and the first thing you've told us that I can agree with." Yet the unthinkable and unspeakable happened for a worker who took those vows. That morning, Leo asked if I was okay, and I was, and so I got ready for fund-raising, but not before one of the girls knocked on Leo's door announcing that Chana was not in her sleeping bag and couldn't be found. Leo assured her that I had fallen asleep in his closet, and not to worry about it. The next night, Leo asked if I wanted to spend the night again, and wanted to know if I would freak out by him asking me. I answered that I would freak out if he *didn't*. It didn't happen again for a while, at least not with me, but women started going missing more and more when it was time to rise for the morning routine. "That wasn't the only thing that was rising," jokes Saadya.

First Mahlia quotes Matthew 7:15: *"Beware of false prophets who come disguised as harmless sheep but are really vicious wolves. You can identify them by their fruit, that is, by the way they act."* Next, she quotes Psalm 76:11: *"Make vows to the Lord your God, and keep them."* Then she asks, "How did you justify that gross deviation from the vows you took?" I believed I was acting as a loyal wife. I had been led to feel this way over the few months I was at the ashram. We had always been reminded to be loyal and to submit, and not to question authority—I thought I was behaving in proper King agent fashion, in such a way that would benefit my spiritual life. Leo, on the other hand, began to take the liberty of sleeping indiscriminately with one and sometimes two girls, though not at the same time. Much later on, he actually confessed this to all of us. He admitted he hadn't been reciting the mind-numbing King phrases for days at a time. Yet he attributed engaging in sex life as part of his responsibility of keeping the women enlivened.

TUG-OF-WAR

"WHAT ABOUT THOSE DREAMS?" Saadya is curious. In the recurring dreams, the theme is the same. I am trying to escape. The circumstances vary only slightly. The people involved are the girls from the ashram as well as the male agents, but especially Leo. These were the people whose presence I was always in and whose company I always kept. I had to perform as an agent whose only objective was to embrace the mission.

Within that context we could be genuine with each other, and I came to feel really comfortable with several girls in particular. We had to be good agents, which meant following the instructions we received from the authority, whoever that was and whatever they said. We were all in the same boat, so to speak, so obedience was a given. Since we shared the ups and downs associated with fund-raising, we had much in common.

"What did you dream about?" inquires Mahlia. The essence of the dream is always the preparations I am making to leave the ashram. I am worried that my inner thoughts will be discovered. I felt I had to make the break without having to explain to the others that I had made up my mind to leave. In the dream, I no longer believed I would be doomed if I left. My plan to leave had to remain clandestine. I just needed to make a break for it without being noticed. I was fretful that the others would find out. I was sure, if they did, I would be talked out of it. Leaving would be an act of self-preservation. It was an expression of inviolability that had been compromised all along. I knew I would be coerced into staying by giving in to the rhetoric. Mahlia attests, "You were in a dream state of virtual tug-of-war." The only way I would be doomed, if I planned to leave, was if I stayed. Those feelings are identical to the feeling of entrapment I had experienced the first few weeks.

"That's exactly what happened when you actually wanted to leave and you were talked out of it each and every time," recalls Saadya. That is exactly why, in the dream, I especially dreaded Leo finding out. If he found out I was planning to leave, it was definite that I would be talked into staying. Saadya grasps the probability of it being much worse since Leo was unpredictable. I just knew, in my gut, I would never be able to leave the WORKS if Leo found out.

Mahlia says, "You also had to hide your hankering to leave from the other girls. If they knew, it would get back to Leo."

"So, basically, you would never get out of there," Saadya emphasizes. Then Mahlia comments, "I wonder if the other girls wanted to leave and could say you were responsible for talking them out of it?" Actually, there were instances when other girls wanted to leave and were simply not permitted to. One evening at the San Bernadino Airport, one of the girls was physically carried out of the airport and into the awaiting soul-saving van, on Leo's instructions. He had learned from several of the other girls that Lorraine was planning to leave. When I spoke to her some time later, she told me she didn't actually want to leave the WORKS; she just didn't want to be a part of the soul-saving group any longer.

During that conversation, I tried to convince her that Leo really cared about her, and that she should stay because there was no place else for her to go. The day she was whisked out of the airport, when she returned to the ashram, she was knocked across the room by Leo. Although she stayed, she was taken off soul-saving and remained at the ashram to take care of the housekeeping duties. This seemed to make her happy. Mahlia continues by noting with disbelief, "So physical abuse was supposed to keep her in the King mindset with the objective of preventing her from leaving." It worked.

THE YELLOW BRICK ROAD

OUR INDOCTRINATION WAS PROGRESSIVE. The abnormal became the normal. Austerity became the standard. Austerity became my way of life. It was the only way I could transcend the physical plane of existence to become truly spiritual. Anything less would be devastating to my opportunity of living the spiritually minded life existing only in a King Center. Now that I had true spiritual knowledge of the King of creation, I had to reconcile myself to accepting the requirements of strict adherence to the authority who interpreted what it was King required of me. The group promised a far superior way of life on this exclusive path to achieving immortality. One afternoon at the San Bernadino Airport, Leo actually said the time for us to stop following his instruction was when he asked us to smoke marijuana. That statement was made three years earlier. However, by this time, proving our loyalty to him through blind obedience as our sole means of making spiritual advancement was ingrained in each of us. Mahlia points out, "You were just following the yellow brick road."

SWALLOWING THE PILL

IN ORDER TO LEARN MORE about God and to ensure my spiritual advancement, I had to commit myself to this lifestyle of austerity as it was prescribed daily, with new austerities constantly being introduced. Along with austerities came deviations. Evidently, Leo thought his duty in King Service was to keep the girls out soul-saving in any way he could. You already know he began sleeping with us, and after he crashed into a truck, he began dispensing his codeine tablets to some of us. Once, when I asked him what he had given me the night before, he simply answered, "Medicine." One of the girls had become extremely ill the day after she snorted cocaine with Leo on her day back from soul-saving. I knew about this because she had confided in me. Not everyone else knew.

None of the girls was aware of what Leo was doing when he was in the kitchen, stirring the large pot of bean soup, while it was being heated on the stove, and before it was served to the girls. We didn't know he was spiking it with a pharmaceutical.

The evening he gave me a codeine tablet—at least that is what I came to believe it had been—was at a very late-night fraternity-type atmosphere in a club at a college; there were people making merriment, and I just didn't feel like I fit in. The pill helped.

I found my groove and resumed hitting up the partygoers, and in no time, the donations started coming in. I was with another girl, who had decided not to take the pill Leo gave her. It hadn't occurred to me that I had an option or that taking the pill was breaking one of the standards, the one about not taking drugs. I had come to think of Leo as beyond questioning.

I had been trained from the very beginning to come to understand that, to make spiritual advancement, I simply needed to follow the instructions of my authority. Mahlia grows impatient. "You already told us that." Well, I cannot say it enough. Interestingly, early on, Leo had spoken about being able to trust him because he was not breaking any of the vows or standards. By the time Leo *was* breaking those standards and having us do so, it was too late for any of us to question him, or so I thought.

METHODOLOGY

BEING A PARTICIPANT in the WORKS made me feel special because of those spiritual standards. "Oh, what were they again? The ones you were breaking not before long," Mahlia points out. The standards were to separate the WORKS agents from the influence of the physical energy and from being deceived by temporary enjoyment that had yielded no benefit in making spiritual advancement. I was led to conclude that the World Organization for Righteous King Service was the only place, and the only way of life in which God would smile upon me. Now that I knew about the dogma, to follow a path outside of WORKS would surely usher in my soul's demise. This was the only information I received, time and again.

Saadya declares, quoting from Oswald Chambers, "Mom, when God gives you a clear determination of His will for you, all the striving to maintain that relationship by some particular method is completely unnecessary." I thought it was God's will, and I didn't want to fall short. Saadya quotes from Romans 3:23, *"We all fall short of the glory of God.* That's because He's holy. We're not."

Then Mahlia reassures me, "But God makes a way where there seems to be no way." That's a relief!

Yet it was *fun* in the beginning, before it became such serious work. Leo had a way of striking a balance for us. It was a worthwhile and worthy self-sacrifice. If I chose anything else, I wouldn't be able to afford regulars the opportunity to come into contact with a King agent, in order to give them a chance at making spiritual advancement, even if they didn't know it. Mahlia says, "You resigned yourself to living according to the practices laid out for you." They were laid out for all the workers, and for the most part, the agents at the Center were very well-behaved.

Saadya remarks, "Except for what went on behind the ashram door."

LEO'S PROFILE

"WHAT DID YOU KNOW ABOUT this character Leo, or whatever his name was?" asks Mahlia, both sarcastically and skeptically. He had spent time in prison for committing robbery at gunpoint. He had many prison stories and delighted in telling them. "You can't make this stuff up," Mahlia says, and cringes. I'm not. He told us that he'd begun reciting Righteous King phrases in prison. When he was released, he'd immediately gone to a WORKS Center and joined the Organization. He gained notoriety within the WORKS by his unorthodox methods of fund-raising. He had an ex-wife on the outside of the Organization and a son by that marriage. He was also married to Michele before they both joined the Organization as a couple. Leo was paying child support, and more than likely alimony, to his first wife, for which he skimmed off the top of his collections, as an unauthorized expenditure. This was an ongoing practice.

By the time I arrived in 1976, he was in charge of the women's soul-saving group at the Barstow Center. There were enough women, so that even if someone stayed back at the ashram, there were still plenty who would be out fund-raising each day. Michele received no special favor or privileges from Leo. She lived in the ashram and slept on the floor like the rest of us. Only, her sleeping bag was positioned closest to the closed door of the room Leo slept in. But they were not sleeping together.

Leo was the only man who had direct ongoing contact with any of us. More importantly, he was the only male it was acceptable for the women to speak to or have anything to do with. I was encouraged to strive for obscurity within the group of women, who were isolated from many other aspects of all the various Center activities.

At one point, Leo had the idea to break off our ties with the Barstow Center and travel worldwide to the Orient—Hong Kong, Japan, the Philippines, and so forth—collecting money, supposedly, to send to Manila, where the WORKS was building a new and extravagant Center in honor of Sir Supreme. This was in accordance with the vision of constructing a spiritual city. Leo began canvassing each of us, to find out who among us would remain loyal to soul-saving in this new arrangement. Mahlia adds, "But this really meant who would be loyal to Leo."

She then asks, "So what did you tell Leo when he asked if *you* would break away?" I told him what he wanted to hear, that I wouldn't even consider it any other way. I saw no other alternative. Right from the beginning, it was Leo who made me feel like I belonged. He was my main source of information about King Service and my link to the King mindset, more and more with the passing of time.

THE TIDE TURNS

SUZANNE, AN AGENT IN THE ORGANIZATION for five years, had left her husband and the New Zealand Center, where she had originally joined the WORKS, to do soul-saving in Leo's world "famous women's soul-saving fund-raising group," as we were referred to throughout the Organization. Saadya recalls, "She's the girl whose nickname was Mary Gold." She also was the girl who subsequently had to return to New Zealand because of her momentous exposé of Leo to the Barstow Center authorities. Mahlia proposes, "She was ostracized for being a traitor." Conducting ourselves according to King standards had morphed into being loyal to Leo, and it was way more serious than mere ostracism. When we learned who had turned against Leo, Suzanne could no longer live in the ashram because several of the girls had threatened that they would kill her, and they meant it.

After exposing Leo's deviations, and his absolute power over the women, Suzanne (or Mary Gold) remained at the Barstow Center for only a few more weeks, and not in the ashram, which had been her home for two years, but in an apartment down the street with several unmarried women from the Center who did not go out on soul-saving activity routinely.

No longer considered a member of the women's group meant Suzanne was disqualified from using any of the soul-saving vehicles. She was also banned from the San Bernadino Airport. This left only downtown San Bernadino for her to continue to fund-raise and pass out books.

One afternoon, she spotted me driving one of the Center cars. I had been on an errand in downtown Barstow. Suzanne was returning from her soul-saving activities for the day. She asked me if, in the future, I would be able to give her a ride into downtown Barstow, where she could catch a bus to go to San Bernadino—graciously adding, if it wasn't out of my way. I told her I would have to ask Camila, who at this time was in charge, in order to get permission. I thought this would only be a technicality and that of course Camila would allow Suzanne to get a ride in one of the soul-saving vans or cars. But this was not the case.

Mahlia is incredulous, not only that Camila refused to give her permission, but that I had to ask it. Camila's refusal came as a surprise, and much to my chagrin. Camila reeked with vengeance and wanted to make life miserable for Suzanne. I questioned her decision, saying that we should help any worker who wanted to serve Sir Supreme, especially by going out on soul-saving activity. Camila's rationale was that Suzanne was no longer a member of the group and should have thought about the consequences of her action before taking such extreme measures against her authority. According to Camila, it was *King* who would not allow her to associate with the more sincere and dedicated soul-saving sisters. Mahlia concludes, "Suzanne was trying to live up to the standards set in the WORKS and instead was blackballed as a traitor."

DECEIVED BY THE DECEPTION

SOMETIME BETWEEN THE EXPOSÉ and Suzanne being threatened and relocated, the Center leaders began an investigation of the activity going on in the women's ashram. I found it rather comical when sitting on the floor at the Center with a select group of male agents. They were trying to investigate and verify what they had been told. To remain chaste, my head was covered down to my eyebrows, and I dared not make eye contact with any of the men. I admitted that I had slept with Leo.

"Were you being interrogated as fact finding?" Saadya inquires. They were calling to my attention their concern that Leo was coming late to the morning worship, sometimes missing it altogether. Their show of concern was surprising, since I thought anything Leo did was sanctioned. He was supposed to be above any reproach.

We were led to think that the leaders appointed by Sir Supreme were similarly above any disrepute.

In the same way, any time my conversion faltered, I was reminded of the obligatory and absolute approach to good and evil. You showed allegiance to the WORKS, or you were doomed. Well-merited righteousness existed only in the WORKS and only for the loyal agents. Within the boundaries and definition of "totalism," there is the tendency for an all-or-nothing emotional alignment. The lines had been drawn for the soul-saving sisters. Either you were for soul-saving activity, or you succumbed to your rebellious nature. This morphed into either being for Leo or against him.

DEFENSE

2 SAMUEL 16:18: *"I'm here because I belong to the man who is chosen by the Lord."*

Mahlia's curiosity is still piqued. "Didn't the Center leaders know any of Leo's deviations before this time?" Right about the time that Sir Supreme stepped down and delegated authority to ten of his original agents, a girl from a Canadian Center was visiting the Barstow Center. She wrote a letter to the Board of Authority (BOA) accusing Leo of various deviations from the WORKS standards of behavior. We, the women in the soul-saving group, were all asked to write letters to the BOA in defense of Leo's treatment of us. Each of us came to his defense, and we were glad to. We were all still on his side. We had been convinced that loyalty to Leo was a measure of how sincere we were in our service to King. The entire program was geared to educate us in how to remain loyal servants to our spiritual monarch. To remain loyal was pleasing to Sir Supreme, and that meant to any one of his representatives. Mahlia comments, "That would be Leo."

Of course I wrote a letter on Leo's behalf describing his own loyalty and unflinching devotion to soul-saving and book-gifting. My letter listed everything he did as being motivated by his sincere desire to promote the mission. We were told what the visitor had reported, first to her husband, then to her Center's president, and finally to the WORKS' BOA.

It astonished us all. We could not believe that Leo would be so foolish as to say or do the things that she alleged. It simply would have been taking too much of a chance to take this girl into his confidence, risking the possibility that she could not be trusted. However, we all felt that

Leo was capable of doing all the things she reported. Perhaps he thought that, if he confided in her, she would begin to feel an allegiance to him, the objective being for her to join the group. "Or perhaps he had delusions of grandeur, and he thought he was King's gift to women," Mahlia asserts.

Regardless, his plan had backfired in his face.

She claimed that he tried talking her out of her marriage and instead into joining the Barstow women's soul-saving group. Throughout the time of her visit, Leo was unrelenting in trying to persuade her to move to the Barstow Center. He promised her security and protection. He would be like her husband, only he could offer her more excitement. This was due to his adventurous spirit when it came to keeping us enlivened.

THE STRIKE

MAHLIA POSES THE NEXT QUESTION: "What was adventurous about going to the airport when you weren't catching a plane?" It wasn't just about where we went. It was about what we did when we were there. For instance, Leo invented the strike. Mahlia humorously and protectively asks, "You mean you went on strike?" No. The strike was when the whole vanload of girls charged into a diner, a bar, any type of store or venue where there were gatherings of people seated at tables, making them an easy target.

Saadya is appalled. "You mean people were sitting ducks!" They were easy to approach, and we did just that, asking each person for a donation, until all of us realized everyone had been hit up, and then we would scram out of the place. We paid little to no attention to any security personnel insisting that we leave the premises. We would not leave until everyone had been approached. We were totally psyched up before jettisoning out of the van. We couldn't hesitate because there wasn't very much time spent in any one place. The regulars liked it too, because, even for them, it electrified the atmosphere. We were in and out before anyone could realize what was happening. After vacating the premises, we would head for the van, making a quick getaway, only to be dropped off at the next location.

HE ADMITTED IT TO ME

ONE DAY, DURING THE TIME that the girl from Canada was visiting, Leo remarked to me that he felt an immediate attraction to her, and that he had told her so. He told her that he already had more than one wife. This news must have shocked her. But by then, I had already accepted Leo's infallibility, convinced that he could do no wrong. "Of course," says Mahlia, "he was above the law." We were duly saturated with hearing about the seriousness of loyalty to him as the stepping stone to spiritual advancement. But she did not fall for his spiel.

Initially, Leo couldn't figure out what the Canadian visitor's motive was in reporting him. The way he presented it, his behavior aligned perfectly with the standards of King service. As a matter of fact, Leo claimed he had been set up.

He contended that other workers in the Organization were jealous because the women in the soul-saving group collected so much money. Saadya quickly reminds me, "Don't you mean Ora?"

I do; I did. Now *you* are confusing me, and I add the "you" as emphasis. I enjoy this type of banter with my daughters, and I have always made it a point to stop what I am doing, make eye contact, and show Mahlia and Saadya that I am listening to them, just as they have been listening to me as this story unfolds. It turned out that everything the girl from Canada said about Leo *was* true. Yet when the BOA was investigating her allegations, Leo had us lie for him, just as he had lied himself, thereby making *her* out to be a liar and a fool.

CLOSING IN ON LEO

SAADYA ASKS, "AND THAT WAS THAT?" All I ever heard about it. Yet a little while after this incident, while Leo was on the road but due back shortly from a trip to Mexico, the newly appointed leader of the Santa Barbara Center, Sir Kabos, came to the Barstow Center to speak with the Barstow soul-saving girls. He wanted to personally explain to us what had to be done. Leo had, he said, hit rock bottom, but we didn't have to worry because we were still considered okay in our King Service, since we were surrendering every day by going out on soul-saving. All we really needed to concern ourselves with was to try to help Leo by listing everything that had gone on in violation of the WORKS standards. Little did we realize, they were closing in on Leo. Many things that had remained behind closed doors up to then started coming out, as the women spoke of the deviations Leo engaged in—some with individual sisters that we had not been aware of even among ourselves.

Mahlia inquires, "Could it have gotten any worse?" We learned that Leo was addicted to codeine and was forging prescriptions, taking dozens of pills each day. He'd also begun smoking marijuana. I knew of the episode when he snorted cocaine with one of the women on a day when she remained back at the ashram instead of going out to fund-raise. Saadya asks, "That girl got sick to her stomach, didn't she?" She told me she had learned her lesson, but it wasn't the lesson we had both needed to learn.

POLYGAMY POLICE

(DEUTERONOMY 17:14-20): *"THE KING MUST NOT take many wives for himself, because they will turn his heart away from the Lord."*

We began to talk openly about Leo's polygamy and his cheating on his wife Michele. All the things that had made us miserable in King Service we now attributed to him.

However, things only got worse after the BOA made Leo move out of the women's ashram. Saadya asks, "What happened to him and the girls afterwards?" He moved into the men's ashram and the women had a hard time submitting to the leadership of another woman. Sir Derek remained too distant, and the women lacked having a personal relationship with a man. So it was decided that we should renounce men altogether and become so-called "widows," never to be married. One of us, who was unwilling to do that, was married off to a male worker. Soon afterwards, she had a baby. There definitely couldn't be single and unprotected women at the Center. Everyone in the WORKS knew that women needed to be protected. After all, Sir Supreme said so.

The entire ashram underwent an upheaval. I think the person who suffered the most, and in silence, was Leo's wife Michele.

Michele loved Leo and was loyal to him to the end. She never uttered one word against her husband. She was supposed to be spared most of the sordid details of his antics, but on that day, as all the women were assembled together with Sir Kabos, Michele took a seat on one of the bottom steps of the staircase just outside the ashram living room. She was very pregnant, and the last thing she needed was to hear about her lying, cheating husband and father of her soon-to-be-born baby. "So they started sleeping together," assumes Saadya. Not really; it happened during the time Michele was reassigned to do the ashram's housekeeping. Thus seated within earshot, Michele sat silently listening to everything being said.

The next day, when Leo returned to the Barstow Center with the girls he had been traveling with in Mexico, Camila and Belinda began to poll each of us to find out if we were with or against him. Mahlia says, "Clearly, Leo put them up to it." Never mind that Leo was deviating from the WORKS standards; it was either you were for Leo or against him.

The loyal ones covered up for him, and the others contended that the consequences of his misbehavior were for his own benefit. "So the ones who were involved in exposing Leo's interpretation of King Service thought *they* were the ones being loyal," Saadya concludes. Yet the women who chose to perpetuate the cover-up had no tolerance for any other perspective. It was all about whether or not we were being loyal to Leo.

THOU SHALT NOT

THOSE CHOOSING TO REMAIN LOYAL to Leo hated that Suzanne and Paula had spoken out against him and had them disenfranchised. They believed the two had betrayed him, their speaking out an act of treason. Paula was the one who'd invited me into the separate room that first Wednesday dinner. She made perfectly good sense when she explained to me that all the things that Leo was doing, and having us do, were not true to our vows. Most of us stood by, while she and Suzanne were ostracized and basically excommunicated from the ashram with all its benefits. "Was Leo out of the picture altogether?" Saadya asks. Not entirely at first.

When Leo first returned from Mexico, he was still left in charge of the women as he had been all along. Only a few small changes were made. He would live in the men's ashram, so the Center president, Clarke, could keep an eye on him.

However, the situation grew absurd as Camila ran over to see Leo first thing in the morning, to bring him a cup of herbal tea and to see if there was anything else he needed. In the evening, Camila visited him again late into the night. I still have no idea how they pulled that off.

Then Leo was with us again for the morning routine, when we assembled to recite phrases. He still conducted Superior Text class. Under these circumstances, and when all this was first coming out in the open, he took advantage of the situation by ridiculing all the girls who had been questioned by Clarke and the other men. It was embarrassing being ridiculed in front of the other girls. Leo made it sound as if we were to blame for his downfall into sex life.

Mahlia asks, "How did he manage that?" Several of us were ridiculed for saying we were remaining spiritual even when we engaged in the sex-life fiasco. We were even above the vows we had taken on becoming members of the WORKS.

"What exactly did you have to vow?" Saadya asks. We would not drink alcohol or take drugs, have no sex outside of marriage, and not gamble.

Mahlia says, "Those are healthy practices a lot of people follow. They don't make you spiritually special! Weren't you also a vegetarian?"

Saadya calculates, "One out of four isn't bad."

No one knew which girls Leo bedded down with, and which remained on the sidelines. But to have my name mentioned dispelled any doubt, and the others knew for sure that I had fallen down in spiritual life. One morning, Leo announced the foolishness of a statement I had made during the investigation—that I actually considered he had not been acting according to the physical energy.

I wanted to portray him in the way I had been led to think of him—acting in accordance with the importance of the mission. After Leo told me that I had been one of the first, which I found flattering, I was terribly embarrassed when he declared that I had said the stupidest thing, when being questioned—that sleeping with Leo was spiritual. Outraged, Mahlia declares, "Well, of all things! That maniac wanted you to believe he was your husband, and then embarrasses you to mitigate his own behavior."

Suzanne often looked over my shoulder when I was recording the scores to present to Clarke to be read aloud at the morning announcements.

Suzanne explained to me why she used to review the scores kept in the ledger. She told me that Leo had told her sleeping with a soul-saving sister was intended to boost her fund-raising score. By checking the scores, Suzanne was able to determine that, when she slept with Leo, it was *not* increasing her collections on the ensuing days.

Suzanne offered me her humility one particular morning, and I bowed down as we both recited the phrases honoring Sir Supreme. Without another word being uttered, we both knew why.

Saadya exclaims, "She either offended you or was forgiving you for having offended her, right?" This time, it had nothing to do with an offense. The night before, Leo had asked me to summon her to join him right after I had been with him. He saved himself for her.

Saadya can't help herself saying, "Ugh, that's disgusting," and she's right.

THE INTERROGATION

I WAS ONLY CONCERNED WITH THE MISSION of telling others about the benefits of King-mindedness. I did what was expected of me. "You wanted your service in the WORKS to be accounted to you as righteous," Saadya states. "You were just trying to be a good agent and save the world." Leo's reign over us was complete and total.

I really did not understand the politics involved at the time. I remember Leo calling me to the front of the van, where he was seated behind the steering wheel, to ask if I would stick with the group if we broke off from the Barstow Center and continued doing only TSS. This is when he had the idea for the girls to travel around the Orient. This was just one of his many bizarre ideas. It occurred on the afternoon Michele's pregnancy was announced. After all, they *were* married. Yet Dulce, one sister in particular, had a difficult time handling this news. She could not hide the fact that she was jealous.

It was only a short time after this polling of the women that Leo was exposed. I was surprised the investigators had no idea of what was going on in the ashram. Mahlia says, "At least they *pretended* not to know while the money was rolling in." I am not sure of that exactly. But I did think they were being naïve to think that it was not bound to happen. The Center president received much of the blame. Mahlia asks, "For being so naïve?" For not having more control over Leo. Supposedly, Clarke was being appeased by the large amount of money coming in that he rarely questioned Leo's methods.

"Probably," says Mahlia, "it was when Leo started getting too big for his own britches that the Center president and others in charge got concerned." When they found out about Leo conjuring up plans to take the women's group away from Barstow to travel and collect, they realized the income from our collections was threatened. "They were in jeopardy of losing you to the scheme Leo was already devising," concludes Mahlia. Thereupon, we began to be interrogated one by one.

I was called into Clarke's office one weekday morning when it was understood that we were all staying back from soul-saving that day. I did not know ahead of time what to expect—only that it was my turn and I would find out, according to Sherine when she passed the baton to me.

When I entered the office, I was motioned to sit down, completing a circle on the floor formed by Clarke and two other men. I kept looking down at the floor, as Leo had trained us to do. I remember thinking they must be thinking how well trained I was by not looking a man in the eye, so we would not be attractive. Mahlia asks for clarification. "Do you mean emotionally or physically?" I mean sexually.

Saadya can't help it and says, "I hate to say it, but those boys must have been a horny bunch." I think this is why the men wore very tight underwear. Now both my daughters are laughing hysterically. But it is no laughing matter.

Clarke and Harley were handling me with kid gloves, not wanting to say anything that might upset me or cause me alarm. Actually I was relishing all the attention for being a part of this controversial group of women within the WORKS. The purpose of the meeting, they said, was to help Leo, because they were concerned with his spiritual welfare. If he was breaking any rules in King Service, his spiritual advancement was in jeopardy. They wanted to hear it all.

I tried to explain how I viewed sleeping with Leo. I didn't think it was wrong. I didn't think we had broken any rules because we were still loyal to the mission. Leo preached that to be loyal meant we needed to show our loyalty to him, as our conduit for spiritual advancement. Therefore, Leo had us thinking that sleeping with him was honorable, and that it pleased the spiritual monarch.

"What pleased him?" asks Saadya. How, by being loyal to Leo, we were strengthening our loyalties to Sir Supreme, and this, after all, was the only way we could advance in King Service.

"You mean *Leo* was pleased when you turned in a pile of money in exchange for the pile of crap he was dishing out," Mahlia says.

I told the interrogators that we had been taught to consider ourselves married to Leo. So I never thought that we were breaking any rules since it was alright for man and wife to be intimate. Mahlia is quick to say, "Yeah, all twenty-five of you."

Saadya sums it up. "So being loyal to Leo was part of a bigger picture." I just needed to communicate this to Clarke and the two other men.

THINGS HEAT UP

THE REAL TROUBLE BEGAN when Leo did not heed the warnings of the BOA, because he had previously been warned about sleeping with the women and he continued doing so. I covered up for him when I was asked by Center authorities, at another of their investigations, when I had last slept with Leo. I knew very well it had been after they told us Leo had been warned to stop, so I just said that I didn't remember. They couldn't have believed me, because it was so evident that it was a lie. When I walked out of the room, another sister was called in. We basically took turns lying for Leo.

Mahlia conducts her own investigation, asking, "Why was Leo allowed to remain in the girls' ashram after they first found out about his shenanigans?"

I pause as I give her a moment to consider the alternative. In a flash she realizes, "It was *still* all about keeping the fund-raising scores high. The Center authority was willing to take another chance because of what was at stake. They didn't want to jeopardize the Ora flow."

However, those next few days, Leo was meeting with other male workers in charge of even him. They were "single men" who had taken a vow never to marry. Being removed as head of our group caused Leo a great deal of embarrassment and he took out his vengeance on those he thought betrayed him. So Suzanne and Paula, who had taken it upon themselves to go to the Center authorities to discuss the deviations, including but not limited to sleeping with the girls, were blackballed.

Enthralled by the soap opera, Saadya asks, "What else was Leo getting away with?"

Mahlia answers, "Don't you remember the fasting for two days at a time, and what about the drugs?" Didn't I tell you about withholding funds for unauthorized expenditures? "You did."

In addition to being banned from the ashram, it was made nearly impossible for Suzanne and Paula to engage in soul-saving activity. No longer were any accommodations to be made for them in any of the usual fund-raising spots. The Center didn't provide them with any transportation either. It was left entirely up to them to find a location to engage on soul-saving. Despite continuing to want to make spiritual advancement, they had to make their own arrangements to engage in this highest service to King.

Consequently, Suzanne and Paula were soon relocated for fear that some harm might come to them. Belinda told me that she would kill one of the "stool-pigeons," and I could tell she meant it.

SIR DEREK ON THE THRONE

AS TIME WENT ON AND I WAS WELL into my third year in the WORKS, a complete transference of power within the women's soul-saving ashram took place. Despite Leo now not directly in charge, his influence continued to permeate the tone in the ashram, and strict adherence to fundraising continued to determine the climate of soul-saving fervor among the women. When Camila was first put in charge, going out to collect every day remained the way that we could prove our continued loyalty to Leo. Camila always reminded us of this. After Leo was dethroned and Camila was also out of the picture, Belinda was placed in charge, and the affections of the remaining girls of the soul-saving group were transferred to Sir Derek, according to the hierarchy and his authority. Mahlia doesn't miss a beat when she says, "He was both designator and designee."

Then, under Sir Derek, several of the girls in the Organization for a longer time than the others were taken off of soul-saving to stay behind and help run the ashram. It was still understood to be necessary for the girls out on soul-saving to be able to have someone to talk to if they were having any difficulty. They could call the ashram and speak to one of the girls to get support and a boost for their morale.

The benefit was in knowing we had someone to talk to when we needed encouragement. However, the decrease in women collecting put added pressure on those of us who were still going out.

Saadya declares, "*More* pressure for the girls! That is the last thing they needed."

Many actually began to crack under the pressure. By then, it had been several weeks since Leo was dethroned. It was uncomfortable for me to ascribe to, and cooperate with, the random transference of power and authority to Camila. Trust in the authority began to waver and wane for each of us. This certainly did not help us on soul-saving. The atmosphere was growing toxic.

RIVALRY IN THE RANKS

TO ADD TO THE ALREADY TOXIC ENVIRONMENT, it soon became obvious that Sir Derek didn't like Clarke. Evidently, there had been a long-standing rivalry between them. It became difficult for Clarke, who had been president at Barstow for four years by then, to accept all the changes Sir Derek was making. All along, we had been led to believe that Clarke was such a faithful agent, so spiritually elevated and capable of managing the affairs of the Center.

Saadya laughs aloud. "Mom, he was not managing *all* the affairs, Leo was." That's amusing, but what's not is that Clarke was being discredited although he was respected by the other agents of the Center. He often conducted Superior Text class as part of the morning routine and his classes were intellectually stimulating.

During the time he was president, Clarke was running the business end of the Center. He had a lovely wife, Lilly, from London, whom we all liked. Mahlia recalls, "It was Lilly who was compassionate when she heard you were made to fast for two days for busting up the van." It was only a few scratches.

Sir Derek, now in the picture as head of the leadership, seemingly out of the blue, waged a campaign against Clarke when, according to Sir Derek, Clarke had become attached to the physical energy because he didn't want to assume "single-man" status, which required more austerity than he was accustomed to. Specifically, it required him to denounce his marriage to Lilly.

As a result, Clarke left the Center with his wife, and he was soon replaced. Several reasons were given by Sir Derek, now in full control of the Southwest Sector of the WORKS. We were told the change had taken place because it had been determined that the Barstow Center had been thriving, not because of Clarke's business prowess or expertise at management, but because it was easy to handle the business of the Center due to the large amount of money coming in on a "regular" basis—no pun intended. When collections dropped, Clarke, although well-liked by the workers, basically got fired.

Suddenly, with him out of the picture, the barrage against his reputation ensued. We were told how impure Clarke had been all along, and how incompetent. Under Clarke's tenure, there had been more than enough money not only to maintain the Center, but to remodel it, as well as renovate—and that is exactly what was accomplished at the Barstow Center—because of the fund-raising, not because of him.

I remember Leo telling us that the granite used for steps leading up to the altar for the carved figures had been imported from Mexico. After all, King deserved the best.

SIR DEREK'S PALACE

(2 SAMUEL 5:11): *"Then King Hiram of Tyre sent messages to David, along with cedar and timber and carpenters and stone masons, and they built David a palace."*

Sir Derek's house was no exception for extravagance. It was immediately to be painted and professionally decorated. When it was announced that he was officially making the Barstow Center his residence most of the women were not at the Center but on the road for traveling soul-saving. Sir Derek had been traveling at this time, but in his case around the world with some other male agents. Also at this time, Camila, our fearless leader, had been on TSS, as a van driver, but she'd flown back to California ahead of schedule to take charge of preparing the house. She was in charge of overseeing color coordination and decorations.

While Clarke was still president, he and Camila had joined forces to prepare the house for Sir Derek's much-anticipated arrival. They shopped for all-brass pots, pans of varying sizes and depths with matching utensils, ladles, carving knives, spoons, and other paraphernalia to be used for Sir Derek and his closest cohorts. Camila bragged to us that, on that shopping spree, two shopping wagons had been filled with merchandise. While the first wagon was being checked out at the cash register, the second was wheeled outside. All its contents were quickly transferred into the nearby car without paying for any of it.

Camila told us, when they went to the exclusive brass store, the real thrill was wheeling out that second shopping cart. Regardless, the items that were paid for amounted to over four thousand dollars. The rationale was that shoplifting, which is what it amounted to, was sanctioned, because it was done in service to Sir Derek, who, we were told, had been appointed directly by Sir Supreme to be our new spiritual monarch.

"So in King Service it was okay to steal?" Saadya asks in unbelief that people who claimed to be religious could justify breaking the eighth commandment, Thou shalt not steal. Since everything belonged to King, it was not stealing. They were just repossessing what was rightfully his, to be used by and for God's own representative. That was the justification. However, on the contrary, this episode left me feeling very uneasy.

Similarly, other behavior in the WORKS did not conform to the norms of society. Saadya declares, "Forget about norms—this behavior was criminal, and is punishable by law." It was before security cameras, though, and they didn't get caught. "Mom, you know the expression 'what you sow, so shall you reap,'" she adds. I know. There were many repercussions over the years throughout the WORKS. Saadya and Mahlia agree it is better for them to Google what these were, since it has been decades since my involvement.

Another incident of theft was when a group of girls were traveling in Japan. I heard that they entered a jewelry store as several of them were eating open containers of yogurt. While the proprietor was intentionally distracted getting an item for one of the girls, another slipped a diamond ring into her yogurt and stood by, watching the jeweler going crazy looking for it, as she continued eating yogurt right in front of him. Mahlia and Saadya have their eyes wide open and their mouths agape.

REALITY TESTING

HAGGAI 1:8: "GO TO THE HILLS and bring wood and build the house, that I may take pleasure in it and that I may be glorified, says the Lord."

The traveling sisters, including me, returned to the Barstow Center only a few days before Sir Derek was expected to arrive. We had fun pitching in to help with the house preparations. We scrubbed floors and painted walls. Foam padding was placed on the floors from wall to wall for people to sit on when they came to hear him speak. The kitchen was stocked with all the brass pots and pans and utensils. A professional designer had created the curtains for the bedroom. Although the spiritual monarch was supposed to be the most austere, he was the only agent allowed to sleep in a bed.

Saadya says, "I thought he was supposed to be transcendental and not affected by physical comforts like that." In spite of that, knowing that Sir Derek deserved this type of special treatment was enough justification for us. I even heard it had brass bedposts.

The entire floor in the main room was covered, as I mentioned, with rolls of foam rubber padding, and some of the women were allowed daily to straighten the sheets, so the padding would be neat and tidy when guests came to hear a pure being speak about the benefits of making spiritual advancement through the lifestyle as an agent in the WORKS. This was an impossible task. "I bet it was!" says Mahlia. "People coming from the outside were able to go home to mull over what they were listening to, unlike you, who by staying behind at the ashram never had the opportunity."

Mahlia, misunderstanding the context of my statement, was shedding light on one of the primary techniques the Organization relied on, which profoundly affects the individual and yields the result of a mind controlled by the group. The group, being the entity, defined our reality.

Saadya piggy-backs on this, saying, "Your curiosity turned into an eagerness to learn what they believed in, so they became your teacher. This morphed into the WORKS as the sole entity you could listen to."

After realizing that my daughters are grasping what I have been telling them, I explain that I was merely referring to the impossible task of straightening out the sheets.

"Hm!" says Mahlia. First, there was no room to pull, tug, and tuck the edges of the sheets so they could remain straight, because we had to crawl on the padding as we straightened, so wherever we stood or knelt, that area was left with our imprint, and smoothing out the sheets became a never-ending task that resulted in one area remaining wrinkled.

"That is our human condition unless we know the One who is without wrinkle, spot, or blemish," Saadya remarks. Mahlia is amused. I am not.

What *was* amusing was for us to be engaged in house preparations, for a change of pace. We thought we were doing something extremely special because we were doing it for Sir Derek, who was coming to live in such close proximity to us, not like Sir Supreme, who had spent most of his time in the Philippians.

Even after Sir Derek took residence, the care and maintenance of the house were left to the women, so that on days off from collecting you could expect to find yourself cleaning the house or going to a fruit and vegetable market to buy the necessary tofu and other ingredients for Sir Derek's special cuisine, which we ourselves did not partake in.

UNSTRUCTURED

NOW THAT SIR DEREK WAS AT THE CENTER, music, worship, reciting phrases, singing, and dancing would ensue and persist for hours into the evening. This created a disruption in our schedule. We were accustomed to a very rigid one. With this carrying on, after a full day of soul-saving, we would then have to hurry back to the women's ashram to lie down so that we could get as much rest as possible before we began reciting the King phrases all over again.

Mahlia gasps, "You still had to get up, recite, and go out the following morning? Didn't you ever want to sleep in?" It was not usually an option. Even if we were up past 11:00 p.m., we were expected to rise the next morning by 2:00 a.m. and were rarely given a chance to catch up on any of that sleep. There simply was no time.

Instead of sleep, we were supposed to feel honored to be in a position to serve such an exalted soul. Honor was supposed to dissipate our fatigue. Much of the time it did. But other times our exhaustion put us into the world's mindset, and we suffered for it.

Mahlia is listening and searching her phone. She looks up, and Saadya prods her, but Mahlia waits to establish eye contact with me before telling me, "We are given the example to follow in which Jesus tells John, *'Don't worship me. I am a servant of God, just like you and your brothers and sisters'*" (Revelation 19:10). Illuminating the distorted practice of bowing and worshiping self-imposed gods in the WORKS, she adds, "We are told to worship only God." I thought I had been.

DISSONANCE

SIR DEREK'S HOUSE CLEANING HAD TO BE DONE in the early morning, while the place was vacant. This matter created yet another disruption in the routine. It meant that several of the girls had to miss much of the morning program and, worst of all, the Superior Text class, which was vital for us to hear. It would keep us in the King mindset for the day while we were fund-raising.

Yet with all the frivolity, we had to carry on with austerity and severity, even while Sir Derek and the others in charge had, to our knowledge, minimal discomfort. The girl who remained behind at the ashram always seemed to be having fun, while the soul-saving sisters were continually on guard against the world and its potential alluring influence that could undermine our efforts. In contrast, we had to remain serious and steadfast. We were compared to front-line soldiers fighting in a war.

Meanwhile, it wasn't always easy striking a balance.

The contradictions we witnessed going on within the ashram and as part of Center life created dissonance for us. Yet to question or doubt authority would impede our spiritual advancement. The way I had been trained to deal with this cognitive dissonance was to recite King phrases on my own or to be preached to about how fortunate I was to be in the highest service, even if it demanded the most austerity. If I endured, my immortality was guaranteed.

To which Mahlia supportively states, "All the agents thought this." This statement is pivotal in Mahlia assuming a more understanding demeanor. She is growing less critical.

One particular episode stands out as a time when there was a major thrust for all the agents to go out on soul-saving. All other activities around the ashram, Sir Derek's house, or the worship center were curtailed to increase collections during the electrified Christmas season. The regulars were going to be in the Christmas spirit and in general more generous, which would make donations easier to collect.

We were supposed to be so enlivened as to be enlivening for them. It was up to us to attract people into giving a generous donation. The goal was to increase our scores by capitalizing on the season of giving. While Camila was still in charge after Leo was somewhat out of the picture, she opted out of collecting during the Christmas season frenzy, declaring that she needed to remain at the ashram to be accessible by phone, in case one of the soul-saving girls needed to talk.

It was difficult to understand why Camila would remain at the ashram. We were already all psyched up, and we had other sisters in close proximity who we could talk to if we needed a quick fix to boost our morale. When I brought this to her attention, she screamed and carried on that, if I thought I could run the ashram better than she, I could stay behind to deal with all the individual personalities and see to it that everyone was happy in King Service. I declined.

CAMELOT

CAMILA WAS ALREADY MARRIED in the WORKS by the time she came to the Barstow Center. Her husband used to beat her, but she still wanted the security of being married. Camila proved herself to be one of the biggest book-gifting agents in her heyday. Her path crossed Leo's on a trip to the Barstow Center to learn new techniques for engaging people on soul-saving activity. When Leo found out that she wanted to return to her husband, he talked her into staying at Barstow, and they were married by a justice of the peace. She became Leo's right-hand girl, assisting him in all aspects of running the ashram, and of course keeping the women motivated. Mahlia states, "Leo couldn't stand the thought of losing such a big fund-raiser." Maybe at first, but then they grew very close—so close that he took her off soul-saving and she remained at the ashram with him to be available to speak to any of the girls who might need a pep talk while out on soul-saving. Clearly, we did need some reassurance now and then, to be sure: The real difficulty was in having to fund-raise with no end in sight.

"So he married someone who was already married," Mahlia notes with a mixture of surprise and disgust. In fact, Leo was married to four of the women at one time. He was already married to Michele from before joining the WORKS. I did not know that he took Camila as his second wife. Yet I wasn't surprised when I found out.

Another girl Leo married was Natasha, the top fund-raiser in the WORKS, collecting close to a thousand dollars a day. She came to live at the ashram soon after me, and after three years of being a top collector, she refused to follow Leo's instructions and even went so far as to announce that she was no longer a member of the soul-saving group. He took her on a trip to Mexico; they were gone for three days. He married her in a civil ceremony in Mexico. His rationale was to keep her loyal to him and to soul-saving. I did not know they'd gotten married, but I did notice her spending more time with him and once again being compliant to him.

Darlene, another top fund-raiser, who consistently collected over five hundred dollars a day, had been expressing her desire to get married. Saadya says, "Let me guess." She goes on to brief us: "He didn't want to lose her to one of the male agents who would distract her from going out on soul-saving." She became Leo's fourth wife.

A CRY OF THE HEART

LEO'S BEDROOM HAD A DRESSER, the only piece of furniture in the entire ashram. It was there that I found a hand-written note from Lady Kaylah, a burn victim. Before joining the WORKS, she and her husband had been trapped in a burning automobile. Her husband perished in the fire, and she'd spent a year in the special burn unit of the hospital. Someone had brought her Superior Text books, and she had read about how she was not her body. Under the circumstances she could relate to that, and it offered her hope, since she was only twenty-three years old at the time.

I came across her letter on Leo's dresser—an impassioned note about how envious Kaylah was of the other girls who were not scarred, and how she wanted desperately to feel married to Leo. She thought her scars prevented this from being a possibility. My heart broke at her sentiment and the realization of what she went through on a daily basis.

This was not an unreasonable request because Leo cultivated in us the feeling that we were as good as married to him. Not only I, but each of the others, was prepared to share him. Lady Kaylah had the most beautiful blue eyes and she consistently did well on fund-raising. The amount of her collections surpassed that of many of the others. But this was not enough for her, as her note illuminated the cry of her heart.

LEO'S POLYGAMY

LEO'S POLYGAMY WAS EXPOSED at the same time as the general upheaval. Several of the girls began speaking among themselves, whereas before, everything had been kept secret even from each other. Leo had boasted that Sir Supreme had actually told him during one of Leo's visits to Manila that polygamy was sanctioned. The only caveat was that Western society was not ready for it. If the WORKS outwardly endorsed the practice of polygamy, it would trigger too much criticism of the Organization. Therefore, Leo felt his behavior was sacrosanct, having been wholly sanctioned by Sir Supreme, and had no misgivings about having multiple wives. Saadya accurately declares, "He already considered himself the husband of all the women in the soul-saving group." To the extent it served his purposes.

Mahlia challenges me by saying, "You were willing to put up with all of this—but why?" Nothing was more important to me than the mission and its far-reaching benefits. I had nothing to do but go out on soul-saving. After all, the essentials of life were provided by the Center, and everything else was looked upon as extraneous and a frivolous waste of time. There was nothing I thought I lacked. I was supposed to be devoid of the desire for physical things. Yet my psyche was implanted with a constant focus for collecting money. "You mean so someone else could acquire physical things," Mahlia emphasizes.

INCONSPICUOUS

A SINGLE-MINDEDNESS AND DETERMINATION to always increase our soul-saving results was constantly being cultivated. This required more of us and from us, as well as more disregard for common sense. Also being cultivated was our obscurity within the Center when we were on the premises. The cunning way we were controlled afforded the leadership an advantage over every other facet of my life. Chastity meant more than covering my head with the tunic scarf. It was a state of mind. If I didn't see others, I assumed I wouldn't be seen and hoped others weren't looking.

I considered myself protected in the WORKS. In this way, I would be shielded from distractions that might impede my spiritual growth. When Leo adopted "single man" status, I, as well as the other women, agreed to regard ourselves as widows.

Our only desire in life was to stay focused on the mission of spreading King Awareness. Soul-saving, high scores, perseverance, not falling under the influence of physical energy, and submitting to whoever was in charge defined our service in the mission. By passing out books, we were promulgating knowledge of King and his kingdom. We were spreading love of God. Saadya advises, "Mom, the irony of the matter lay in the fact that, in your fervor to spread love of God, you had no opportunity to experience it for yourselves."

LEO'S BETRAYAL

MAHLIA WANTS TO KNOW, "WHAT HAPPENED when Leo moved into the men's ashram?" He became an ordinary male agent at first. While he was living there, news got back to us that he talked about us among the men, asserting that none of them could have remained staunch for as long as he had because the temptation was so great. He'd even gone so far as to insinuate that the fault lay with us. Mahlia says, "He set himself up to be some kind of a martyr."

We had to counter the embarrassment of knowing that Leo was revealing these things about us. We agreed we had to overcompensate for the exposure. So when the subject of our lifestyle was discussed among ourselves, we agreed as a group never to marry. Saadya asks, "Was this so you would honor Grandma's request?" I wish I could say that. As a group, we were still functioning under a tightly knit, interwoven network of discipline and obedience. By positioning ourselves in the back of the worship room for sing and dance worship during the morning routine, we would be out of Leo's field of vision, as well as that of most of the other male agents. We remained toward the back of the room to avoid causing distraction to any of them. Saadya alleges, "This sounds like the women actually felt responsible for Leo's downfall." That's what he had us believe.

Mahlia responds, "It's obvious you all stopped thinking critically." Or for ourselves. All our spirituality amounted to was being inconspicuous.

"Yeah, like a kitten at the ashram and a tiger out on soul-saving," Saadya says, recalling Sir Supreme's analogy.

The problem the Center authorities faced concerning Leo and us was not resolved by isolating him from us by having him live in the men's ashram. We still belonged to him. We were his soul-saving group. Furthermore, his relationship with Camila was already firmly established.

LEO IS ELEVATED

WITH SIR DEREK RUNNING THE SHOW and Leo's behavior out in the open, it was initially decided that Leo be given two alternatives, or so we were told. He could either forgo any ongoing relationship with us, and take "single man" status, or he could leave the WORKS altogether. He opted to stay.

As a "single-man," he gained a position of prestige and honor. It was so ironic that, immediately after his downfall for the most serious infraction an agent in King Service could commit, descending into sex life, Leo was now elevated to a position of reverence. The agents, both men and women, would fall to their knees to prostrate themselves when he passed. This was the proper thing to do—men with that status were supposed to typify an exalted soul who was choosing to decline any form of sensual pleasure. Mahlia notes, "The workers, or agents, or whatever you called yourselves, fell into sex life and then fell to your knees, all because you fell for this nonsense!"

This was the culmination of Leo's hegemony over our group; now he had even the men kowtowing to him.

None of us women were supposed to speak to, or look at, Leo in his new status. Yet we spoke *about* him with one another. We reminded each other that we still had to please him through our soul-saving results. Mahlia observes, "You must have been in love with him." It was different. It was more an allegiance than a commitment. Leo exerted a strong influence over us, and it was his style of leadership that created a desire to win his approval at the end of each day. The only way to please our leader was to collect money on a daily basis, with no expectation of any reward than a barely noticeable nod of approval. Mahlia addresses this sentiment, "You wanted your service in the WORKS to be accounted to you as righteous." Before I can say a word, she quotes, Romans 11:6: *"But if it is by grace, it is no longer on the basis of works."* "Anyway," I interrupt, "Leo's reign over us was complete and total."

CAMILA IN CHARGE

CAMILA WAS SUPPOSED TO BE more advanced than the other women because she had been in the Organization longer than any of the others and had direct contact with two of the other newly appointed leaders. When Leo was still in charge, he claimed that a woman could not be in charge of other women. It was Sir Supreme who was attributed with saying that a girl could not maintain authority over other girls because of jealousy. There had to be a man in charge. This had been Leo's rationale for exerting so much power over us.

Nonetheless, Camila was placed in charge, and we were told to obey her just as we would Leo. We were to respect her as an authority figure because she was supposedly being empowered to know exactly what to do and say to keep the fund-raising group running smoothly, just as it had been under Leo's reign. Saadya emphasizes, "In reality it hadn't been going that smoothly!" It had, in the beginning.

Yet what ensued was the full-fledged rivalry among the top fund-raisers, which meant there was animosity among the top collectors. Several of the top collectors would not stop fund-raising when the signal was given to meet at the van. They would simply continue approaching regulars for donations. Their supererogation had an ulterior motive. They knew the more people they asked, the more they would collect. Anyone who collected the most would be rewarded by being allowed to bring the money over to Sir Derek at midnight. This competition was not meant for all of us, because some were not even in the running compared to these two top collectors. Natasha and Darlene began collecting somewhere around eight hundred dollars each, daily. They persevered and were super-charged at the prospect of bringing Ora over to the spiritual monarch in his palace. Saadya remarks, "It wasn't about the money for the girls, because they didn't get any of it. It was about getting a higher score, so they would get attention."

Mahlia adds, "They loved the extra attention, and Sir Derek loved the money."

Consequently, all the quibbling and squabbling among us, the jealousy, and Camila's own insecurities became too much for her to handle. There was an enormous amount of responsibility being placed on her, and as a result she flipped out. She used to scream at the top of her lungs for anything to get done, and no one listened to her when she got to that point. One morning she reached her breaking point. By then, she had been sanctimoniously preaching about how we had to immerse ourselves in our service, or we would be deceived by the physical energy into wanting to get married and have babies.

The thought of getting married was not prominent in my mind, and it felt awkward to hear Camila speak about it as much as she did. On the contrary, the more we heard this notion, the more it sounded appealing. Getting married started presenting itself as a viable alternative to fund-raising.

BEHIND THE SCENES

CAMILA WAS SUPPOSED TO HAVE HAD the highest scores in soul-saving before she was delegated to be Leo's right-hand girl. Her performance years earlier, while she was at the Carlsbad Center earned her this reputation. However, by having to assist Leo in keeping the girls motivated, she had not been out on soul-saving activity for two years. One day she admitted to me that she was deathly afraid of it. Saadya opines, "That is the epitome of hypocrisy."

Camila was experiencing so much conflict because she had to maintain a semblance of confidence in order to be able to influence the other women to continue going out day after day. Leo had been her support; without him, she was running on empty, and it began to show. We were no longer a fund-raising group, because, although we were still fund-raising, our efforts were void of a group effort.

Camila was under so much pressure because she knew she was losing her grip. She had been in love with Leo, and even in his status of "single-man," he kept calling her, though he was supposed to be forfeiting any relationship with women. If anyone at the ashram other than she answered the phone, he would hang up. Several times, I answered the phone when this occurred. It struck me as odd. When I mentioned this to Camila, she merely told me not to worry about it. Later I learned that it was Leo on the other end who was hanging up if anyone other than Camila picked up. Leo was running things from behind the scenes.

CAMILA CRACKS

SO WHEN LEO WAS REMOVED, Camila assumed his role at the ashram. She was the logical choice since we were accustomed to listen to her. Mahlia pauses. "Leo found a clever way of maintaining his communications, though, given the fact that they were secretly still involved." That is exactly how it played out. She would assign girls to various places for collecting and see to it that breakfast and lunch were arranged. But Leo was still running the show.

Camila would do anything for Leo, and, just as I had once done, she summoned the girls when it was their time to spend with him. It was treated like a big joke. One night, she was even going to call a motel for Leo to take me to. She said it would be fun, but I didn't want to go. Even when he had taken "single-man" status, he was not only calling, but also secretly meeting with her.

It increasingly became too much for her to handle the responsibility of keeping the girls motivated to go out on soul-saving every day while she doubted her own abilities. She was experiencing extreme anxiety in having to preach to the women, having to keep everyone else's morale up by telling them how all they needed to do was remember the benefit of dutiful service when she herself could not. The strain started showing on her face. She began to chew on her lip.

Previously, it had been easy for her to preach to us because Leo had her back, so to speak. With no Leo to back her up, Camila realized she was powerless. At this time, yet another change occurred. Leo was demoted from his elevated position, in which the agents bowed when he passed by. Undoubtedly, Sir Derek prevailed as to whom the women would venerate. Leo was promptly stripped of his elevated status and was now to be considered an ordinary worker just like the rest of us.

According to Sir Derek, Leo was no longer worthy of being held in high esteem. He told us this was King's way of punishing Leo for all his wrongdoing. In essence, Leo was being cut down to size. Saadya says, "So everything Leo did was supposed to make the girls go out to collect donations, and then he was maligned by Sir Derek." We started getting used to this pattern. Whenever someone left the Center, they were spoken poorly of. We were told they were not sincere enough, and King had therefore kicked them out. Camila was no exception. She eventually left the ashram and returned to live with her parents.

Saadya also considers Sir Derek's motives. "In his attempt to replace Leo in the eyes of the women, he maligns Leo, just to 'drive the nail into the coffin,' so to speak." You can say that for sure. First and foremost, Sir Derek wanted to be kept on a pedestal when it came to the girls.

Mahlia asks, "How did Camila come out in all of this?" Sir Derek spoke malevolently about her as well. We were told she had fallen off her own pedestal due to her physical attachment to Leo, causing her to fall out of the King mindset and to lose her King mentality.

CAMILA AND THE CAR

"IS THERE ANY MORE TO THIS STORY about Camila?" inquires Saadya. As I said, Camila wound up moving back to Carlsbad, where she was originally from. During the time Leo was functioning in the capacity of a worker, just like us, he was arrested for not paying the bill on a rental car he had used for soul-saving. He'd rented it in his own name to "strike" fast-food and drive-through restaurants. The Center refused to pay the bill, so Leo was left responsible for it.

Saadya is quick to catch that term. "I remember you told us about the strike. The girls would just storm into a place and ask everyone for a donation. They would move around so fast, and talk so fast, there was no time to go into any details about who, or what you were collecting money for." The regulars simply got caught up in the excitement, and it would be more fun to give a quick donation than to be a "stick in the mud" by turning down the request.

Mahlia says, "The regulars probably figured it was something sanctioned, and even if it wasn't, it was better than just sitting in their car waiting for a hamburger." Exactly. We created the energy.

Saadya reflects, "Going out on strike meant hitting up everyone in sight quickly, and then disappearing as quickly as you appeared."

Mahlia reflects upon the car rental: "I guess Leo forgot to use the money he collected to pay the bill." My guess is he turned in all his collections to get a higher score.

When Leo could not put the money up because he had none of his own, the Center disavowed any knowledge of his activities. Since the car rental company pressed charges against him, he was arrested. The way the whole episode was justified to us was that all the deviations Leo had committed were catching up with him. Actually, most of the girls were glad that Leo was getting a taste of his own medicine. However, Camila put up the bail for Leo from money her parents gave her.

AFTER THEIR DEMISE

WHEN LEO'S POWER WAS USURPED, coupled with Camila's departure, we were soon left in the hands of yet another one of the girls, this time under the auspices of Sir Derek. Mahlia and Saadya are wrought with anticipation as Saadya demands, "Who was it this time?"

Mahlia says, "Must have been Belinda." Yes, and under her jurisdiction it became apparent that, as Leo had said many times, girls will take direction from a man more readily than from another girl, and he was right.

There was more than one problem with Belinda being in charge after the dissolution of Leo and Camila's reign. It was not easy for us to take direction from her and even more difficult to even acknowledge her as an authority. Additionally, Sir Derek also took another top fund-raiser off soul-saving to run the ashram. Mahlia acknowledges the ramifications: "So that put more of a burden on the remaining soul-saving girls," shaking her head incredulously from side to side.

Now, with Belinda and Dulce in charge of overseeing the soul-saving girls, no effective authority figure directly monitored our attitude toward soul-saving. As a result, Sir Derek's feeble attempt at replacing Leo and Camila with Belinda and Dulce failed. Both were poor choices, and as a result the system in the ashram continued to unravel.

Many of us were running on empty. We were told it was because we weren't reading the books for ourselves and were thus falling under the influence of the physical energy. This explanation was supposed to reassure us and encourage us to believe that, by reading the Superior Texts, we would again be psyched up about soul-saving. If we could just give these books out, if we could just get them into the hands of the people we encountered, then they too would be enlightened. Yet many of us did not know what was in the books other than what was taught during a Superior Text class.

We were told that, as a result, we struggled because we did not wholly understand the philosophy for ourselves. Saadya is quick to say, "I'm glad you didn't say theology."

Mahlia nods. "That was certainly *not* theology." The books taught about life with King in the kingdom and the benefits of leading an austere life.

My daughters make eye contact, and there is a gleam in their eyes. I ask, "What?"

Mahlia is bursting to say—but Saadya beats her to it— "Mom, there is only one book that speaks of the one true God and the kingdom of heaven."

I bow my head, and my eyelids close gently. I hear myself whisper, "Is this yet another clever deception?"

BEATING BELINDA

MAHLIA CONTINUES, "TELL US what happened after Camila left and Belinda was put in charge." Belinda would preach about how we could trust her because she was not under the influence of physical energy, as Leo and Camila had been.

Unlike most of the other girls, I was able to resume my soul-saving endeavors. Belinda said it was because I'd had a year to read and study when I was staying back full time to edit some WORKS literature. The fact was, that I, surely, could not listen to Belinda's harangues about soul-saving. They were empty words. She did not have that kind of rapport with any of us, and there had been a personality conflict between her and me. Previously, when I brought this to Leo's attention, he'd said half-heartedly,

"Belinda eats nails for breakfast."

My personality does not do well with people of that temperament. Both of us were headstrong, and she had come to the Barstow Center only a few months before me, so she did not have much seniority over me. Belinda had been the person who chased after me at Riley's at Los Rios Rancho in the Oak Glen area. Saadya caps it by saying, "And she was the one who caught you just as you were going to eat a piece of cheese."

"You were trapped like a rat!" Mahlia says.

So was Belinda. In the past, she had thrived on Leo's attention, even when it came in the form of beating and bruising. We didn't know the specifics, but I am pretty sure it had to do with surrendering her will. Beating Belinda was Leo's way of keeping her humble. I can tell you the sound of it. I know the sound because I heard it as it was taking place. I was on the first floor and could hear the thrashing around of her body. I could hear her body crashing into walls in his room on the second floor as she absorbed the blows from Leo's fists.

The result of Belinda's lesson in humility was two black eyes and a swollen lip. She stayed in the ashram for a few days and used dark glasses to hide the bruises until they began to heal, though not completely. We all knew because the sunglasses she wore could not conceal her black eyes from the side. Neither, Leo or Belinda ever explained it in any detail—only that it had been necessary to keep Belinda humble. The beating was supposed to have been for Belinda's own good.

SHOT IN THE ARM

"WERE YOU SCARED OF LEO?" ASKS SAADYA. No, not scared; we always thought whatever he did was for our own good, and trusted that that was his motive. We believed that if Leo resorted to using his fists on a sister, it was for the good of her spiritual life. Anything Leo did was supposed to negate the influence of the physical world. His theory was that, when a soul-saving sister succumbed to her own will, she needed to be knocked around.

Mahlia emphasizes, "So Leo was literally trying to knock some sense into Belinda." Unfortunately Belinda was beyond common sense, as we all were. Fortunately, not all of us were abused in that way. I wasn't punched because my behavior and attitude didn't warrant it.

Saadya has to send an email and excuses herself. Seeing the look of disappointment on my face, she reassures me, "I'll be right back."

I continue with Mahlia. At least my attitude didn't warrant getting hit, in Leo's estimation, until one Wednesday dinner. "Oh, no! What happened?" Mahlia is girding herself for the atrocity.

I came back to the ashram a few minutes later than the others because I was hitting up the Philippine families who had come to the midweek dinner. I was collecting money from everyone I asked. Leo didn't know this, so when I passed him near the entrance to the ashram, he punched my arm. It felt like I'd gotten a flu shot in the deltoid muscle of my left arm. I immediately questioned him, "What was that for?"

He was quick to say, "For not coming back on time."

I told him that was not necessary, because I was not like the other girls. He could have just told to me—and he never hit me again. Mahlia barks, "Creep!"

Saadya returns to say, "I know Mahlia has to be talking about Leo. What did I miss?"

"Leo was taking liberties," Mahlia explains, "and began throwing punches at his discretion to humble the girls."

Saadya is quick to say, "You mean to abuse the girls."

Mahlia continues, "In any case, he misapplied this technique after a mid-week event, when Mom returned to the ashram."

Saadya wants the specifics.

Leo met me at the doorway to the ashram. I told him I had been collecting donations from everyone I asked. He told me to go upstairs and rest up. As I passed in front of him, he slugged me on the arm. Saadya says, "I guess he couldn't help himself."

"He was getting in the habit of doing so," Mahlia agrees, "so yeah, he couldn't help himself."

"You were an easy target in so many ways," Saadya concludes. I scurried up the stairs. I am embarrassed to tell you that, later, I offered humility to him as an act of contrition for initially feeling that punching me in the arm was uncalled for. I was so convinced that Leo always did things for our own good, and this was no exception.

Saadya impulsively says, "Mom, you were really messed up!" She's harsh but right. If one of us lost her focus, we understood that drastic measures needed to be taken. Leo was doing whatever he thought would do the trick. It had all gone to his head.

PROTOTYPE

"IT'S NO WONDER LEO HAD TO BE cut down to size," Mahlia asserts. While Sir Derek garnered our allegiance and Camila stuck by her man, all the responsibility that went along with running the ashram fell to Belinda. As I said, she ate nails for breakfast, and I didn't: That seemed to explain the difference between us, and I was barely able to tolerate her temperament. In general, we did not resonate with each other.

Belinda being put in charge made no sense, since she didn't have our respect in her own right. She had just been one of us. I guess her reputation and tough demeanor had elevated her to the position of authority. Dulce was nice but just too soft-spoken. This delegation of power and authority occurred just after Camila returned to her parents to get money to bail Leo out of jail.

The mere fact of Belinda being put in charge was supposed to be enough to maintain us as a cohesive group. But it couldn't, and it didn't. The rationale was that the only input we received about King Service had come from Leo and his teaching and preaching. We never had enough time to read any of the books. The girls began to crack because they did not have a foundation strong enough in the theory of King Service, written about in the Superior Texts, to solidify their identity as workers without Leo's prodding. The solution was for us all to take time off from soul-saving activity. Thus, we all stayed back for days at a time to do things around the ashram and use that time to read from the Superior Texts. However, the time off only made matters worse.

UPHEAVAL

WE GIRLS WERE NOT STRONG ENOUGH without Leo. We reacted to losing him as our guide and mentor for which we had needed him on our fund-raising and soul-saving service. We needed a male authority figure. This was soon very evident. Sir Derek assumed the role, but our interaction with him had to be limited. Therefore, this arrangement proved inadequate to fill the void. After all, he was an elevated soul in charge of the entire Southwest sector of the WORKS, and he had "single-man" status.

Saadya contends, "So there was no pretense about being married, and you didn't have the day-to-day interaction with him that you had with Leo." After a short time, a few of the girls said that they wanted to get married.

There was further disruption within the ashram because, as it turned out, Renee, yet another one of the girls chosen to stay back, was also a top fund-raiser. When Natasha, *the* top fund-raiser, refused to collect and instead would just sit in a phone booth at the airport, none of the other women could sustain her own focus to collect either. Natasha, one of Leo's wives, was under the influence of the physical energy, and the rest of us lost our incentive. The whole fraudulent undertone of the operation was becoming obvious, and we didn't know how to deal with the upheaval. Saadya notes, "Fund-raising in the guise of saving souls was being revealed as a sham."

"More like a scam," says Mahlia.

THE KICKER

ON THE OTHER HAND, I felt relief that I could now focus on the mission. I proceeded with renewed energy. When I asked why the others were having so much difficulty, it was Belinda who presented the leaders' well thought-out explanation that, by going out every day, the soul-saving sisters did not have enough time to read from the Superior Text books for themselves. When you read them, you were supposed to experience a transcendental transformation while plunging into the sweetness of King's mercy, the vastness of King's love, and the reality of his kingdom.

I especially enjoyed reading about the universe having emanated from the thoughts of the great and righteous King, as was explained in the first chapters, along with colorful pictures depicting the events of the cosmos as they were supposed to have occurred. Saadya says, "It's a spin off. All you have to do is read the Bible and you will see for yourself."

"Okay," I say placating Saadya, "maybe I will."

The fact is, we did accept unquestioningly, having abandoned our trust in the element of society, parents, siblings, friends, and especially scientists, who were supposed to be the worst of all due to their ungodly hypotheses. All of the above were drawing faulty conclusions from faulty perceptions of the world around them, ignoring that they are not their physical body, which is the basic premise in the King philosophy. Mahlia nods vigorously. "Once they get you to agree to this premise, they could always bring you back to it as a way to get you to acquiesce to everything else subsequently required of you." This was the kicker.

Now, with Belinda in charge, several of us did go out on soul-saving with fervor, feeling that at last everything would be as it should in the ashram and for us, as sincere agents on a mission just trying to make a difference in the world.

Mahlia realizes I use the word "out" when I speak of leaving the ashram to engage in soul-saving activity, and deduces, "Every time you went out, you were leaving the shelter of the ashram and the Center, venturing into the world of the physical." We could easily be enticed back into that world by the allure of its false illusion. We were thoroughly convinced that, if we were to allow the grip the WORKS had on us to slacken, it would usher in our downfall.

We were adequately brainwashed into being unable to comprehend that the WORKS was no different than the world, from which it made an artificial distinction. Additionally, I felt betrayed by Leo and Camila. I tried compensating for their falling short by immersing myself even more as I continued to embrace the mission and its importance.

AND THE END

BOUND FOR HOME

MAHLIA INQUIRES, "SO HOW *did* you actually get out, and I don't mean to save souls?"

Saadya pronounces the inevitable: "You have to tell us about the deprogramming."

Ultimately, it amounted to being a rescue. But it didn't take place without a fight. In early January 1979, I finally boarded that United Airlines flight for what I thought would be no more than a four-day visit to see my parents. It had been a long and drawn-out decision whether to return home after not seeing my mother for over two years, and after a total of three years since seeing my father.

Mahlia says, "I thought you were not sanctioned to leave the Center and the company of the other workers." Despite being repeatedly discouraged to by Leo and Camila, and now by Belinda and Sir Derek, whenever I spoke to them about the subject, my parents had been hounding me and had been for months. With Belinda now in charge, I knew she had told Sir Derek I was considering a visit home because, one afternoon when he called the ashram and I picked up, he began to talk about the illusion of family relationships. So every time I broached the subject, I was talked out of it in one way or another, postponing the visit I eventually made in January, going into my fourth year in the WORKS.

"Mom, I think you were getting homesick," Saadya alleges.

Well, just before, in November, I had been in New York with a traveling soul-saving group. I was fund-raising smack dab on Thirty-fourth Street, where my father had his business. Other girls also had to fund-raise in the general vicinity in which they'd lived as regulars before joining the WORKS.

I was warned that I might have some difficulty, but I actually enjoyed being on the East Coast as an agent for King Service.

Mahlia wants to know, "What was enjoyable about it? It's not like you were going shopping. . .oh, yeah, who wants to go shopping and spend money when, instead, you can collect it?" That's what we did, because that's what we were there for. I was not overwhelmed being on the busy streets of New York City. In essence, I was able to say, "No more," to all of it. I had rejected everything known to me as a regular—societal norms, pressures, demands, and the empty promises of physical energy, of more of the same things that could not satisfy or fill a hungry and thirsty soul. Saadya is beside herself when she hears this coming from me. I hear her say, "Whoa!" In an instant her face is turned down to her phone.

Mahlia derides her: "That is not something I have to reference." She recites, from Matthew 11:28: *"Come to me, all who are weary and burdened, and I will give you rest."*

Saadya tells her, "That's not what I had in mind," and continues from Isaiah 55:1, *"Come, all you who are thirsty, come to the waters. . . ."*

Without skipping a beat, Mahlia retaliates from John 4:14, *"But whoever drinks of the water that I will give him will never be thirsty again. The water that I will give him will become, in him, a well of water springing up to eternal life."* I am not sure who is talking, because by this time Mahlia and Saadya have clearly teamed up. *"For he satisfies the thirsty and fills the hungry with good things"* (Psalm 107:9), one of them recites.

All I can think of is, instead of living water, in the WORKS I had affiliated myself with the power structure by which I was isolated from the world outside of the WORKS. I had concluded that this world had nothing to offer but distractions to advancement on my life's journey to attain an eternity defined by the WORKS. We remained on the East Coast for two days; I did not call my parents or anyone else.

MONEY GRABBER

WHAT DID TRANSPIRE WAS A FRENZIED attempt to reach the bank where I knew there were EE bonds, in my name, in a safe deposit box. The bank manager told me I could not gain access without proper authorization, and especially without a key. It was of particular importance to me to access this money, accumulated since I was a child through gifts from my parents, grandparents, aunts, uncles, and family friends. Redeeming the bonds would serve two purposes: I'd be turning the money over to the Barstow Center to be used in King Service, and I'd be severing any remaining connection I had with the outside world.

When I first joined, I had asked my parents for that money. They refused. My mother had not believed that I would use the money on myself or for myself. She had known I'd immediately turn it over to the Center, and she'd been right. I had rationalized that I'd be using the money for my personal use. I had no need for it and wanted nothing to do with it except procure the funds so I wouldn't have to deal any further with the physical world and the things associated with it. Mahlia grasps this. "The money represented your attachment to all that was supposed to be rejected according to the WORKS philosophy."

Saadya adds, "Rejected by the individual workers, but not rejected by the leadership."

So much so that I expressed this concern over the money to Belinda. Saadya recalls, "I thought you didn't have a good rapport with her." She was from Long Island, so, being that we were on the East Coast and we were fund-raising together, in this instance, at the time of this conversation, there was a connection. She explained to me that King already had all the money in the world. He was already rich and didn't need my money. What he was really interested in was me. It was more important that I surrender to the mission and not allow this money matter to interfere with being in the King mindset. Nothing else mattered except that I become pure in this lifetime. "Here we go again," says Mahlia. Although accessing this money had been a major issue for me, I was now able to reconcile, not only that I could stop plotting how I could get my hands on the money, but that I would cease to care about it.

Years later, my mother asked me, seemingly out of the blue, whether I was glad she hadn't given the bonds to me when I had asked for them. "Sounds like Grandma was being kind," Mahlia comments. The expression on my face shows that I'm not sure what she means. "I mean, Grandma was kind by saying you *asked* for the money."

Saadya jumps in. "Yeah, it was more like you were demanding it." I wanted it for what I thought was a selfless reason and higher purpose. When I responded to my mother, I had to be honest, and I was.

"Was what?" asks Saadya.

Mahlia answers for me, "Glad that Grandma didn't give her the bonds." My girls are definitely taking this all in and have their fingers on the pulse.

HOME BOUND

SAADYA INSISTS, "TELL US ABOUT how you finally decided to visit home!" To begin with, it was not that easy because whenever any of us considered a visit home, we were repeatedly discouraged from doing so. This was one of the questions I had stopped asking early on. Wanting to visit family was addressed as a reflection of my lack of sincerity. In addition, I was told I could visit home but first needed to get stronger in King Awareness. So the months turned into years. Now with both my parents hounding me to visit, when I told them I would not, I said so to Sir Derek one afternoon when he called the ashram and I was there to answer the phone. He reiterated his stance that this "business about home" was just an illusion. Our real home lay in the spiritual world, and I belonged at the Center, in the company of the other workers.

I felt good at the time about my decision. I reconciled myself to it whenever I had a disagreement or a full-fledged argument with my mother over the phone. Saadya probes, "What did you talk about in your phone conversations?" They usually consisted of me telling her I was fine and happy. Yet she never seemed convinced, and that frustrated me. Saadya says, "That's because Grandma knew you weren't fine and dandy."

For some time my parents had wanted me to pay them a visit. I told them I would come overnight only, arriving early in the morning and leaving late at night the next day. This is what Camila had decided while she was still in charge and had finally sanctioned a visit, stating that no more time than an overnight was needed. But this was totally unacceptable to my parents, who asked that I stay for at least three days. Months later, when I acquiesced, suggesting a convenient time frame I was willing to make the visit, my mother told me the week I had designated was not good—due to my father's business, he would be especially busy that week and could not possibly take time off.

Mahlia recognizes, "She was just putting you off for some ulterior motive." I obviously didn't know it then, and certainly would never have flown back to Connecticut if I had. The actual reason was that my parents had arranged for a "deprogramming" to take place. When they learned that I was agreeing to come home, but a week earlier than we had discussed, the arrangements with the key players had already been made.

Mahlia double checks: "So far, Grandma and Grandpa's plans were shaping up." It didn't go seamlessly. I agreed that going home for one day was a bit unreasonable, but I knew deep down that it would be difficult for me to be home for a full week. So when it was suggested I come for a week, a week later, due to my father's so called business commitments, I decided not to go home at all. That was when I had that phone conversation with Sir Derek.

It was after the demise of Camila and Leo, and only days after the phone conversation with Sir Derek, that I once again began to contemplate a visit home after I received another of my mother's unrelenting phone calls insisting that it would be only for a quick visit, and that I would be back in California shortly. "I bet you wanted to go home," Saadya suggests. I can say that, deep down, I wanted to get away, at least for a bit, to get a reprieve. The atmosphere in the ashram was toxic. With the visit going to be for four days only, Belinda told me it would be alright to go home, and since she had been put in charge, I felt I had the sanction of an authority figure. The day I was flying home, Belinda had second thoughts, and asked me if I thought my parents would have me deprogrammed.

I answered that I didn't think I was worth all that money because, the way the Center leaders explained deprogramming, it would cost tens of thousands of dollars. We were told that professional deprogrammers contacted parents of workers, telling them terrible things about the WORKS to convince them to have their children deprogrammed. I was told that one of the girls from the Barstow Center, deprogrammed almost a year earlier, must have been forced to eat meat and must have been raped. We were told we could just imagine the terrible things that had happened to her.

On an otherwise typical day of fund-raising, her parents had her forcibly removed from the airport terminal. I was not there to see it. But other girls had, and there had been nothing they could do to stop it. Farrah had been surrounded by men and carried out of the airport lobby into an awaiting car against her cries of protest. Farrah had been abducted according to her parents' bidding, leaving her with no say in the matter.

So of course, we all imagined the worst, and I was no exception. At my own deprogramming, in fact, I was confronted with the terror of what kinds of awful things might befall me in the hands of these atheists, as they were referred to at the Center. I expected everything described at the Center to happen to me.

It didn't. The worst thing was that I realized something terrible had happened to me in the WORKS. Mahlia offers, "You realized you were manipulated." I realized that I had truly been deceived and would now have to come to grips with the reality that my mind had been hacked into and programmed.

The ramifications are far-reaching. I accepted King Service as my way of life, just the way it was doled out. Whatever was presented to me, I had to accept. The sacrifices and austerities were made in increments, so that I wouldn't consider them unreasonable. Since I was supposed to be getting a taste of eternity by being joyful and ecstatic during sing and dance in the temple room at the Center, whenever I experienced any form of mental anguish, I was supposed to remain aloof and unaffected. Those feelings were to be dismissed and suppressed as not worth consideration, to be viewed only as deterrents to the mission of saving myself and the souls of others. Leo knew subconsciously that, if I stayed long enough, it wouldn't take long for me to adopt the mindset. I would fit right into the mold of a King worker. Besides becoming a loyal agent, I also became a transcendental soldier in a transcendental army in a war against the outside world.

THE FRONT LINES

I FOUGHT THIS WAR ON THE FRONT LINES of soul-saving. Previously, at the onset of my indoctrination, all the credit was given to Sir Supreme, who was supposed to be empowering his agents to collect donations. We attributed our success to Sir Supreme. We took vows he said we needed to take. The agents pledged loyalty to him. As time went on, we turned our allegiance and affections over to one of his representatives. I am aware of how bizarre this all sounds, but at the time it made perfectly good sense. Saadya quickly points out, "It's like in a dream—as the events are unfolding, everything makes sense." Only I wasn't dreaming.

And so the ideal image for a worker, as an agent in King Service, was to surrender each step of the way, in full submission to authority. In accordance, I functioned in a state of constant and total self-effacement in which I was not to entertain divergent thoughts or adopt any attitude contrary to fund-raising for Sir Supreme, Leo, Sir Derek, and ultimately King. Mahlia gasps, "Why couldn't you ever just stay at the ashram because you felt like it?" Honestly, I can't recall a time when someone didn't stay back without Leo or Camila giving us permission. We would tell them when we were getting burnt out, and they probably would have already recognized it for themselves, and we would be granted the following day off. Otherwise, we went out on soul-saving.

Except for the time I just couldn't stand being out there: I was miserable to the hilt. I couldn't bear it for one minute longer. This didn't happen often, but that day I had reached the end of my rope. Camila was at the airport, and I implored her to let me get a ride back to the ashram with her. It was still early afternoon, and since she was passing by, she'd just happened to stop in. She wanted me to finish the day fund-raising and offered to let me stay back the entire next day. I refused her offer, insisting that I be excused on the spot. At that point, she knew she should let me leave with her. So, that same day, I finally got some relief.

Mahlia says, "All your efforts were maintained through concentration, cooperation, compliance, and self-sacrifice." All of which eluded me that day.

Saadya adds, "Evidently, there was a clear network in which you all functioned, supposedly laid out for you upon the supreme authority of King." I am so proud of my daughters for their patience with this story, their wanting to hear it all, and their understanding that I had been manhandled into thinking I would always have to answer to an immediate authority.

THE ARRIVAL

"DID YOU EVER VISIT HOME before during your three-year stint?" questions Saadya. I flew home, after a year, for three days. My parents thought that if I saw the family pet schnauzer I would "snap out of it." They were wrong, and I was back to Barstow in no time.

However, the events leading up to my "bout with the devil" ensued at the onset of that second visit home. My parents met me at Bradley International Airport, in Hartford, at 6:00 a.m. on a cold January morning, six hours after I boarded a United Airlines flight at 9:00 p.m. California time at San Bernadino International Airport. I'd boarded it after being reassured by my mother during a phone conversation I made, just before departing, that she was not planning a deprogramming. Mahlia exclaims, "You made Grandma say she wasn't going to have you deprogrammed!"

I didn't make her say anything. I just needed assurance that she wasn't planning to interfere with my being a worker. I actually told her that I was different now that I was a worker, and she cunningly said, "Yes, Robin, I know."

The airplane touched down, and I exited. I walked down the ramp connecting the exit door to the airline terminal. I was immediately overexposed to the frigid early morning air which was further chilled by wind carrying with it an icy mist. Clad only in cotton slacks, a button-down shirt, and a light jacket, I tried to fight off the penetrating cold percolating up my spine. I was being challenged by the freezing temperatures, just as I had been when my journey began and I nearly froze in the cold that first night on the road.

There stood my mother. After greeting each other with a peck on the cheek, my duffel bag in hand, we walked through the swinging doors and stepped out onto the sidewalk. I was visibly shivering while waiting for my father to drive the car from the adjacent parking lot to the arrivals terminal where she and I were standing. We weren't saying much.

I placed my duffel bag on the ground close to the edge of the curb. When I straightened up, my mother secured the collar of the fleece-lined winter coat she had wrapped me in, inside the terminal, insisting that my light jacket was inadequate. She was right. I allowed her to untie the wide coat belt and use it instead to drape my head, making sure that my ears were covered under the warmth of the heavy wool fabric.

Mahlia has been debating whether to say what's on her mind but does: "You're lucky Grandma didn't use the belt to strangle you."

I was fortunate for many reasons, as my parents were prepared to make the financial sacrifice after all. Standing curbside, Grandma clearly wasn't thinking of herself because she wore only her thin all-weather coat. I believe now that she was wholly indifferent to the extreme cold that early morning. Her struggle was not of selfish survival, but of controlling her fears about what the outcome of the visit would be—a mother's concern for the welfare of her daughter.

We returned to the home in which I grew up. I promptly cleared a space on a shelf in the living room where I placed a bronze-plated bust of Sir Supreme and a photograph of Sir Derek. I spent the next two hours reciting the Righteous King phrases while pacing in front of my makeshift altar and reading, as my parents slept endeavoring to get some rest, having received none to speak of the night before in anxious anticipation of what lay ahead.

Mahlia suspects, "Not to speak of all the sleepless nights Grandma spent while you were getting purified." She had indeed spent many sleepless nights remaining awake into the wee hours of the morning, as I later learned, playing solitaire with a worn-down deck of cards. She was wrought with worry, not knowing how to rescue her daughter. Then she started doing some research that led to the undoing of my cult experience.

A LONG TIME TO BE GONE

I THOUGHT IT ODD THAT MY PARENTS were so willing to take me shopping the morning after I arrived. My attitude was, why waste any time? "That was very ambitious of you," Saadya observes.

Mahlia chimes in, "That is an understatement." You're both right. The more I could get my parents to engage in King Service, the more worthwhile my visit would turn out to be.

Then Mahlia parodies, "To shop or not to shop, that is the question."

To which I reply, "The pressing question for me was whether or not my parents would have me forced into relinquishing all that I embraced in the WORKS."

Saadya recaps, "So Grandma and Grandpa were just waiting to hear from you definitely, so they could give the deprogrammers the go-ahead to make all the necessary arrangements."

Exactly. Remember I told you that, the day I was to leave, Belinda asked if I thought my parents would have me deprogrammed. Bethany, who drove me to the airport to catch the flight, also asked me if I thought it was safe for me to return home, implying that I make sure my parents would not attempt a deprogramming. I told her I didn't think my parents thought I was worth the expense. Little did I know, it cost in the vicinity of twenty thousand dollars. Critically, Mahlia says, "You underestimated your parents."

THE RENDEZVOUS

I sat in the back seat of the family car. My mother sat up front while my father drove. We left the house before noon for the Turnpike Shopping Mall in Fairfield. It did not feel especially unusual, at the time, for them to want to take me shopping all the way out to Fairfield, even though we lived in Danbury. We had shopped there many times before, and there were several especially nice boutiques nearby. Over three years of fund-raising, I had come to regard shopping malls as representative of the physical marketplace, in which it was a favorite pastime for the regulars to spend their time and money.

It was after noon when my mother suggested we stop at a diner for a bite to eat. It seemed spontaneous and innocent enough, especially when my father said that he wasn't hungry but nevertheless agreed to stop. At the diner, I asked for some heated tomato juice. My mother ordered a scrambled egg sandwich, and my father asked for a cottage cheese and fruit plate. Both were conscious that a meat dish would offend me.

I learned two years later, from my father, that two of the deprogrammers were in the diner at the time we stopped in. The real purpose for the diversion was to meet up with them at a convenient location. The diner was a point of rendezvous for my father to follow them to the motel. At this time, the deprogrammers called ahead to the motel to confirm that the adjoining rooms that had been reserved were available and had been made ready, in order to proceed with their plans.

Throughout lunch, my mother seemed especially concerned that I not get upset. I sensed her uneasiness and withdrew, regretting that I had ever made the trip. I sat there, in that booth, in some diner somewhere between Fairfield and Danbury, not wanting at all to be there. I began to calculate how much time was remaining in my visit and how I would have to do everything within my power to keep from bursting. I was dealing with unresolved anger towards my parents, especially my mother, who I came to view as being responsible for depriving me, as a child, of opportunities at music, dance, or any other form of self-expression. I was still frustrated by the thought of that. The two people sitting with me in the diner were no longer my parents. They were regulars.

FIRST-HAND ACCOUNT

MAHLIA'S TONE OF VOICE IS ONE OF DISGUST when she says, "These two regulars, as they were called, were willing to spend part of their life savings for you to have a life." In the King mindset, we entertained our family members as coming together only briefly in this lifetime, only to be dispersed like wind-blown fluff in separate directions for all eternity.

I had decided before joining the WORKS, long before I had any idea that I would even affiliate myself with something so destructive, that I was not going to allow myself ever to be manipulated into thinking I was less than who I wanted to be. I was going to remain aloof, so that I would be unscathed by anyone else's perception of me. I had constructed an invisible and impenetrable fortress around myself, barricading myself in. The Center served as an actual fortress. There, my attitude was reinforced and exploited to extremes I never knew existed.

The WORKS offered a viable alternative for me to actualize my ideals, by which I boxed myself in and away from the outside world. I had concluded the world was an empty place, having nothing substantive to offer. It was more important for me to be free. My idea of freedom and independence was not to have to explain myself, or be accountable, to anyone else. I was relishing my independence, which I considered my only valuable possession. Mahlia declares, "What a far cry from what you've been describing in that cult."

Saadya softens this account, saying, "It's the cult phenomenon, and it can happen to anyone if they don't understand what's going on."

Now Mahlia says, "You mean like what went on behind the ashram door!"

But in King Service, I felt safe and secure, tucked away in my little niche. Mahlia notes, "Yes, as long as you were a good obedient worker dedicated to fund-raising." I cherished the guarantee of spiritual enlightenment and held the mission in the forefront as incentive for, and justification of, all I was turning away from. Mahlia remarks, "And that included parents and family. . . . Mom, you didn't theorize all this on your own. WORKS led you to this conclusion." I never considered that the guarantee of enlightenment being promised to me in the WORKS would lead me on a straight path to forfeiting so much through blind acceptance. In exchange for my liberties, I was molded and manipulated according to dogma, practice, ritual, and pressure from within.

"Tell us about the deprogramming," prompts Saadya.

The subject of my deprogramming remains a very sensitive topic. I avoided putting it down in writing for two years after it took place. Just as the events remained fresh in my mind, the experience remained impressionably in recollection. I had, over the course of those two years, responded to very personal questions from people who were concerned, curious, and careful about acquiring accurate information on this extremely controversial topic. I could give them a first-hand account.

FACE TO FACE

MAHLIA SENSITIVELY INQUIRES, "What happened after you left the diner?" I was told we were stopping for my father to take care of some business matter. We had driven only a short distance from the diner when the car stopped, and my mother was insisting that I accompany them inside to meet my father's business associate. I became wary when her voice took on a desperate tone. "Oh, Robin, please don't be that way. Come inside." I had been refusing, unable to understand why I had to go inside while my father attended to his business.

It occurred, in one flashing thunderbolt, as time and space froze and then coagulated, as all my impulses were being bombarded, and then congealed in a stark moment of horror. From being situated in the back seat of the family car to being overcome by a rush of adrenaline from my innate fight-or-flight response, I was catapulted into a state of hyper-alertness, and I was *terrified*.

As it occurred, my apprehension was aroused by the tragedy-laden tone of impending disaster that my mother's voice was conveying. She was scared, and she could not hide it.

I detected devastation and impending doom as the goal, and I was the target. My attention was drawn away from the King book I was absorbed in as I sat with my shoulder pressing against the side door I was subconsciously trying to escape out of long before reaching the motel.

The sight, still unfocused, seeping into my consciousness, entering through the corner of my eye, was that of someone moving uncomfortably closer to me, which I could only make out from my peripheral vision as being a head, which now appeared only inches in front of my own face. It was someone else's face with a beard and mustache, and it scared me. It was someone I did not know, and I did not understand what concern I could be to whoever this was.

Then I understood! I was face to face with the devil himself.

THE GAUNTLET

ONCE I COULD FOCUS, I realized that peering into the back seat were the eyes of a bearded, curly haired young man fixing an unflinching and penetrating gaze, fixed like an ultra-intense laser beam, on me. As this vision came into focus, it began to grow grotesquely out of proportion, its features distorted and indistinguishable. My head began to pound with muffled words resounding deeply in the recesses of my mind: "If we have to, Robin, we'll carry you—come on!"

"Oh, no, oh, no—no, no, no!" was all I could muster up in response.

The adrenalin coursing through my veins pulsed to the racing of my heart.

Mahlia asks, "What were you told at the Center you could expect?" I was inclined to identify with stories I had heard and read about efforts made on behalf of the brother of a Catholic priest whose desire it was to have the priest deprogrammed. Various attempts had been made, according to a newspaper clipping circulated among the agents at the Center, at defiling the priest as well as blaspheming the entire Catholic Church. And I felt as devout as a nun in an established religion. I anticipated violence to my physical as well as my spiritual being.

I froze, unnerved and suspended in that stark moment of apprehension, knowing that I was on my own. I was completely caught off guard as I sat facing the enemy, as vulnerable as any unarmed person can be, confronted with the surety of certain demise. It was to be my ultimate test against the physical energy—in the form of demon deprogrammers whose every effort it was going to be to bribe me out of my King Service and the King mindset. Sir Supreme, his mission, and my identity as a worker were going to be ravaged by hungry wolves, and it was all going to happen beyond my control. I had been led to believe this is what would happen, and it was going to be happening to me. With nothing within my grasp to hold on to, I was floundering. I felt utterly helpless. Who I was as a WORKS agent was not something anyone else cared about but me. I had to be prepared to be raped.

I had let my guard down, and I could think only of my mother's betrayal. I had been lied to and lured into coming, and now I was in this absolutely dreadful predicament.

Once I recovered from the initial shock, I recouped by reminding myself of the Righteous King philosophy. Once I was able to regain my composure, I told myself that nothing would be potent enough to dissuade me, long term, from my allegiance to King and my commitment to being King minded.

Mahlia has tears in her eyes: "How dismal that you were going through all this because you wanted to remember God!" Even as a child, my secret wish, when blowing out the birthday candles, had been a prayer to God: "Please help me remember you." Oh yeah, "And let everyone be happy and healthy."

"That just about covers everything," says Mahlia, as she leans in to kiss my cheek.

Somehow, I thought God had honored this request by bringing me to a WORKS Center.

Mahlia says something that surprises me. "No, Mom, God was not honoring your prayer by using deceptive practices, leading you to believe that there was a spiritual monopoly held by this cult. In God's abundant mercy, He fulfills his plan for us all, and He is not finished with you yet!"

My eyes are open wide, but I still do not see.

All I could think of in the motel room, being held against my will, was, once this ordeal was over, I would resume my duties as an agent in the WORKS. I would return to the Barstow Center as soon as the challenge ran its course. I was prepared to run the gauntlet.

MY BOUT WITH THE DEVIL

MY BOUT WITH THE DEVIL WAS ABOUT TO BEGIN. Saadya inhales deeply, puffs her cheeks, and as she closes her eyes she exhales slowly as if to brace herself.

To begin with, it was a time of devastation, with feelings amounting to nothing less than life and death. I felt powerless, trapped by an inferior adversary who could not possibly understand and would not tolerate the degree and extent of my commitment, and my unwillingness to waver, in the least, from that commitment. These feelings stirred all at once. I was to be in perpetual hyper-vigilance, in order not to succumb to the wiles of the devil.

Mahlia is aghast. "You couldn't possibly believe he was the devil!"

But I was led to believe precisely that. Either you were in the WORKS, or you were an enemy of God. These people were strangers, and I was in a strange place. I resolved to stay one step ahead and beat them at their own game. My very survival depended on it.

I was led into a motel room, thinking somehow I would have to escape or go along with the deprogrammers whom I considered my staunch enemy, remaining up until then nameless and faceless, except for the bearded devil and my parents. The strategy was to follow an instruction I had heard frequently at the Center whenever the subject of deprogramming was brought up. I planned to play along by cooperating, and then *come back*.

Once inside the motel room, my mother accompanied me into the bathroom. That was the only place there was to get away from what seemed to be a room full of strangers—evildoers. This situation was completely beyond my control. So I exerted the only control I thought I had, admonishing my mother to change her mind before any damage was done, and I would forgive her. I didn't want to hate my mother, and I hated harboring any ill feelings toward her. I had received a warning at the Center that deprogrammers might resort to rape—beyond a physical assault, a penetration into my psyche violating my spiritual being by the mere thought of severing my connection with my Righteous King, to which I held fast. I warned my mother that they had better not try to rape me, the worst possible thing that could happen. She was appalled at the suggestion.

Shortly after my mother, I ventured back into the bedroom, Gregory, the devil, said, "You think we're going to rape you? Do they tell you that at the Center? Huh? Did they tell you that's how you would be deprogrammed?" This same Gregory of Toetje's rescue was the devil.

I was speechless, feeling embarrassed, flushed, ashamed, and subtly violated by this kind of talk. Again, I felt betrayed by my mother, who had revealed a confidence to this stranger I loathed.

Expressionless, Gregory told me that the deprogramming would be different from what I had been led to believe by the Center leaders. I would be able to have anything I needed, so that I would not have to compromise my values.

This did not alleviate my terror. In fact, it heightened it, because he gave it a name by calling it what I feared most, a dreaded *deprogramming*. I had expected that they would try to bribe me out of my King Service by catering to my physical comfort. It did not help these demons in gaining my trust.

When I realized that I was to remain completely out of control of my immediate circumstances, and that my ultimate destiny was going to be in the hands of the evil deprogrammers, I began to build a wall between me and them. I was not, under any circumstances, going to allow them to penetrate my psyche, as up until that time my true destiny was laid out for me in King Service. Terror lingered with me in having to face this challenge to my faith, a challenge to the survival of my beliefs and the survival of my soul, totally helpless and alone. The reality of that terror kept wielding its ugly face. The threat that this wall of defense between me and them could disintegrate drove me to dig in my heels with greater resolve. The carpet had been pulled out from under me, the plug yanked from my life support. My very being, my substance, my essence, were spilling out of me. I was one big gushing wound.

JEOPARDY

I HAD TO DEFEND THE KING SERVICE philosophy because it was my religious conversion that was held responsible for my estrangement from my family. It was my dedication and sacrifice that my parents found so incomprehensible. I thought this was what the deprogrammers exploited for their own selfish financial gain.

Mahlia says, "You thought deprogrammers were in it for the money, and that you were not worthy of the expenditure. Yet Grandma and Grandpa thought you were."

I did not think my parents were for me but against me. I did all I could to avoid losing my cool WORKS demeanor. I wanted to remain passionate, to prove that King Service did so much for me and that there was so much benefit in being an agent of God. It was my duty as a worker, and a test of my sincerity, to meet this newest and most severe attack against my King mindset. I did not have a van full of King Service agents to retreat into as I had after a day of soul-saving.

I had made up my mind that I would not waver from allegiance to my devoutness. Nothing could stop me from being King minded. I would have to endure this temporary physical separation from the Organization, the Center, and the agents. I just wanted to get back to the Barstow Center. I had been trained all along to endure, simply by reciting King phrases and adhering to the standards set in the WORKS, as a guarantee of my spiritual survival. I definitely did not want to be in this predicament.

Yet once I accepted it as fact, I decided I had what it took to remain steadfast. I was equipped to persevere under such dire circumstances. After all, I had endeavored so hard to be staunch these past three years.

Mahlia remembers something I had spoken of earlier about reciting the King phrases in jail. "You were taught to keep track of the number of times you recited the phrases on your fingers, just in case you were physically removed from the WORKS." No one could prevent us from reciting, and no one could hold us prisoner. In other words, we could recite phrases to ourselves, and we could escape any threatening situation because we were mentally removing ourselves from it. I just knew I had to maintain my King mindset at all costs. At bedtime I recited the phrases in my mind. Otherwise, my identity as an agent was in dire jeopardy.

SERIOUS BUSINESS

SAADYA BOLDLY DECLARES, "Being King minded really meant being in the WORKS mentality, which meant being mind-controlled." My mind was controlled within the WORKS, which had siphoned its teachings into me. I recalled something attributed to Sir Supreme in reference to the subject of deprogramming: "The workers may even have to eat meat, and King would forgive." I had a simple formula to follow. Mahlia asks, "And what was that?" I thought I could just play along with them and then go back to the Center. I would pretend to be deprogrammed. I also decided that it would be fruitless to try to prove anything to the deprogrammers about having faith as an agent of WORKS. So I remained quiet, did not listen, and did not respond to anything they said. They could talk all they wanted to. They could talk until they were blue in the face. I was not going to engage.

They were saying things to me about Sir Supreme and the mission. I shut them out. Emotionally distant and removed from my surroundings, I sat at the edge of the bed, nibbling on sunflower seeds. But I knew I had to make some concrete plans.

An escape strategy began to take shape the first time I was left alone in the bathroom. I had a ten-dollar bill wrapped up in tissue paper, along with a quarter, for the change I would need for that quick phone call I planned to make to the Center. I secured the package firmly between my buttocks, confident it would not be dislodged. Once I got away, I planned to use the money to contact the Center in Barstow and actualize my plan to return.

Saadya affirms, "It wasn't as if you could just walk out the door." No, I was never left alone, except for brief times to go into the bathroom. Whenever I did, one of the deprogrammers would stand outside against the wall below the bathroom window. I became aware of this when, each time I entered the bathroom, I heard the door to the motel room open and close, and, when I came out, saw one of the guys return from outside. So I was aware of the tight security to thwart my effort to escape or to shout out the bathroom window at passersby.

Besides, calling someone's attention to my plight was impossible and would have been fruitless, since the bathroom window opened only a few inches from the top, on a slant, and the only passersby were in cars speeding on the highway alongside the motel. Saadya observes, "Nor did they want you climbing out the window." I would have if I could have.

Likewise, I quickly learned that I could not feign being deprogrammed. I realized I could not go on refusing to listen and expect to be released from the motel room to go on my merry way. These people could not be fooled. It was serious business.

THE OBJECTIVE

SAADYA WANTS TO KNOW, "Other than offer reassurances and let you eat sunflower seeds, what were these guys supposed to be doing to get you deprogrammed?" It was their job to get me to see for myself how the group had power over me. I had to grasp that the WORKS was not affording me any spiritual benefit, but instead infringing on my personal freedoms, as well as my religious liberties.

I saw the WORKS as the vehicle to enable me to reach heights that I came to understand as spiritual revelations.

Moments of complete immersion in surrender brought me to heights of ecstasy during King worship. The WORKS portrayed itself as having knowledge of God, and this is what kept me going.

Saadya says, "Sounds like an unhealthy addiction." It was certainly a dependency, and it was definitely unhealthy.

It took several days before I began to register the deprogrammers individually. Before then, they were demons and could not be trusted. To alleviate my fears the first night I was in the motel room, they explained what was supposed to happen to me and what was not going to happen to me. Still they were demons. I was told that someone would be coming to talk to me. I was petrified.

Towards evening, Jamison came in, wearing gray slacks and a blue V-neck sweater. Saadya remarks, "I can't believe you can remember what this guy was wearing." I can relive the entire experience of the deprogramming moment by moment. I had no prior experience like this to relate to, so as the events unfolded, each one left a lasting impression.

As I lay near the edge of the bed, head and torso propped up on two pillows, I kept my eyes closed and visualized the Barstow Center worship room. I recalled and fixated my mind on designs, decorations, and details as they were. I was in that motel room in body but not in mind. I postured myself so as not to succumb to the feeble attempts being made to engage me in dialogue. In essence, I was a social and emotional paralytic.

Despite this protective stance, I was able to distinguish that Jamison spoke to me about research into the Church of All United Souls Eternal, CAUSE, and other mind-control cults that friends of his had gotten involved in while he was a student at the University of Hartford. Now, in the telling, I think he was talking from personal experience. He was potentially threatening to me just by being there, but once he left, I realized there was nothing shocking that could be done or said to me. All that the deprogrammers wanted to do was talk. The only thing I wanted to do was not listen.

It took three days of nibbling on sunflower seeds before I realized that the only jarring aspect of the entire deprogramming was that they wanted me to listen. My footing in the WORKS began slipping as I gradually was able to make up my own mind for myself. The notions that strict adherence to the dogma, submission to authority, and exclusivity of spirituality existed only in the WORKS and only for its loyal workers were dissipating.

Yet I still considered myself part of the majority, as one who was privileged to be a part of a universal organization destined to engulf the entire planet in just a matter of time. I had been on a mission of saving souls, introducing others to the privilege of being in the King mindset, and serving the spiritual monarch. Mahlia inquires, "Based on every-thing you've been telling us, how can you say it was such a privilege?" The World Organization for Righteous King Service was the only conduit through which anyone could expect to make spiritual advancement, by breaking the cycle of repeated births into a physical body rather than assuming our intended spiritual identity. I had been frightened of death since childhood. Yet, simply by remaining steadfast to the mission and surrendering to the selflessness required in this lifetime, I had been guaranteed an eternity of bliss with King in his pastoral kingdom. This objective was beyond anything else the world had to offer.

A MENTAL GRIP

THE KING SERVICE LIFESTYLE had the effect of a mind-numbing drug that cut me off from the intuition of my heart. In the motel room, there was no way of convincing my parents or the deprogrammers how wrong they had it. They simply misunderstood the WORKS, my motives, and ultimately me. I was angry, but I didn't let it show. I felt cheated, with nowhere to turn. I remembered seeing a movie about an American soldier—The Manchurian Candidate starring Frank Sinatra as a prisoner of war in a communist prison. He was undergoing brainwashing, a victim of thought reform to turn him into a mindless assassin. In order to maintain his sanity and keep from losing his mind, Sinatra's character began to mentally construct a house by building it brick by brick.

I began to apply this strategy right there in the motel room I was confined to. Accordingly, I had begun to construct a worship room by designating various features and fixtures within the motel room to represent an altar.

I chose three overhead lamps to represent the figures of worship I had grown accustomed to at the Center. The three overhead hanging light fixtures began to emit back the energy I lent them as they morphed into objects for my worship. I was doing the very same thing to these light fixtures that I had done at the Center in a climate in which all the workers' minds had snapped into adoration and worship of a designated carving.

Saadya maintains, "You certainly didn't make it easy for the deprogrammers, and it wasn't easy for you either." I thought the deprogrammers were trying to get me to compromise by talking me into something that was not of God. So I hid in the cacoon I had created for myself in the context of all I had learned in the WORKS.

The milieu in the WORKS was created for us to be under the jurisdiction of the doctrine and practices.

Saadya retorts, "It's more like the espoused dogma was the net that ensnared you." After a pregnant pause, she continues, "It was not your religious persuasion, but coercive persuasion, and how it was applied unsuspectingly against you, making you an unwitting recipient."

I had all I needed in the WORKS, and I thought I could maintain my King-mindedness, even in that motel room. I was not going to gratify the deprogrammers by being one of their success stories. But my feeble attempts to shut them out were ineffective in getting them to back off.

My undoing began when I saw for myself that I was not thinking. I was unable to make a distinction between my sincere desire for awareness of God and the King mindset. My mind was dwarfed, resisting and rejecting all input. The undoing of my one-dimensionality began when I saw that my mind had been tampered with and was not able to function properly.

It gradually began to occur to me that, in the WORKS, I had taken on more than I'd bargained for. I had been duped in King Service. It was the very fact that I was not able to use my mind to process and understand when I wanted to that alarmed me. My mind was doing twists, flips, and turns as the newfound doubts forced me to confront all those delusions that I had been functioning under. When I actually wanted to listen, I could not focus for more than a few minutes at a time. When I wanted to listen, my mind was not working. I could not get a mental grip, even now that I wanted to.

WHO IS WALTER CRONKITE?

MAHLIA ASKS, "SO HOW DID IT HAPPEN?" She sees my questioning look. "I mean, how did you actually get deprogrammed? In other words, how was any headway made if you were being so obstinate at first and now were having so much difficulty?"

The hours grew into days, and I began to realize how I had burrowed myself into what began feeling like a deep, dark cave with no hope for the future if I remained in that cavern. I began to confront my own growing doubts about this group as they surfaced.

When I became able to hear, I tried to listen more to what was being said to me. Although I was only able to pay minimal and fleeting attention, I realized there was no way of getting around the issues being raised. The deprogrammers, Gregory, the bearded one, in particular, were consistent in having me confront these issues with serious consideration rather than keep thinking I would just go back to the Center. I comprehended that, if I did, I would be like a lion's prey, caught between its clenched jaws, being carried back to be devoured by the awaiting pride.

My initial resolve was dissipating. I was gaining an ability to consider myself as distinct from the WORKS. I was beginning to allow myself to process the information with a bit of careful consideration. The threat of having to abandon my love for God was lessening.

And I was also gradually becoming a willing participant in the process. Once I got to this point, I wanted to hear more. I wanted to know what was known about the WORKS that I did not know about, that I could not have known about as a member, whose only input was what I received from within the Organization. For the past three years, my contact with the outside world had been severed. I had not been reading a newspaper. I had not watched the evening news. I had not seen Walter Cronkite in all those years.

In unison, Saadya and Mahlia exclaim, "Who is Walter Cronkite?"

EARS TO HEAR

I WAS SOON AT A POINT OF WANTING to listen, hear, and understand what was being said to me. On the third night, I was presented with some WORKS literature. I began to very carefully read and scrutinize articles from various other cult organizations as well. All the literature seemed so similar in pronouncements about life and death, God, spirituality, and the physical world. Despite my stonewalling having to admit it, it was becoming evident that the WORKS was promulgating rhetoric along the same lines as any of the other cults I was reading about.

That evening, I acknowledged that a process of indoctrination, employing sophisticated mind control and thought reform techniques, is what I had succumbed to at the Barstow Center. Each of the cults being discussed shared the commonality of an authoritarian hierarchy and a spiritual figurehead held in the highest esteem. I had been trained to think of the other groups as cults, so it was easy to agree with Gregory on that point. It was, however, excruciating to categorize what I was affiliated with as a cult no different from any of the others. I had come to view the WORKS as the only group having legitimacy to its claims. I still had to fully grasp how those claims of legitimacy were used against me and to my detriment.

Mahlia asks, "So all this awakening suddenly happened on the third night. What made the third night different?"

Up until then, I had been blocking everyone and everything out by nibbling on those sunflower seeds and visualizing the Center's meditation and worship room. On the third day, my mother had put her foot down.

She gave Gregory, and the only other guy I would listen to, an ultimatum because the days were dragging on without any headway being made. All I was doing was nibbling on sunflower seeds and blocking everything and everyone out.

So when these two guys emerged from the room adjacent to the one I had been sharing with my parents, they snatched away the bowl of sunflower seeds. Well, not exactly snatched, but it felt that way. This was to be a major impetus in allowing me to listen to what was so important for me to be able to hear. In having to relinquish those seeds, I knew they meant business.

SEEDS OF FAITH

MY MOTHER MEANT BUSINESS ALL RIGHT. I began to panic as my initial terror of three days earlier resurfaced. I could no longer be distracted by the seeds I had been munching on incessantly. They had been provided to me as proof from the deprogrammers that I could have whatever I wanted. But in reality, they served to distract me from engaging in conversation. I was doing whatever I could to hold onto strands of what was left of my agent identity. I had never been so committed to anything before, and I was desperate to be worthy of the mission. I was not ready or able to let go, so deep was the indoctrination.

Mahlia cuts to the core of the matter by saying, "You mean so deep was the deception being carried out in the name of God!"

Bereft of sunflower seeds, I was now going to have to pay attention. My mind had been flip-flopping, floating off as if it was immersed in some thick, milky, plasma-like substance. The activity of nibbling sunflower seeds had aided and abetted my effort to avoid absorbing any pronouncements critical of the WORKS. That short episode of emergence, when I wanted to listen, ended as my mind carried me off to a place where I no longer had to face the intensity of the confrontation, especially with Gregory. There I remained under the spell of the mind control from the Center. After all, the deprogrammers were once again demons, the enemy, who could not be trusted. I would not be tricked or talked out of the King mindset. This meant I was not going to be available to anything more they had to say—that is, until the trusted sunflower seeds were taken away.

THROWING OFF THE FETTERS

AFTER MY INITIAL ACKNOWLEDGMENT of the cult aspect of the WORKS, further scrutiny was a great mental exercise for me, whose mind had lain dormant for so long. I experienced mental floating, swimming sensations, unable to exert myself objectively. I couldn't maintain a coherent discussion for any length of time. It scared me to think that something was wrong with me, until Gregory made the analogy that the mind is like a muscle. He explained that a muscle that has not been in use cannot function to its full capacity, and that is what happened to me.

Saadya testifies, "It's like when I broke my ankle. I couldn't put any pressure on my leg. My calf muscle shrank, and I needed some physical therapy." In the same way, my mind had to be gradually restored. And now I was realizing I had to be patient with myself. My mind had atrophied.

Late into the evening of the fourth night, I was again reviewing an article with Gregory. This one had appeared in a CAUSE pamphlet distributed by the Church of All United Souls Eternal in response to the tragedy of Jim Jones' The Peoples Temple. We also reviewed an article published by the WORKS in a *Knowing King* magazine. The articles paralleled each other point for point, so much so that they could have been used interchangeably on the scale of entire paragraphs.

The main points brought out in each article were how the followers of the CAUSE, and the agents of the WORKS, were all willful participants. They were free to come and go. They were not entrapped in barbed-wire concentration camps isolated in a foreign country and cut off from the outside world. They were not followers of a charismatic leader but serious students of scripture. It occurred to me how very similar the WORKS Centers were to the CAUSE Churches, in having the same requirement of intense loyalty to the leader, as the leader was God's representative. I could understand that, in both organizations, the ramifications of those requirements were the same. Their members had been mind-controlled. I *was* in a cult.

Another similarity was made between the intense loyalty I personally experienced and that of the members of The Peoples Temple, in which nine hundred people had committed mass suicide by drinking arsenic- and cyanide-laced grape-flavored Kool-Aid. They were physically isolated in Guyana, and on November 18, 1978, they enacted a drill they had practiced, but now it was in real-world time, and the Kool-Aid was lethal. Nine hundred bloated bodies were discovered when authorities arrived on the premises. Before this, all its members cut off ties with the outside world.

Saadya indicates, "It's puzzling that you spent so much time on the outside and didn't make a run for it more than that one time." It's really not that baffling because I can tell you that, although I was not being physically isolated, I was certainly insulated, and I unmistakably felt cut off from the outside world. Just as Jim Jones' followers believed everything they were told, so had I. The only difference between the WORKS Center and The Peoples Temple is that the WORKS did not have to physically isolate its members.

SPIRIT AND MATTER

THE ACTUAL WORDS I ACCEPTED AS GOSPEL, as a worker, were losing their grip on me. Saadya admonishes me, "Mom, don't say 'gospel' when that is nowhere even close to the gospel." Okay, the rhetoric was no longer having the effect it had on me while I was at the Center.

At this point in the discussion with Gregory, I wanted to continue reading. Seated on the edge of the bed, we plunged into *Through the Cosmos* (TTC), a small paperback in which the eternal nature of spirit, and the temporary nature of matter, are expounded to make the point that human life should not be wasted over concerns with the temporal, but rather that, as human beings, we must take up the real purpose of our human birth to purify ourselves, so as to return to our original and true spiritual natures. Written by Sir Supreme, this book sets forth the difference between spirit and matter.

Mahlia recalls me glancing at some literature at a book display when I first visited the mid-week event. "Was that the book you were reading at the book table?" Not the same book, but it was the same rhetoric. It was what got me so deeply entwined in the WORKS philosophy and lifestyle. While I was a worker, I was reading this material exclusively and hence thinking only as a WORKS agent.

But I was now no longer under the exclusionary grip that the WORKS had held me in. Saadya suggests, "So now you could read the same literature, but thoughtfully, without it having the same effect on you."

Reading the same literature at this time, I could be critical. It did not grip me the same way. Nevertheless, I had gotten entangled, and remained entangled. I began to understand exactly what the writings embodied as if for the first time. I saw for myself that it was rhetoric.

NO OTHER NAME

AT 4:00 A.M., AFTER A LONG, INTENSE NIGHT of study, we halted, needing to get some sleep, but not until after reading a passage in which Sir Supreme explained how the recitation of Righteous King phrases altered brain patterns—acknowledging that the phrases had a psychological effect on the agents. It was making us susceptible to suggestion. Now I understood that I was hypnotizing myself into an altered state of mind. I was experiencing a form of what was being referred to as "mind expansion." Saadya says, "Sounds like reciting was having more of a mind-quelling effect on you."

Then Mahlia remarks, "Sounds to me like reciting was having a mind-controlling effect."

It was supposed to be pure love of God that I was experiencing, yet it was brainwashing, or brain-stifling, instead. Mahlia concludes, "The bottom line is, it was not spiritual but psychological." I clarify: It might have been spiritual, but not from God.

This god spoken of in the Superior Texts required his workers to beg alms and spend their time thinking about him, while he frolicked in a land filled with green pastures. "Or a land of make-believe," retorts Mahlia.

This was King's kingdom. Saadya asks, "You want to know what Jesus tells Nicodemus?"

Mahlia responds for me. "Don't ask, just tell her!"

Saadya speaks up: "Jesus replied, *'I tell you the truth, unless you are born again, you cannot see the Kingdom of God'*" (John 3:3).

Next, Mahlia quotes from John 3:5: *"Jesus replied, 'I assure you, no one can enter the Kingdom of God without being born of water and the Spirit. Humans can reproduce only human life, but the Holy Spirit gives birth to spiritual life.'"* Having spoken their piece, my daughters allow me to continue.

We could only imagine what King's kingdom would be like. Yet, being in King Service was not all that it was cracked up to be. Saadya says, "Well, whatever it was, you were now able to see it for what it was not."

For me to have even entertained this notion, after all that time as a King agent was monumental. I was overwhelmed by the fact I had been so duped. I needed more time to digest what had just occurred, and I had to get some sleep.

"Then what?" asks Mahlia.

I was eager to resume the next day. I felt better than I had in years. My defenses slackened, and as I let them down enough to continue to listen, I was not so quick to reject what might disprove the King Service philosophy. At the onset, I had a knot in my gut that tied and bound me into disavowing any identity beyond being an agent in the WORKS. Yet now, physically removed from the WORKS, I grew increasingly more assured that I was not going to be gobbled up by the powerful forces waiting to devour me outside of the WORKS. I was no longer being force-fed by the intricate hierarchical structure at the Center having us believe our demise was imminent if we chose not to remain under the spiritual umbrella of the WORKS.

IN MY RIGHT MIND

AS PART OF THE DEPROGRAMMING PROCESS, I BEGAN to grasp more and more. I came to terms with the idea that the process I was undergoing was not an attempt to disprove the existence of God. I was not being asked to abandon my ideals. But I no longer had to be a worker in WORKS to be a candidate for spiritual life. Saadya seizes this moment. "You were not only a worker. You and the others were turned into workaholics, which has nothing to do with pleasing God."

Mahlia adds, "You guys were workerholics." Very funny!

Throughout the deprogramming I was not at all expected to compromise my values. I saw that what was being restored to me was rightfully mine. "Life, liberty, and the pursuit of happiness," Saadya says. Yeah, kind of like that, but it was more of a freedom to be the person I was intended to be rather than going through the motions as a King Service worker. She replies, "So your mind was being restored to you." In my endeavor to be in the King mindset, I was unaware that I was being required to forfeit my very own psyche.

Mahlia says, "You surrendered more of you, increasingly, over time." Overall, having to yield more meant I had to yield more of me within the context of more yielding in general—except now I was in the process of regaining my right mind.

SINKING SAND

REALIZATION MOUNTED UPON REALIZATION. They were crashing in on me like a battering ram. Being revealed before me was my God-given right of self-identity, as well as nourishment and intuition of the mind. Mahlia says, "Mom, you understand that work is inspired by love."

Saadya piggy-backs on this, paraphrasing from Hebrews 6:19: *"Mom, not by works, but by God's grace you have a hope as an anchor for your soul, firm and secure. It enters the inner sanctuary behind the curtain."* I surmise the inner sanctuary is where God dwells, and the curtain is the veil that separates us from the holiness of God. This kind of hope was not available behind the ashram door. "It's no wonder the morale of the girls in the ashram was disintegrating," Mahlia concludes.

"Endurance is inspired by hope, and the ashram had none because the WORKS was built on sinking sand," Saadya declares.

Nevertheless, as I was being awakened and reacquainted with thinking for myself, my liberty to question and consider was now subject to constant scrutiny from the voice within. "You mean you were still confused," suggests Saadya. I was challenged to distinguish my own voice from the one coming from the WORKS telling me that I had failed miserably as a worker. No longer under the protective umbrella of the WORKS would ultimately mean that I was beyond redemption.

Embracing the magnitude of this, Saadya states, "That would mean you could not escape from the cycle of karma." Escape was indeed the goal, and I am glad you are taking this seriously. For the past three years someone else had been in charge of me, and now I would be plagued with self-doubt stemming from having succumbed to this milieu of control.

Understandingly, Mahlia offers some reassurance, reminding me, "Anyone would have succumbed, had they been subjected, and you were—by ploy of dinner, and doing the right thing for yourself and for others." I needed to clarify this. I was not plagued with self-doubt from having been suppressed by a power that was exerted over me, but because it demanded so much of me to relinquish any attestation of myself.

I would chide myself for rejecting the WORKS philosophy and the King mindset dogma. I felt equally guilty for continuing to be attracted to the Organization and for not being a good little worker.

I was able to communicate this to Gregory, who reassured me that I could hold onto the ideals that were still meaningful to me. For example, just as when I was a teen, I could not understand why people were walking around ignoring God, by pretending that He was not there, and even worse, that He didn't exist. He permeated my thoughts and I still wanted to know Him and about Him.

A BLOODLETTING

AS I EMERGED FROM THINKING the deprogrammers were evildoers and I was at their mercy, revelations continued to shatter my defenses.

I admitted that I had been manipulated, as I began to see into the mechanism of mind-control and have glimmerings of awareness that that was what had happened to me.

However, this did not negate having to face the challenge of desperately wanting to maintain faith as I had come to know it. I was to be on my own, no longer in the company of others with the King-mentality. As I was becoming unfettered, I had to face the fact that I would be moving on and forward.

Yet the core of my being was holding steadfast to the system I had been following within the WORKS. I remained skeptical of the efficacy of the deprogramming. Mahlia, who is very close to her grandmother, tells me, "I'm sure Grandma and Grandpa were nervous also." They were nervous about the outcome and any backlash, while my only consideration at the time was for how I would make it on my own.

Over the course of the five days in the motel room, I survived being left behind in a helpless situation. It was as if I was in the middle of a churning ocean during a tempestuous storm on a moonless night without a raft. Now I felt vulnerable, exposed and raw in a new and different way. No longer a WORKS agent, I felt as if the carpet was pulled out from under me. Whatever was left inside me had been squeezed out even more. I was withered and weary, left high and dry. All my life force, my substance, had been drained out from me. I had undergone a blood-letting.

REHAB

"SO THEN WHAT HAPPENED?" asks Mahlia. The rehabilitation was a time for me to be together with others in a similar predicament.

Saadya is now munching on baby carrots and, between bites, asks, "You mean others who were in a cult?" Others who were becoming reacquainted with the intuition of the heart and the instinct of the mind. It was too soon for them to just go home after what had happened to them within the cult, and after having undergone a deprogramming.

For the short term, we had been rescued. However, there were reservations about the long-term outcome, spontaneous reversion to the mindset, and worst of all, actually returning to the cult. More time was needed to truly be free, so we could once again be on our own. This was written for my fellow rehab mates:

The memory fades of the treachery we bore. We know what must be done and are at peace because there are others who un-

derstand and care. When we shared and shared our love; that is the only reality I know of. It's just so nice to be able to talk, emerging from the shadows of doubt that were cast by what happened to us in the past. Then together we can be as we are; we did get hurt and torn apart as our world; the one that no longer exists was thrown askew. It seems some damage was done; some effect has taken place.

As we did what few have dared—we gave up all, that which is valued by man, disregarding our friends, our family, our home, to venture forth into what we didn't know was unknown, forfeiting our God-given rights of a life of liberty, and in our search we found a joy that promised to all, if only they'd come.

But this we've been told, and we're coming to learn, was only surreal. We acknowledged Him above all else, so we turned to those who claimed to have the truth, and we followed as if untold. Now we must question, "How can each one be right, when all they'd have us believe is not black and white?" The truth be told, yet we wonder if there be but one, and was I among them? We are left to rediscover the highest of heights and the loneliest of nights, while never letting go, in our search for home.

IN LIMBO

MAHLIA GLANCES AT HER WRISTWATCH, slides her cell phone out from her purse, taps out a quick message, and looks at me before asking, "How did you get to the rehab?"

I realize she has just postponed plans she had with a friend; flattered she prefers to remain home to hear what I have been waiting all these years to tell.

The afternoon that I left for the rehab house, I was accompanied to the airport by my mother and Gregory. She had driven us there, but Gregory was to accompany me on the flight to the rehab house in Chicago. Obviously, I could not be left alone, especially in an airport. I soon bade farewell to my mother, and she departed. Gregory and I made our way through the terminal for the departure gate. It was the first time in three years that I was in an airport when it was not incumbent upon me to approach every passerby. Saadya catches on. "You weren't seeing people as regulars in need of giving you a donation." Not quite, not just yet. Walking through the corridor to get to the departure gate, I spotted a military boy in uniform. My inclination was to approach him. I had to fight the impulse to walk right up to him, smile, and ask for a donation. I knew the military boys always had a lot of money on them.

Mahlia quips, "You were trained to screw them out of their money without having to go to bed with them." Actually, contrary to the things I've read that have been written about Leo's soul-saving group, the women never prostituted themselves.

Yet I continued through the airport on automatic, sizing people up in my mind, considering who would be a good prospect. I realized how dangerous it would have been if I were left on my own so soon after the deprogramming. I was in a state of limbo. I felt that if I was not a worker, then I would have to be a regular, which had come to mean that I was subject to the laws of nature, in opposition to spiritual laws. I could not relax. I was wound up like a rubber band ready to snap.

I felt guilty about not approaching people, and guilty about letting all that potential money slip by. It was almost as if the money was just slipping out of my hands, and I couldn't help thinking that souls were being lost.

Gregory encouraged me to keep walking. He knew what I was thinking. It was his job, and he did it well. Not being actively engaged in King Service was a new experience for me. I did not know what would happen, how I would feel, or what I would come to understand as time went on.

Matters at hand were within my reach but beyond my grasp. I needed some control of my life, so I decided that I would remain a vegetarian and, in my mind, always be serving God, doing what I thought was the upright thing to do. Disturbed, Saadya tells me, "I am saddened that you still thought you had to earn your way into heaven." Doesn't everybody? "Then it wouldn't be *grace*." Saadya makes the point in a lilting tone.

AT A CROSSROAD

MY MIND CONTINUED TO HAVE THE PROPENSITY to slip into the King mindset, meaning the mind control—one minute I could be me, and the next I was an agent. I had the tendency to assume an "us-against-them" mentality. I was still being very much vexed, and that meant that the WORKS still had power over me. My newfound freedom was still quite tenuous. I had an inner struggle of fighting tooth-and-nail to maintain my semblance of a person who made God a priority. It was not yet okay for me to grant permission for God to be on the back burner, which is what I needed to prevent from happening. Every morning I woke up in rehab, I was at a crossroad.

Although I was coming to grips with the cult aspect of the WORKS, within the context of the "us-against-them" mentality, I had now become the "them." It mattered to me, because those I left behind, still at the Center, had been my friends, associates, sisters, and comrades for a substantial amount of time. We cared for each other. We watched out for each other. We were comrades-in-arms. Mahlia confirms this only to an extent: "They cared for you as long as you were a cult member."

Nevertheless, I got to know the girls individually and had relationships with them, spoken and unspoken, as we shared so many unconventional experiences, fiascoes, shenanigans, and uncommon adventures. Together, we had gone through mountain-top experiences, but we had gone through the valleys as well. I thought of some of the girls as confidantes. We shared a common power source driving us from within and controlling us from without.

When I didn't call anyone to pick me up at the airport at the date and time I was supposed to return, I knew Bethany, Belinda, Kaylah, and the others would know I was being deprogrammed. I knew they would realize I wasn't coming back. I knew they would be crying out to King for me at the first sign of me not contacting the ashram. It is true that I would not be returning at all, but as in the past when one of the girls had been physically whisked out of the airport lobby, the Barstow Center agents would beseech King for my return, just as they had done for Farrah.

In the agents' estimation, I had defected, and I also knew they would think the worst of me for having done so. In their eyes, I had walked away from the only hope of ever making spiritual advancement. In order to have done so, in the agents' eyes, I was nothing but an ungrateful, meat-eating regular, motivated only to please my physical desires and willfully subjecting myself to spending eternity on a horrendous treadmill of spiritual decline. I could not bear the thought of admitting to myself that I had defected to the other side, and that I no longer would be protected by Righteous King. Saadya reassures me, "Mom, you knew better than that." But they did not know better. Saadya continues, "You knew what they would think because of what they were indoctrinated to think." Precisely, and I was trained to think the way they were trained to think. Although I was no longer apt to slip back into the mindset, I still needed to be at the rehab.

DIGGING MY WAY OUT

THE REHABILITATION WAS A TIME FOR ME to come together to share my re-socialization in a supervised environment, and to better understand the techniques used in the WORKS first to indoctrinate, and then control, its adherents.

I understood rehab to be an opportunity to take time for myself to read and re-experience the flow of life without the fear, guilt, and shame of not being at the Center. I had to get comfortable with not affiliating with the Organization or associating with the girls at the ashram.

Mahlia asks, "Mom, at this point, you were still not able to admit you had joined a cult?" I needed to do exactly that. It was going to be a long road.

I had to sort out my own feelings and either find a new identity for myself or become comfortable with my old one. I was drifting on a sea of uncertainty. My first night at the rehab house, I needed to be reminded why I was there, what I needed to do, and that it was going to take time. I was reminded I would have to be patient, in order to get on with my life. It was not only my life that needed definition, but life in general. In other words, I had been stripped of my assignment.

I had been blinded by the haze that offered only a false promise. So I guess that made me a blind fool. "Mom, don't say that!" I am admonished by Mahlia. "You were not the only one, and worse things have happened to people who were subjected to these types of tactics." The bottom line was, I had to cope with large-scale disillusionment and disappointment. Mahlia puts her arm over my shoulder and pulls me close. I feel the gentle squeeze of her hand followed by a single-handed back rub. I am comforted by this brief interlude.

There were several other young adults at the rehab house from all over the country who had been in other cults. We'd been hoodwinked by the cult dangling before us a carrot stick of exclusivity for which we would do almost anything. One of the girls spoke of being in the Gift of All Love (GOAL), prostituting herself to win converts. Two of the boys had been in the CAUSE. Another had been in Love of God Omnipotent (LOGO). One girl had been in Beauty of Forever Faith (BFF), but only for three weeks. Yet another had been involved in a meditation center known as Souls Up-Right Everlasting (SURE). We had one thing in common—once we visited the cult, we were unable to leave. Even if we did, we could not escape the cult's rhetoric already so deeply embedded in our psyche. The cult had such a deep-rooted grip on each of us. We had to rid ourselves of this hold. No one else could do it for us.

Yet another boy who'd been in the CAUSE had come to the rehab house prematurely, as it turned out. He escaped from the rehab house in the middle of the night, climbing out a screen window in the boys' bedroom. He did what he'd been told and went right back. I remember the look on his face that night when we were sitting around the dining room table. No one else saw it, and I didn't speak out. We were engaging socially, but he perceived the situation as serving no purpose. In this boy's eyes, conversing was not purposeful, and we were lost souls. I could tell the stronghold of the CAUSE had gripped his thinking back into the cult totalitarian mindset.

I had been just like this boy. So when I washed, cleaned read, ate, you name it, I tried to remember that I was doing it to serve and to please God. Although I had rejected the idea of living at the Center, I knew I must not concede myself to being regarded as lower than low, subject to spontaneous spiritual decline. This gnawed away at me. "Is that what you thought would happen to you?" asks Mahlia, who finds it hard to believe that, in the back of my mind, the thought festered of what my former god-sisters must be thinking of me. It wasn't about them as much as about me having walked in the shoes they were still wearing. It was as if I had an alter ego. It would require the rehab to lend time, support, and understanding for me to deal with that alter ego, so that what it was telling me would no longer matter.

DAYS AND DAZE IN REHAB

THE TIME SPEND IN REHAB WAS BENEFICIAL. However, that very first night, I was lying in bed, uncomfortable at being physically comfortable. Lying on a mattress was not austere. Psychologically, I was in a dark abyss, lying in stark space. I felt I didn't belong anywhere. I did not know who I was. I needed help to avoid concluding that my own short-comings were the raw underpinning for my disaffection with the Organ-ization. I was lying in bed feeling abandoned in my abandonment. Regarding people outside of the WORKS, I couldn't fight them and I couldn't join them. I couldn't be a loyal agent in WORKS, and I couldn't be a regular.

Saadya points out, "It was a double whammy." I was being shaken like a rag doll, tossed and thrown to and fro. I was alone with and without myself, and this daunting notion gripped me. It left me in a daze.

Yet as the days wore on, a definite and increasing rift grew between me and the agents still at the ashram. I was less dogged by the hold mind-control had on me. Yet it bothered me when I thought about all the girls still in the ashram. I remembered each of them. I was coming to grips with the emotional, psychological, and humanistic reasons for which I'd joined, and knew it was impossible to tell them about their own victimization. I cared that they were still subject to the intimidation tactics at the WORKS Center confluence, where I had been one of them. Now their perception of me, affected by a very tightly woven dogma, prevented my ashram sisters and me from being able to relate to each other. I was no longer disposed to the King Service mindset. We did not have that in common. Mahlia and Saadya declare in unison, "Thank God!"

Mahlia recites from Psalm 142:5: *"Then I pray to you, O Lord, I say, "You are my place of refuge. You are all I really want in life."* I hope this applies to me. "It does," she assures me.

While rehabbing, I was caught in old ways of thinking about myself and old hang-ups. Mahlia reflectively says, "Mom, you mean insecurities, and everyone has them. Maybe you were more normal than you real-ized." Yet I was still rising early and bobbing up and down to music I listened to on headphones. I was chronically caught between my past and my past as a worker. Both personae were alien to me now. It was the first time since my joining the cult—there! I said it, happy now? Mahlia replies, "Mom, this is not about me and how I feel. It's about you and how honest you are able to be with yourself."

Thank you, Mahlia darling. This is also about how honest I am being with you and your sister. There is an inside of me that I want you to know about. I no longer want either of you to misunderstand, although I realize there will be those times; but for now, I want to say all this to you in my endeavor to share myself with you both. Then I say what needs to be said no matter what. The love I have for you is beyond description.

"We know," they reply. What might have been awkward for each of us has turned out to be a heartfelt moment for the three of us.

"So, as you were saying—please go on," Mahlia coaxes. Not having to be out fund-raising afforded me time I had not had in a long time. Rehab was the first place I could simply sit quietly, the first time in three years to reflect on my involvement.

At the beginning, rehab seemed the lesser of two evils. I willingly went to rehab because living in the ashram was out of the question, I did not have anywhere else to go, and staying with my parents was not even an option. I would've done anything to avoid having to settle in and settle down to an ordinary and mundane life. I absolutely did not want to be lulled into complacency. That probably would've driven me right back. "Don't say that, Mom. You can't possibly mean that!" Mahlia admonishes me.

Saadya joins in, "It wasn't prudent for you to go home yet." I just couldn't, and this is understood. I could not adopt my parents' lifestyle, and I wasn't expected to. Still, I was plagued by having been denied some form of self-expression.

"Poor me," I say, putting words into my daughters' mouths. Mahlia and Saadya are visibly touched. Saadya reassures me, "Mom, you are entitled to have these feelings." Mahlia nods in affirmation. I never felt more validated in my life.

Immediately following my deprogramming, I surreptitiously felt I needed to prove myself, to prove that my motives were real, and my intentions genuine and honorable. I came to understand, and I wanted my family to understand, that I had meant no harm and was not at fault for what had happened to me.

Saadya discloses, "What happened to you is a prime example of the expression, 'the road to hell is paved by good intentions.'" I wanted to be exonerated of any personal responsibility of what transpired over the first several days, weeks, and months, which turned into years, at the Righteous King Center. Everyone at rehab felt the same way. We knew what had happened to us was serious messing with our minds. We spent time at rehab talking about thought reform. We read from Robert J. Lifton's book, *Thought Reform and the Psychology of Totalism.*[2]

It had been beyond any of our wildest dreams that we were being subjected to thought reform and succumbing to it. Our parents knew they were up against an entity that employed sophisticated indoctrination techniques. My parents knew I was not functioning autonomously, so it wasn't really necessary for me to convince them that I had been manipulated. They already understood the circumstances that create susceptibility.

Mahlia scrolls through her phone and reads from Psalm 34:5: *"Those who look to Him for help will be radiant with joy; no shadow of shame will darken their faces."* Then she tells me, "That's a promise from God just for you!" It *is?*

---

2. Robert J. Lifton. (1986) *Thought Reform and the Psychology of Totalism.* Chapel Hill, NC: The University of North Carolina Press.

FRENZY

SAADYA REMARKS, "IT CERTAINLY SOUNDS like it was a process. What about the recurring dreams you started to have?"

Mahlia prods, "Can you give us an example?" Saadya nestles up to me and rests her head on my shoulder. This show of affection is endearing. It always is with my daughters. Feeling the pressure of Saadya's head on my shoulder evokes this one dream that I had in particular:

I am back in the WORKS, at a luxury hotel. We stayed there, the male and female agents of the Barstow Center. We were all in the lobby, waiting to return to the Center.

The bus stop that I needed to catch the bus that would bring me to the airport is not far from the hotel entrance. Amid this chaos, as the workers await the arrival of the Center vans for our satchels to be loaded, I try to slip into obscurity with my handbag secured by the strap pressing on my shoulder (similar to how Saadya has nestled on that same shoulder). I find out that I need to get on bus #00 which will take me to the airport, so I can get on that United Airlines flight my parents have reserved for me to fly home.

Mahlia says, "That sounds like a solid plan."

Except that, terrifyingly, I realize I do not have my handbag any longer. I have lost it along with my wallet, which has all my identification. I am in a frenzy of desperation. Where did I lose my handbag, my identification? I cannot elicit anyone's assistance.

Saadya recognizes, "If you do, you will be revealing your intentions."

No one is trustworthy to help me. Bus #00 pulls up, I see it from the lobby, yet I cannot board. I am in a no-man's land, caught between opposing forces. I am wrought with anxiety. I have lost my identification. I have no identity.

STILL BEING UNDONE

I HAD TO BE REPEATEDLY REMINDED why I was at the rehab and what I was supposed to be doing there. I didn't belong to the WORKS, Sir Supreme, Sir Derek, not even to Leo. I didn't have to submit to an arbitrary authority figure. However, I persisted in pursuing a self-imposed mission. I did not understand that it was enough just to be myself. Whenever I came into contact with any of my emotions or identified myself separate from the WORKS, I would immediately feel worthless, inferior and impure. This was consistent with how I had been trained. You were either a pure worker in the WORKS or the only other alternative, an unholy regular.

I was still feeling the tug on me from far beyond the four walls of the ashram. This duress had me subconsciously believe I would fall prey to the force of physical energy, and I fought with every fiber of my being to prove to myself that I was worthy without the WORKS and its mission. At that point, I was the only one who even cared. I was awake before 4:00 a.m., getting up and out of bed, just as when I was at the Barstow Center, to dance and prance to music I listened to, but now on headphones, so as not to wake the other rehabbers or staff that early in the morning. Mahlia declares, "You were so used to rising early at the Center before going out on fund-raising." Saadya confirms, "You were trying to maintain the early-morning routine." I got called out on that by my fellow rehabbers. I tried to explain to them that I was doing it for exercise, and I was. But I was also doing it as an act of austerity and to set my mind on things above—although I was listening to music by Billy Joel.

ANSWERED PRAYER

SO, IN REHAB, I BEGAN RISING before anyone else was up. If I stayed in bed longer and got up any later, I would feel as though I'd lost a grip on the day. It was not possible for me to stay in bed just to languish. Upon my awakening, I was revved up and ready to rock 'n' roll. My nervous system was still overexcited.

It took some time before I was able to sleep deeply at the rehab house and feel really rested. Functioning in a rested manner took some getting used to. At the ashram, when I woke up, I would have to drag myself around, not in a stupor, but in a frenzy of excitement. The effect this had on me and the other girls was that we stopped getting our periods. We took it as King's mercy that we wouldn't have to deal with that monthly nuisance. One of the first months I was staying at the Center, I did get my period and had no sanitary pad or tampon. Jayda suggested I pray to King. So I did.

I then reached up onto a closet shelf and swiped my hand along it as far back as I could reach, and to my amazement, I found some pads. It was an answer to my prayer. Soon enough, after following the early-morning rising and frenzy of the lifestyle, and over-stressing my nervous system, I no longer needed to pray that prayer because, like the other girls, my period stopped coming.

When I lay down to rest up at the ashram, I would wake up again just a few hours later, picking up where I had left off. There was no break in the routine. We were constantly on the go, with no place to go. We viewed life on a continuum. It was difficult to discern where one day ended and another began. I had no solitude, no privacy, no time for reflection, no time but for King Service and a totalitarian authority figure who dictated my every moment and oversaw all my activity.

At the King Center, I heard and learned about King's omniscience and omnipotence. We discussed this among ourselves in the ashram. Finding the pad was the first experience I had with attributing this glory to King. Saadya maintains, "You found a sanitary pad, and you thought it was heaven-sent." I thought King had answered my prayer. This confirmed for me that King was real and existed in the WORKS.

I ascribed the incident as an example of God's omniscience and consequently submitted myself to those who claimed sole propriety to God. It seemed that, if I were to feel God-minded, the only place for me was in a King Center.

DIVINE INTERVENTION

AT REHAB, ALTHOUGH I KNEW I had been subjected to coercive persuasion, choosing not to be a member of the WORKS did not preclude me from still thinking I had to be good enough, and work hard enough, to earn favor with God. I continued entertaining the philosophy that a mind absorbed in the spirit realm was superior to one lived on the physical plane with all its prominence tugging on the heartstrings of sinful man.

"No one can be good enough on their own merit, "'But we are all as an unclean thing, and all our righteousness are as filthy rags,'" Saadya quotes Isaiah 64:4. She explains, "God makes this a distinction of His holiness, and without some divine intervention we are lost. God himself intervenes and makes the way." Too much information, I tell her.

It was a daunting task not to construe my self-worth as propagated solely from being held in esteem by the god of the WORKS. Active engagement in the World Organization for Righteous King Service, and the requirement of strict adherence through our daily endeavors, was the only way to effectuate approval from King.

Now far removed from the WORKS, I no longer had an overriding philosophy for life. The WORKS infrastructure and totalitarian power structure no longer provided me with answers to questions I had not stopped asking.

Saadya insists, "It helps to remind yourself to '*seek God with all your heart, mind, soul, and strength,*'" according to Luke 10:27 and Deuteronomy 6:5. I am totally caught off guard, being cut to the heart, realizing how penetrable is this message, and not only the message, but that my daughters have such conviction.

I thought I had to do the right thing to get close to God. I thought I had to do the right thing to earn recognition. Serving made us think we could get close to the Divine. Saadya shakes her head. "No one needs to earn God's love. His love for us is unconditional, in and through our imperfect temporal condition." I lift my right hand, palm facing in, placing four fingers upward, thumb tucked in, to cover my mouth. As I squint, taking this in, Saadya fixes her gaze on me, and Mahlia's eyes fill with tears, as both my daughters focus on how I am reacting.

The bottom line is that I was confronted by the magnitude of what happened to me in the cult, and after being removed and rescued, I still needed to rid myself of the lingering toxic effect. "On your own you can do nothing when it comes to your innate imperfections," says Mahlia, no doubt paraphrasing some scripture. I fight off my initial perplexity and become annoyed. "Mahlia, you make it sound so simple," I tell her.

She replies, "It *is* simple." Huh? "You can repeat a simple prayer," she suggests. It may be simple, but it is not easy for me to do.

FAMILY FEUD

Saadya senses that this conversation, for the first time, is not going well and steers it back on track, commenting, "Thanks to Grandpa and Grandma, they did what they had to do."

Mahlia adds, "They most definitely were left with no alternative, and

I can imagine how difficult it must have been for them." The deprogramming was a heart-wrenching process for all concerned. It was a trying time for my family because no one could be sure of the outcome and everyone knew they would have to live with its aftermath and dreaded that it might turn out to be a botched effort.

My mother would have none of that. She put her foot down just at the right time, with me and with the deprogrammers. I had to live through the painstaking reality of disillusionment, and my parents had to live through it with me.

It was common for girls at the ashram to discuss our life as regulars prior to joining the WORKS. We would reflect on the inevitability of our joining. We concluded that, being left with no possible alternative in the outside world, King had orchestrated events in our life to bring us to the exclusive truth found only in the WORKS.

Many of the soul-saving girls held grudges against family. Sherine, the one I did fund-raising with at Binghamton University, had been traveling up and down the California coastline. She encountered Clarke when he was soul-saving. Sherine came back with him to stay at the Barstow Center, having nowhere else to go. She came with her only possession, her sleeping bag, in which she rested up on the floor of the women's ashram.

It proved to be a good thing for the Center. Sherine went on to be a loyal worker, a staunch member of the fund-raising group, engaging in soul-saving activity every day, collecting close to three hundred dollars daily. Belinda, who was from Long Island, moved to California and joined the Barstow Center. She was hardened by the vicissitudes of life. She deplored the upper middle-class values she'd grown up with on Long Island. Those forces opposed her openness and eagerness to embrace austerities as a King agent. Belinda's animosity was palpable.

One afternoon, Belinda's father came through the airport lobby to catch a flight, presumably after a business trip to San Bernadino. Belinda was furious when she saw him there. She completely ignored him, and he passed her, ignoring her as well. As he passed me, he remarked in utter contempt, "When are you girls going to wise up?" Belinda was absolutely infuriated when I told her what he'd said.

Saadya explains, "They were so estranged from each other as to ignore each other, reflecting the emotional distance between them from even before she got involved in the WORKS." That is exactly the point. Their unequivocal lack of engagement stemmed from a family feud.

SENSE OF PURPOSE

IN A NUTSHELL, WE WERE ALL SPIRITUALLY HUNGRY. We were searching for God. Mahlia says, "Unfortunately, you wound up looking in the wrong place." This is why I needed to be deprogrammed.

Saadya adds, "You also needed to be in rehab because you were so uptight, unable to function." I did; and I was. In rehab, I began to experience the scents and feelings that I had known previously, before my involvement in the cult. Different sights and sounds would evoke feelings that I had disavowed. I would ignore or dismiss sensory stimulation as being a millstone around my neck, dragging me down into the dregs of life. Up until then, I turned my nose up at what others seemed to be enjoying. I certainly did not participate in a drinking fest at the rehab one late night. It really was in good fun, and the next morning the others were talking about the funny things that had transpired the night before. I had slept through it.

Several of us in rehab went roller-skating one night. Up to then, I was not able to enjoy myself. It was out of the question. I had to safeguard myself. My ability to enjoy anything beyond activities sanctioned by and in the WORKS had been sabotaged. Within the group, I was assured a sense of purpose and deserving of recompense based solely on being an agent of King.

If I was not in the WORKS, I would lose out on all its benefits. The ability to enjoy myself was limited to activity related to King Service. Therefore, at rehab, I was cautious in everything I did throughout the day. I had to rationalize that I was serving God in some way. Risking any enjoyment at the roller-rink might qualify me as being pugnacious, branding me as insincere.

But this evening was different.

As I was moving through space along to the music, I was enjoying the simple activity of roller-skating. Mahlia notes, "It sounds like you were having a breakthrough." I didn't feel I was contradicting some edict against making spiritual advancement. Feeling jubilant at moving through space on roller skates, gliding along to the melodious upbeat tempos, the rhythmic music, simply enjoying the moment, not feeling that I was breaking some rule or regulation for spiritual advancement, was monumental. "Mom, you were having fun," Saadya assures me.

LARGER THAN LIFE

As time went on, I began piecing together the events leading up to the actual deprogramming from bits and pieces I learned through inquiries to various members of my family. I learned that my parents had been admonished not to discuss things with me when I first came home from rehab. As a result of this advice, they were afraid they might say the wrong thing to me. Subsequently, whenever I made some reference to a specific incident or experience, my family members would grow awkwardly quiet. I detected their uneasiness whenever I mentioned anything about the Organization. Mahlia says, "You mean cult."

"Mahlia!" Saadya exclaims.

I assure them both, "That's okay." As a result of my parents' restraint, I stopped bringing up the subject. The door to this type of communication had been shut, and it continued to remain so.

Until one afternoon, when I decided to be open and honest with my mother, and told her things that'd bothered me as a child and what effect they had had on me. Surprisingly, she welcomed this exchange. She had been reluctant to reveal her feelings to me because of warnings from other parents with children involved in cult activity. Evidently there was some kind of networking taking place.

My mother feared she might say something to trigger the mental flip-flop that would drive me right back to a WORKS Center. *"God is not a God of disorder, or confusion. He gives us peace and a sound mind,"* Mahlia paraphrases from 1 Corinthians 14:33. My mother was not at peace. She thought I might not be able to handle a discussion, that it might stir up a cache of memories. All this was conjecture on her part and that of other parents.

Whatever their reasoning, my family thought it best to keep my experience as an agent in King Service an off-limits topic. The irony is that, all along, they wanted to ask questions, and I would have welcomed them.

Instead, their reticence only fueled more dysfunction. I would have felt acceptance from them and acceptance of them had they given in to their desire to know more. I would have welcomed their expression of interest, curiosity, or willingness to hear and talk about specific incidents. Not asking or listening when the subject was broached only served to create more of a chasm between us, at a time when I needed the rift between myself and my family to close forever.

Their reluctance to engage made me think they were trying to erase the entire experience for me by denying it, and consequently denying a part of me, which is what had driven me into the open arms of the WORKS to begin with. This added to my resentment. I wanted to be taken seriously—if not by them, at least by myself.

Those three years were substantive, and my entire experience did not warrant being ignored. I did not want it to be erased or deleted, as if I, or it, was some kind of a computer virus. Saadya reassures me. "Mom, your diligence, steadfastness, and commitment were honorable. You were exercising a form of self-expression."

Mahlia elucidates this: "The mission was something larger than life."

SETTLING DOWN

I WAS NOW EXPECTED TO "SETTLE DOWN." That catch phrase held a negative connotation for me. I could not visualize myself in any situation settled down. Mahlia smiles, finding humor in my resistance. Our eyes lock, the corners of my mouth curl, and we smile.

Saadya turns with a smile on her face as well, clutching in her hand a cluster of blood-red globe grapes from the refrigerator. This moment highlights for me how special this conversation with my two dear darling daughters is turning out to be. I will treasure it always! Saadya begins to rinse the grapes at the sink under a stream of clear running water. As she shakes off the excess water, holding the stem in hand, one of the grapes falls to the floor. She picks it up, turns back to the sink, and dips it into a bowl of water. Announcing, "Five-second rule," she pops it into her mouth.

Mahlia proclaims, "Save some for me."

After twelve weeks at the rehab house, six as a rehabber and six on staff, it was time for me to go back into the real world. By then, I was ready. When I first returned to Connecticut, I went to live with my youngest brother, but he grew increasingly territorial in his small studio apartment, so I went to live with my oldest brother.

"Was it any better with Uncle Henry?" Saadya asks. "He's always been on the quiet side, and a bit of a loner himself." In fact, Uncle Henry was the most available for discussion, making this time more tolerable. He too had a studio apartment, so I slept in a sleeping bag on the floor in an alcove between the clothes closet and the bathroom. I was thankful for having a roof over my head.

During this time, I found myself with two months of summertime in which I spent writing and reflecting. It was time I had for myself and by myself. Mahlia asks, "How was it, not living with a bunch of people?" I pause at Mahlia's astuteness. It was an adjustment and required some getting used to. Communal living ensured a steady dose of company. There were times I missed having people around me, while, at other times, I savored my solitude.

I had some episodes of loneliness when they crept up on me. I longed to be good enough, having to silence the voice within telling me I was otherwise. As a result, I wrote dozens of poems in an attempt to reconcile myself to the imposed limits set on me in the cult and the intrigue at the ashram.

This is one of my reflections.

My memories shine bright as I take in the sights, of the park, plaza, and people on parade, registering within what I said and what I heard. I was there, and so were they. It meant so much. I remember as if it were yesterday. Although no longer considered dear, those times are now so far away, yet still so near.

DEISTS

MAHLIA REFLECTS, "YOU HAVE TO GIVE your parents credit for their courage." I did, and I do. Under the circumstances, they needed to do what had to be done. I am grateful that they took measures to rescue me from a situation it was not possible for me to extricate myself from. I still wonder what has happened to the other girls who remained in the confines of the dogma, their minds contorted to conform to the apparatus that is the WORKS as it existed for me and the fund-raising group.

Something I don't have to wonder about is how mind-control evolves from conformity and envelops us, swallowing us whole. I understand how the tenets of the dogma trickle down through the culture created within it. Their intended purpose is to reform our thoughts and acculturate us for strict adherence to the system.

We were deists. Like so many religions, we had a system. Like so many religions, we tried to get into God's kingdom through works. Saadya says, "In your case, literally." I abandoned the religiosity, and I was rid of the system. However, it left a void.

LIVING WATER

AFTER THE WORKS, WHENEVER I FELT what I had come to regard as the presence of God, I hungered to know more. Whatever technique was the latest fad, I was open to it. I tried various types of meditation. But these techniques left me feeling like an outsider looking in—I sensed there was always more. I even became a member of the neighborhood synagogue. When I heard the congregation utter, in Hebrew, "Yeshua," I quickly referenced the English translation. Yeshua means salvation. Why was Jesus being spoken of in the Jewish scriptures? I was in turmoil.

On the other hand, there is peace that permeates my daughters. It is perceptible, some kind of a presence. If I am not mistaken, it is as an "unction"—but from what, or from where?

Mahlia rummages through her purse, and I can't imagine what she is looking for with such urgency. She plucks a folded piece of paper the size of a business card from her wallet, and hands it to me. It's light pink stationary with a border of purple calla lilies along the bottom and left side. I accept it and stare at it. Mahlia's chin protrudes ever so slightly, and she lifts her eyebrows, prodding me to read the message on the card. I am holding it between the index finger and thumb of each hand. I stare at the calla lilies. Mahlia stands beside me. I sense her gazing along with me at what I am looking at. She nudges me with her right elbow.

I am comforted by the touch of our arms and shoulders. Reflectively, in a hushed tone, I begin to read, *"Jesus stood and said in a loud voice, 'If anyone is thirsty, let him come to me and drink. Whoever believes in me, as the Scripture has said, streams of living water will flow from within him'"* (John 7:37).

This must be the reason for that presence I perceive in my daughters. It is more than their faith, but what? I ask, "Is this what Jesus does for us?"

Mahlia is quick to reply, "Those are his exact words, and if He says it, He does it. The Holy Spirit will open the eyes of your heart." Interesting.

THE AFTERMATH

SAADYA WISELY ASKS, "WAS IT over after rehab? Did this chapter come to an end?"

Yes, but the dreams kept coming, the recurring dreams that had a theme of entrapment and escape that was always thwarted, although I had the whole escape planned out. Mahlia says, "You never seemed to be able to dream yourself out of the WORKS." Instead, those feelings of entrapment kept resurfacing. But I was one of the fortunate ones, because when I awoke, I was out. Upon reflection, I wrote:

At the height of my climb, I cling and scream, wedged in the rubble of my mind, mercifully supported, out from the hewn stones of disenchantment—culpable for thwarting my nature, trapped while clutching at feeble straws. Shouting out, surrounded, engulfed in flames of fiction—simple answers, sure solutions to the dilemmas of life: Adherence absorbed me from within, surrender wrung me dry, chewed me up, and spit me out.

I am, according to the depths of my joy, equally crushed as the grapes of wrath from the lack-lusterless-ness of lurid lies.

Soothed not by solitude, teetering on perceptions limited by pinnacles of pernicious passion, I cling, screaming, Where were you then, where are you now that I need you to take a hold of my hand? Yet I refuse to admit defeat. I can face the challenge now. I aligned myself to a truth that made false promises but could not promise the Prince of Peace.

After rehab, I immediately began to persevere with confidence and persist with deliberate enthusiasm. I began making long-term plans and fashioning short-term objectives. The details of an activity were no longer a matter of life and death. As a WORKS agent, the execution of the means was equally important to the fulfillment of the ends. Gone was the mission. Therefore, my most important realization was that life, after all, still held meaning.

It often seems there is something to be said, even when there is nothing to say without the words getting in the way. I had to be patient and not force things to happen. My thoughts would fire and manifest the logic that God did not condone the living conditions in the WORKS. Words never were as conspiring as what I had been told in the WORKS about what to feel passion for. The mind-bending contortions I had been put through upon crossing the portal of the WORKS Center were unfathomable beforehand.

As a WORKS agent, I had shared a lifestyle because I shared a theology. "More like an ideology," Saadya says, "with loopholes—a sieve that sifted its adherents out of their own mental mechanism and landed them in the machinations of mind control." There was persistent emphasis that we had the absolute truth. Any confusion we might have about this could be clarified by the certainty of the dogma. Being committed to the mission gave us the same purpose. Anything less or else was proof that we were not being God-minded and, therefore, needed to be even more committed. Mahlia offers, "It was a false doctrine and a godless ideology." I wrote this a few weeks after the rehab:

> *I plummet through hollowed-out hollers, through echo chambers in that place where the ice of life tries to freeze me, from out of that place where I was kept under lock and key, for someone else had been in charge, where I was hidden, especially from me.*
>
> *My desire is to be, just as I would have others see. Fright beheld when I find myself alive and alone, like Alice in the looking glass, I belong to no one; I am part of nothing that exists. Yet in my magical mystery space where gold is golden and love is molten, I dissolve and turn from those who might have design to spite me, in spite of my warmth and tenderness.*

I was lost in the process of trying to find myself when it wasn't me who I was looking for. My heart had melted into molten lava. It burned within me, and I longed for it to be reshaped into what God intended.

Now Mahlia interjects, "God doesn't set us up for failure, Mom. He ensures our success." Mahlia reflects the light that shines within her quoting from Psalm 103:8: *"The Lord is compassionate, slow to anger and filled with love!"* I can't help but say, "That's the kind of God worthy of worship. "

CITY SCENE

I WROTE THIS ON AN AFTERNOON EXCURSION to New York City, sitting in a plaza near Rockefeller Center while taking in the sights:

> *There are people dressed to kill, put together, come as you*

*are, out of town, down and out, or ain't got nothin' else. There
are bike riders, roller skaters, truckers, trotters, strollers. People
can be seen eating pizza, pretzels, yogurt, ice-cream, passing on
the left, and right, fountain, subways; don't walk—walk signs,
flashing yellow—caution, stop signs, construction, destruction,
do not litter signs, movies and restaurants featured from England,
Italy, France, Brazil, women wearing skirts with slits up the front,
sides, and back; high shoes, low shoes, clogs, no shoes; art gal-
leries, photography studios, Radio City Music Hall.*

*Some people going someplace, to a place, another place, any-
place—no place. Walking and talking and buzzing, people stop
to eat, grab a bite, a bite to eat, bite of a dog, curb your dog, some
people are sitting and resting, some moving and grooving. Some
people riding in cars, taxis, buses, Rolls-Royces. Those people
pulsate and jive, creating the beat, and they go on and on and on.
Each one living and dying, provocatively smiling, and crying out,
under a façade, of maybe I'm cool! But sometimes I hurt, or
maybe I just don't know who I am. All this while they can be
seen creating the beat, and they go on and on and on. The beat
pulsing, don't come too close, or else you'll see me, but please
reach out and touch to feel me.*

UNSCATHED

NOT VERY LONG AFTER REHAB, on a chance encounter, I came across
Suzanne fund-raising in New York City.

Mahlia recollects, "She was the stool pigeon who orchestrated the
turn of events for Leo."

Saadya recalls, "She was the girl who offered you her humility, realizing you had stepped aside to make room for her and Leo." Well, she
wasn't offering me her respects now. But she did tell me that she'd re-

united with her husband after she moved from the Barstow Center back to New Zealand, and had rejoined the Righteous King Center in Wellington.

This would be the safest place for her because she would not be a burden to any of the other WORKS' Center authorities. They were aware of the ferocity of the hatred the other girls, especially Camila and Belinda, had for Suzanne. I learned from Suzanne that, for the past year, she had been traveling around the world with the traveling Mardi Gras carts to all the major cities that welcomed the WORKS' participation in the parade. Mardi Gras was also a Righteous King Service-celebrated festival that drew attention to the World Organization in many cities. Mahlia comments, "I bet they loved the crowds of people they could fund-raise in."

Saadya asks, "What happened when you saw her?" It was I who approached Suzanne and inquired of her about the Barstow women. At first she was amenable. I could tell she did not know what to think or how to react at seeing me. I knew she thought of me as a regular, now that I was no longer an agent in the WORKS. We both kept our composure, and she told me they, the Barstow soul-saving sisters, were being broken up as a group and paired off with the men to be married. She told me she'd heard what happened to me. I started to tell her that, to realize the actual omnipotence of God, I didn't have to be a member of the WORKS. She fired back that she knew I was trying to talk her out of her King-mindedness, and that I couldn't.

Then she reached the point where she could no longer hide her true feelings. She reacted exactly how I had expected. I cringed at seeing the snag that had kept me there for three years still having a powerful hold on Suzanne. It sickened me to see that, on her own, Suzanne could not opt out of living among the other agents, thinking she was gaining merit in her quest for God. Although she didn't know it, indelibly stamped on Suzanne's mind was an errant allegiance. Suzanne and the other workers were misguided into trusting the cult's dogma, which made life as a WORKS agent their only option. The cult's tactics left them devoid of the ability to consider anything else as a feasible alternative.

I knew that Suzanne felt pity for me because I was now living a meaningless life destined for a lower life form.

Mahlia assures me, "You knew that was what she was supposed to think, because you lived through it, got out of it, and were the wiser for it."

Actually hearing Suzanne's response and seeing her react viscerally caused me to see how irrational she was, mitigating the impact her mini-tirade had on me. She accused me of being disloyal and a snake filled with poisonous venom. This encounter assured me that the grip of mind-control was very real, and that I was thankfully no longer under its sway.

I had turned away from King Service, and now I turned away from Suzanne, alert to the fact that there indeed was no talking to her. She shouted after me in one last attempt to save my soul, and I could hear her impenetrable cry, "Righteous King," as I walked away. Mahlia confirms, "Mom, you were above it now. It didn't have an impact on you. You were able to walk away unscathed."

THE TRUTH WILL SET YOU FREE

EZEKIEL 13:20-23: *"I WILL LET THE SOULS whom you hunt go free, the souls like birds. Your veils also I will tear off and deliver my people out of your hand, and they shall be no more in your hand as prey, and you shall know that I am the Lord."*

"It's getting late," Mahlia says with sweetness in her voice. My daughters take a few steps closer to me. Each one gives me a kiss. Embracing this intimacy, my eyes close as I hold on tightly to this moment. At first I think my daughters are excusing themselves. But when Saadya says, "Mom, you should get some rest," I realize that they're thinking of me.

Mahlia goes on to say, "But before you go, we want you to know in Joshua 14:8, Moses said, *'For my part, I wholeheartedly followed the Lord my God.'*" She adds, "We think this is the sentiment you embodied while embracing the WORKS ideology." Saadya is nodding in agreement. I am thoroughly moved by how genuinely precious and darling my daughters are. I can't help but tell them.

Referring to that scripture, I make a declaration, "That is what I want as my epitaph. This is what I want as my legacy."

"No worries, Mom," I hear, and I am not sure which of them said it, because the lump in my throat, growing increasingly tighter, is about to burst, and the tears welling up in my eyes are ready to overflow, from emotion at the epiphany that my husband and these two daughters of mine are my life.

Mahlia presently reads from Hebrews 11:27: *"It was by faith that Moses left the land of Egypt, not fearing the Lord's anger. He kept right on going because he kept his eyes on the one who is invisible."* "Our Father in heaven," she goes on to say.

I attest to their faith, saying, "I wish I had your faith, but after this deception—"

Before I can finish, Saadya tells me, "You can't have my faith." This catches even Mahlia by surprise, and she glances at her sister, eyes narrowing. "You can't have my faith—you have to have your own."

Now it is I who speak. "I know God is real, and I know that you both know far more than that. But I am still not sure what that is."

"You're not sure who that is," Mahlia declares, but she offers a dose of assurance. "Let's talk about it some more tomorrow. It really is getting late."

I admit I am weary, but at the same time relieved and gladdened. Saadya now reads off her smart phone from Isaiah 57:10, before placing it on the marble top kitchen counter, *"You grew weary in your search but you never gave up. You strengthened yourself and went on."*

This clinches it for me, and I burst into tears. The three of us embrace.

GIMME SHELTER

IN MY DREAM, I WAS BACK AT THE ASHRAM. *The other agents were scurrying about performing one type of activity or another. I knew the plan. I had to catch a bus and get over to the airport, but I had to wait for the signal. The time had to be right. Before the signal could come, I was found out. I knew I was found out because the gold-trimmed, black leather journal of my life was not in the place I usually kept it. I was panic-stricken. My secret life had been revealed. They knew I had two daughters. They knew I had a life. I was found out because, although I was still at the ashram, in order to have had this life, I would have had to have left the WORKS. If I had not left then, I would never be able to leave, ever again. This would be my last and only chance. I would not have another chance of having the life I have—no husband, no Mahlia, no Saadya.*

My duffel bag was empty. I had no possessions. I had nothing to call my own. The only item of any worth was that gold-trimmed journal that gave an account of my life. I grabbed it and held it close, and without any hesitation protectively stuffed it into the duffel bag. I was barebreasted. Realizing I was exposed, I donned an extra-large T-shirt, plucking it right off a hanger out of the ashram closet, to cover up.

I left. No one seemed to notice until word got out. Then someone was looking for me. It was an exceptionally sunny day. I was being followed by an unknown woman driving a car. She was chasing after me, intent on bringing me back. I began running down a steep incline. I needed speed to stay ahead of my pursuer. A gust of wind lifted my feet off the ground, giving me the sensation of flying. With my feet only inches off the ground, I was able to navigate the steep incline, gliding along several streets lined with parked cars.

Finding myself at a dead-end street, I could go no farther. My objective was not to be seen. I hid under the gold-trimmed down feather comforter that I plucked out of my duffel bag, previously empty other than for my journal. It had the same gold trim as the journal of my life.

With unexpected suddenness, the weather grew mysteriously cloudy. Then there also was a young man in the front seat of the car, searching for me. I found myself wrapped in the comforter. It covered me, protected me, provided warmth and, along with the cloud covering, concealment. When they arrived, peering out of the windshield of the car they used in hot pursuit of me, they looked left and right, then peered directly at me but couldn't see me. I was invisible to them. Then, for no apparent reason, the tires on their car went flat. They were utterly confused. At that moment, I knew they had lost their grip on me.

FREE INDEED

I AWAKE, GO DOWNSTAIRS TO THE KITCHEN with pen and paper in hand, and begin to write down my dream. I notice Saadya's phone where she left it on the kitchen counter. I use it to find out about the meaning of my dream, searching: *wind; cloud; comforter in the Bible.*

I read from Psalm 91:1, 3-4: *"He will cover you with his feathers, and under his wings you will find refuge; his faithful promises are your armor and protection."*

I read from Exodus 14:24-25: *"But just before dawn the Lord looked down on the Egyptian army from the pillar of fire and cloud and threw their forces into total confusion. He twisted their chariot wheels, making their chariots difficult to drive."* This explains my dream.

I then read from John 3:16: *"For God so loved the world, that he gave/sacrificed his own son [being in the likeness of man, yet fully God], so that none should perish, but have everlasting life."* It makes sense that humans beget humans, so God begets God. My heart melts at the stark contrast that it is not what *I* must do, but what God has *already* done and makes available as a gift to all, if only we receive it.

I grasp the contrast between a heavenly Father who alone fulfills his purpose by playing out in human history the role needed for the era, rather than a god needing me to accomplish a mission through my toil. He is a faithful Father who calms the wind and storms of life, who provides a cloud covering from the scorching elements as he did for the Israelites in the wilderness; a Comforter, God's Holy Spirit, a guide to understand the things freely given to us by the Father; and a Son, whose unique and perfect character is the only acceptable sacrifice, once and for all, to delete our imperfections, not to condemn us, but to allow us to spend an eternity in God's loving embrace, with all its benefits, starting now!

I bow my head and lift my arms in realization that the Comforter in my dream is not a what, but a Who. I realize my daughters were not forcing their faith on me. Instead, they were introducing me to the Almighty who knocks on the door of our heart, yearning for passionate intimacy with us, his kindred spirits. I may have been rescued from a cult, but I still needed a relational God, a personal God, not of my own making, who came not to condemn but to rescue.

I had left the WORKS with the ashram door forever closed behind me and walked through the veil of the Temple of the living God. In the light of grace, I entered the Father's sanctuary and was no longer concerned with birth leading to death. In that moment, I passed beyond death and became able to grasp the greatest mystery—a life abundant and everlasting!

My daughters know that I sought the Lord, but they don't yet know that I finally found Him. Mahlia and Saadya are now fast asleep. I can't wait until I see them in the morning, so I can tell them.

EPILOGUE

"Now I stand on solid ground, and I will publicly praise the Lord" (Psalm 26:12).

I can't bear the thought of ever parting from my husband, my darling daughters, or any of my loved ones, let alone the reality of an eternal separation from the One who loves me most, Almighty God. God is spirit and His spirit is the Holy Spirit. He is not a God to be merely held in awe, as in most religions, or induced through auto-suggestion by reciting a mantra.

"What is his name—what is his son's name?" the writer asks in Proverbs 30:4.

He is Yehovah (The Lord), El Shaddai (The Almighty God), our Protector (Yehovah Jireh), our Healer (Yehovah Rephaka), our Righteousness (Yehovah Tzidqenu), the Lord who is always there (Yehovah Shamah), and he is the Sar Shalom (The Prince of Peace). Still another of God's names is Salvation, Yeshua, translated into English as Jesus, who bears witness to the Father's heavenly Kingdom and makes its attainment a reality for all!

It would be remiss of me not to ask you to ask God for His living water and see if he does not pour His Spirit into you as the Great I Am revealed! His abundant love I cannot deny.